MznLnx

Missing Links Exam Preps

Exam Prep for

Macroeconomics

DeLong & Olney, 2nd Edition

The MznLnx Exam Prep is your link from the texbook and lecture to your exams.
The MznLnx Exam Preps are unauthorized and comprehensive reviews of your textbooks.

All material provided by MznLnx and Rico Publications (c) 2010
Textbook publishers and textbook authors do not particpate in or contribute to these reviews.

MznLnx

Rico Publications

Exam Prep for Macroeconomics
2nd Edition
DeLong & Olney

Publisher: Raymond Houge
Assistant Editor: Michael Rouger
Text and Cover Designer: Lisa Buckner
Marketing Manager: Sara Swagger
Project Manager, Editorial Production: Jerry Emerson
Art Director: Vernon Lowerui

Product Manager: Dave Mason
Editorial Assitant: Rachel Guzmanji
Pedagogy: Debra Long
Cover Image: Jim Reed/Getty Images
Text and Cover Printer: City Printing, Inc.
Compositor: Media Mix, Inc.

(c) 2010 Rico Publications

ALL RIGHTS RESERVED. No part of this work covered by the copyright may be reproduced or used in any form or by an means--graphic, electronic, or mechanical, including photocopying, recording, taping, Web distribution, information storage, and retrieval systems, or in any other manner--without the written permission of the publisher.

Printed in the United States
ISBN:

For more information about our products, contact us at:
Dave.Mason@RicoPublications.com

For permission to use material from this text or product, submit a request online to:
Dave.Mason@RicoPublications.com

Contents

CHAPTER 1
Introduction to Macroeconomics — 1
CHAPTER 2
Measuring the Macroeconomy — 22
CHAPTER 3
Thinking Like an Economist — 40
CHAPTER 4
The Theory of Economic Growth — 52
CHAPTER 5
The Reality of Economic Growth: History and Prospect — 60
CHAPTER 6
Building Blocks of the Flexible-Price Model — 74
CHAPTER 7
Equilibrium in the Flexible-Price Model — 90
CHAPTER 8
Money, Prices, and Inflation — 95
CHAPTER 9
The Sticky-Price Income-Expenditure Framework: Consumption and the Multiplier — 109
CHAPTER 10
Investment, Net Exports, and Interest Rates: The IS Curve — 122
CHAPTER 11
The Money Market and the LM Curve — 133
CHAPTER 12
The Phillips Curve, Expectations, and Monetary Policy — 142
CHAPTER 13
Stabilization Policy — 154
CHAPTER 14
Budget Balance, National Debt, and Investment — 170
CHAPTER 15
International Economic Policy — 182
CHAPTER 16
Changes in the Macroeconomy and Changes in Macroeconomic Policy — 195
CHAPTER 17
The Future of Macroeconomics — 209
ANSWER KEY — 224

TO THE STUDENT

COMPREHENSIVE

The *MznLnx* Exam Prep series is designed to help you pass your exams. Editors at MznLnx review your textbooks and then prepare these practice exams to help you master the textbook material. Unlike study guides, workbooks, and practice tests provided by the texbook publisher and textbook authors, *MznLnx* gives you **all** of the material in each chapter in exam form, not just samples, so you can be sure to nail your exam.

MECHANICAL

The MznLnx Exam Prep series creates exams that will help you learn the subject matter as well as test you on your understanding. Each question is designed to help you master the concept. Just working through the exams, you gain an understanding of the subject--its a simple mechanical process that produces success.

INTEGRATED STUDY GUIDE AND REVIEW

MznLnx is not just a set of exams designed to test you, its also a comprehensive review of the subject content. Each exam question is also a review of the concept, making sure that you will get the answer correct without having to go to other sources of material. You learn as you go! Its the easiest way to pass an exam.

HUMOR

Studying can be tedious and dry. MznLnx's instructional design includes moderate humor within the exam questions on occassion, to break the tedium and revitalize the brain

Chapter 1. Introduction to Macroeconomics

1. The GDP gap or the _____ is the difference between potential GDP and actual GDP or actual output. The calculation for the _____ is Y-Y* where Y* is potential output and Y is actual output. If this calculation yields a positive number it is called an expansionary gap and indicates an economy in expansion; if the calculation yields a negative number it is called a recessionary gap and indicates an economy in recession.
   - a. Output gap
   - b. AD-IA Model
   - c. ACCRA Cost of Living Index
   - d. ACEA agreement

2. _____, 1st Baron Keynes was a renowned economist from Britain whose many ideas on economic and political theories as well as on many governments' monetary policies influenced America. He advocated a government that played an active role in the lives of people regarding business, economy, etc. In this role, the government would use fiscal measures to reduce the consequences of recessions, economic depressions and booms.
   - a. Adolph Fischer
   - b. John Maynard Keynes
   - c. Adam Smith
   - d. Adolf Hitler

3. The _____ says that it is naïve to try to predict the effects of a change in economic policy entirely on the basis of relationships observed in historical data, especially highly aggregated historical data.

   The basic idea pre-dates Lucas's contribution, but in a 1976 paper he drove home the point that this simple notion invalidated policy advice based on conclusions drawn from estimated system of equation models. Because the parameters of those models were not structural - that is, not policy-invariant - they would necessarily change whenever policy - the rules of the game - was changed.
   - a. Peak-load pricing
   - b. Demand management
   - c. Lucas critique
   - d. Dahrendorf hypothesis

4. _____ is a branch of economics that deals with the performance, structure, and behavior of a national or regional economy as a whole. Along with microeconomics, _____ is one of the two most general fields in economics. It is the study of the behavior and decision-making of entire economies.
   - a. Nominal value
   - b. New Trade Theory
   - c. Tobit model
   - d. Macroeconomics

5. _____ is a branch of economics that studies how individuals, households and firms and some states make decisions to allocate limited resources, typically in markets where goods or services are being bought and sold. _____ examines how these decisions and behaviours affect the supply and demand for goods and services, which determines prices; and how prices, in turn, determine the supply and demand of goods and services.

   Whereas macroeconomics involves the 'sum total of economic activity, dealing with the issues of growth, inflation and unemployment, and with national economic policies relating to these issues' and the effects of government actions on them.
   - a. New Keynesian economics
   - b. Microeconomics
   - c. Recession
   - d. Countercyclical

6. In finance, the _____s between two currencies specifies how much one currency is worth in terms of the other. It is the value of a foreign natione;s currency in terms of the home natione;s currency. For example an _____ of 102 Japanese yen to the United States dollar means that JPY 102 is worth the same as USD 1.

Chapter 1. Introduction to Macroeconomics

a. interbank market
b. ACCRA Cost of Living Index
c. ACEA agreement
d. Exchange rate

7. The traditional definition of _____ is considered to be the ability to use language to read, write, listen, and speak. In modern contexts, the word refers to reading and writing at a level adequate for communication, or at a level that lets one understand and communicate ideas in a literate society, so as to take part in that society. The United Nations Educational, Scientific and Cultural Organization (UNESCO) has drafted the following definition: "_____' is the ability to identify, understand, interpret, create, communicate, compute and use printed and written materials associated with varying contexts.

a. 100-year flood
b. 130-30 fund
c. Literacy
d. 1921 recession

8. _____s is the social science that studies the production, distribution, and consumption of goods and services. The term _____s comes from the Ancient Greek οἰκονομῐ́α from οἶκος (oikos, 'house') + νόμος (nomos, 'custom' or 'law'), hence 'rules of the house(hold)'. Current _____ models developed out of the broader field of political economy in the late 19th century, owing to a desire to use an empirical approach more akin to the physical sciences.

a. Inflation
b. Opportunity cost
c. Energy economics
d. Economic

9. _____ refers to the actions that governments take in the economic field. It covers the systems for setting interest rates and government deficit as well as the labour market, national ownership, and many other areas of government.

Such policies are often influenced by international institutions like the International Monetary Fund or World Bank as well as political beliefs and the consequent policies of parties.

a. ACEA agreement
b. ACCRA Cost of Living Index
c. AD-IA Model
d. Economic policy

10. The term _____ refers to government debt, expenditures and revenues, or to finance (particularly financial revenue) in general.

- _____ deficit is the budget deficit of federal or local government
- _____ policy is the discretionary spending of governments. Contrasts with monetary policy.
- _____ year and _____ quarter are reporting periods for firms and other agencies.

a. Bucket shop
b. Procter ' Gamble
c. Drawdown
d. Fiscal

11. In economics, _____ is the use of government spending and revenue collection to influence the economy.

_____ can be contrasted with the other main type of economic policy, monetary policy, which attempts to stabilize the economy by controlling interest rates and the supply of money. The two main instruments of _____ are government spending and taxation.

a. Sustainable investment rule
b. 100-year flood
c. Fiscalism
d. Fiscal policy

12. In economic models, the _____ time frame assumes no fixed factors of production. Firms can enter or leave the marketplace, and the cost (and availability) of land, labor, raw materials, and capital goods can be assumed to vary. In contrast, in the short-run time frame, certain factors are assumed to be fixed, because there is not sufficient time for them to change.
   a. Price/performance ratio
   b. Productivity world
   c. Diseconomies of scale
   d. Long-run

13. _____ is the process by which the government, central bank (ii) availability of money, and (iii) cost of money or rate of interest, in order to attain a set of objectives oriented towards the growth and stability of the economy. Monetary theory provides insight into how to craft optimal _____.

_____ is referred to as either being an expansionary policy where an expansionary policy increases the total supply of money in the economy, and a contractionary policy decreases the total money supply.

   a. 1921 recession
   b. 100-year flood
   c. 130-30 fund
   d. Monetary policy

14. A _____ is a package or set of measures introduced to stabilise a financial system or economy. The term can refer to policies in two distinct sets of circumstances: business cycle stabilization and crisis stabilization.

Stabilization can refer to correcting the normal behavior of the business cycle.

   a. Stabilization policy
   b. Capacity Development
   c. New International Economic Order
   d. Volunteers for Economic Growth Alliance

15. _____ is the increase in the amount of the goods and services produced by an economy over time. It is conventionally measured as the percent rate of increase in real gross domestic product, or real GDP. Growth is usually calculated in real terms, i.e. inflation-adjusted terms, in order to net out the effect of inflation on the price of the goods and services produced.
   a. ACCRA Cost of Living Index
   b. ACEA agreement
   c. AD-IA Model
   d. Economic growth

16. _____ is an economic situation in which inflation and economic stagnation occur simultaneously and remain unchecked for a period of time. The portmanteau _____ is generally attributed to British politician Iain Macleod, who coined the term in a speech to Parliament in 1965. The concept is notable partly because, in postwar macroeconomic theory, inflation and recession were regarded as mutually exclusive, and also because _____ has generally proven to be difficult and costly to eradicate once it gets started.
   a. Real interest rate
   b. Stagflation
   c. Chronic inflation
   d. Price/wage spiral

Chapter 1. Introduction to Macroeconomics

17. The term _____ refers to economy-wide fluctuations in production or economic activity over several months or years. These fluctuations occur around a long-term growth trend, and typically involve shifts over time between periods of relatively rapid economic growth (expansion or boom), and periods of relative stagnation or decline (contraction or recession.)

These fluctuations are often measured using the growth rate of real gross domestic product.

- a. Tobit model
- b. Business cycle
- c. Nominal value
- d. Consumer theory

18. _____ is that which is owed; usually referencing assets owed, but the term can also cover moral obligations and other interactions not requiring money. In the case of assets, _____ is a means of using future purchasing power in the present before a summation has been earned. Some companies and corporations use _____ as a part of their overall corporate finance strategy.
- a. Hard money loan
- b. Collateral Management
- c. Debt
- d. Debenture

19. The _____ was a worldwide economic downturn starting in most places in 1929 and ending at different times in the 1930s or early 1940s for different countries. It was the largest and most important economic depression in the 20th century, and is used in the 21st century as an example of how far the world's economy can fall. The _____ originated in the United States; historians most often use as a starting date the stock market crash on October 29, 1929, known as Black Tuesday.
- a. Jarrow March
- b. Wall Street Crash of 1929
- c. British Empire Economic Conference
- d. Great Depression

20. The _____ is a concept of economic activity developed in particular by Milton Friedman and Edmund Phelps in the 1960s, both recipients of the Nobel prize in economics. In both cases, the development of the concept is cited as a main motivation behind the prize. It represents the hypothetical unemployment rate consistent with aggregate production being at the 'long-run' level.
- a. Robertson lag
- b. Natural rate of unemployment
- c. Real Business Cycle Theory
- d. Romer Model

21. In economics, the _____ is a historical inverse relation between the rate of unemployment and the rate of inflation in an economy. Stated simply, the lower the unemployment in an economy, the higher the rate of increase in nominal wages in the economy. Rate of Change of Wages against Unemployment, United Kingdom 1913-1948 from Phillips (1958)

William Phillips, a New Zealand born economist, wrote a paper in 1958 titled The Relationship between Unemployment and the Rate of Change of Money Wages in the United Kingdom 1861-1957, which was published in the quarterly journal Economica.

- a. Phillips curve
- b. Lorenz curve
- c. Demand curve
- d. Cost curve

22. In microeconomics, _____ is quite simply the conversion of inputs into outputs. It is an economic process that uses resources to create a good or service that is suitable for exchange. This can include manufacturing, storing, shipping, and packaging.

Chapter 1. Introduction to Macroeconomics

a. MET
c. Red Guards

b. Solved
d. Production

23. In economics, _____ is the total supply of goods and services produced by a national economy during a specific time period. It is the total amount of goods and services in the economy available at all possible price levels.

a. Aggregation problem
c. Aggregate supply

b. Aggregate demand
d. Aggregate expenditure

24. In economics, _____ is a sustained decrease in the general price level of goods and services. _____ occurs when the annual inflation rate falls below zero percent, resulting in an increase in the real value of money -- a negative inflation rate. This should not be confused with disinflation, a slow-down in the inflation rate (i.e. when the inflation decreases, but still remains positive.)

a. Tobit model
c. Price revolution

b. Deflation
d. Literacy rate

25. _____ is a decrease in the rate of inflation. This phase of the business cycle, in which retailers can no longer pass on higher prices to their customers, often occurs during a recession. In contrast, deflation occurs when prices are actually dropping.

a. Disinflation
c. Reflation

b. Mundell-Tobin effect
d. Stealth inflation

26. The _____ is a monetary system in which a region's common medium of exchange are paper notes that are normally freely convertible into pre-set, fixed quantities of gold. The _____ is not currently used by any government, having been replaced completely by fiat currency. Gold certificates were used as paper currency in the United States from 1882 to 1933, these certificates were freely convertable into gold coins.

In the 1790s Britain suffered a massive shortage of silver coinage and ceased to mint larger silver coins.

a. 1921 recession
c. 100-year flood

b. 130-30 fund
d. Gold standard

27. _____ in economics and business is the result of an exchange and from that trade we assign a numerical monetary value to a good, service or asset. If Alice trades Bob 4 apples for an orange, the _____ of an orange is 4 apples. Inversely, the _____ of an apple is 1/4 oranges.

a. Price war
c. Price book

b. Premium pricing
d. Price

28. A _____ is a hypothetical measure of overall prices for some set of goods and services, in a given region during a given interval, normalized relative to some base set. Typically, a _____ is approximated with a price index.

The classical dichotomy is the assumption that there is a relatively clean distinction between overall increases or decreases in prices and underlying, e;reale; economic variables.

a. Discretionary spending
c. Price elasticity of supply

b. Discouraged worker
d. Price level

Chapter 1. Introduction to Macroeconomics

29. In economics, a _____ is a general slowdown in economic activity over a sustained period of time, or a business cycle contraction. During _____s, many macroeconomic indicators vary in a similar way. Production as measured by Gross Domestic Product (GDP), employment, investment spending, capacity utilization, household incomes and business profits all fall during _____s.
   a. Recession
   b. Monetary economics
   c. Leading indicators
   d. Treasury View

30. The _____ is 'the basic residential unit in which economic production, consumption, inheritance, child rearing, and shelter are organized and carried out'; [the _____] 'may or may not be synonymous with family'.

   The _____ is the basic unit of analysis in many social, microeconomic and government models. The term refers to all individuals who live in the same dwelling.

   a. Family economics
   b. 130-30 fund
   c. 100-year flood
   d. Household

31. _____ and Keynesian Theory) is a macroeconomic theory based on the ideas of 20th-century British economist John Maynard Keynes. _____ argues that private sector decisions sometimes lead to inefficient macroeconomic outcomes and therefore advocates active policy responses by the public sector, including monetary policy actions by the central bank and fiscal policy actions by the government to stabilize output over the business cycle.

   The theories forming the basis of _____ were first presented in The General Theory of Employment, Interest and Money, published in 1936.

   a. Deflation
   b. Rational choice theory
   c. Market failure
   d. Keynesian economics

32. The term _____ used by politicians and economists to measure broader social effects of policies, such as the effect that reducing graffiti or vandalism might have on the wellbeing of local residents.

   Two widely known measures of a country's liveability are the Economist Intelligence Unit's _____ index and the Mercer Quality of Living Survey. Both measures calculate the liveability of countries around the world through a combination of subjective life-satisfaction surveys and objective determinants of _____ such as divorce rates, safety, and infrastructure.

   a. Quality of life
   b. Culture of capitalism
   c. Genuine progress indicator
   d. Compliance cost

33. The _____ is the largest national economy in the world. Its gross domestic product (GDP) was estimated as $14.2 trillion in 2008. The U.S. economy maintains a high level of output per person (GDP per capita, $46,800 in 2008, ranked at around number ten in the world.)
   a. AD-IA Model
   b. Economy of the United States
   c. ACCRA Cost of Living Index
   d. ACEA agreement

Chapter 1. Introduction to Macroeconomics   7

34. In economics, the term _____ of income or _____ refers to a simple economic model which describes the reciprocal circulation of income between producers and consumers. In the _____ model, the inter-dependent entities of producer and consumer are referred to as 'firms' and 'households' respectively and provide each other with factors in order to facilitate the flow of income. Firms provide consumers with goods and services in exchange for consumer expenditure and 'factors of production' from households.
   a. Circular flow
   b. 1921 recession
   c. 100-year flood
   d. 130-30 fund

35. _____ is a common concept in economics, and gives rise to derived concepts such as consumer debt. Generally _____ is defined by opposition to production. But the precise definition can vary because different schools of economists define production quite differently.
   a. Foreclosure data providers
   b. Cash or share options
   c. Federal Reserve Bank Notes
   d. Consumption

36. _____ is a branch of applied statistics focusing on the collection, processing, compilation and dissemination of statistics concerning the economy of a region, a country or a group of countries. _____ is also referred as a subtopic of official statistics, since most of the _____ are produced by official organizations (e.g. statistical institutes, intergovernmental organizations such as United Nations, European Union or OECD, central banks, ministries, etc.). _____ provide the empirical data needed in economic research (econometrics) and they are the basis for decision and economic policy making.
   a. Economic statistics
   b. Event study
   c. Indirect least squares
   d. ACCRA Cost of Living Index

37. In economics, the term _____ refers to the microeconomic analysis of the behavior of individual agents such as households or firms that underpins a macroeconomic theory (Barro, 1993, Glossary, p. 594.)

Most early macroeconomic models, including early Keynesian models, were based on hypotheses about relationships between aggregate quantities, such as aggregate output, employment, consumption, and investment.

   a. Technology shock
   b. Minimum wage
   c. Microfoundations
   d. Fiscal adjustment

38. A variety of measures of _____ and output are used in economics to estimate total economic activity in a country or region, including gross domestic product (GDP), gross national product (GNP), and net _____

There are three main ways of calculating these numbers; the output approach, the income approach and the expenditure approach. In theory, the three must yield the same, because total expenditures on goods and services must equal the total income paid to the producers (Gnational income), and that must also equal the total value of the output of goods and services (GNP.)

   a. Volume index
   b. GNI per capita
   c. Gross world product
   d. National income

39. _____ use double-entry accounting to report the monetary value and sources of output produced in a country and the distribution of incomes that production generates. Data are available at the national and industry levels.

Chapter 1. Introduction to Macroeconomics

The NIPA summarizes national income on the left (debit, revenue) side and national product on the right (credit, expense) side of a two-column accounting report.

a. Current account
b. Net national product
c. Gross private domestic investment
d. National income and product accounts

40. In economics _____s are goods that are ultimately consumed rather than used in the production of another good. For example, a car sold to a consumer is a _____; the components such as tires sold to the car manufacturer are not; they are intermediate goods used to make the _____.

When used in measures of national income and output the term _____s only includes new goods.

a. Goods and services
b. Luxury good
c. Substitute good
d. Final good

41. The _____ or gross domestic income (GDI), a basic measure of an economy's economic performance, is the market value of all final goods and services produced within the borders of a nation in a year. _____ can be defined in three ways, all of which are conceptually identical. First, it is equal to the total expenditures for all final goods and services produced within the country in a stipulated period of time (usually a 365-day year.)
a. Countercyclical
b. Market structure
c. Monopolistic competition
d. Gross domestic product

42. A _____ is an object whose consumption increases the utility of the consumer, for which the quantity demanded exceeds the quantity supplied at zero price. _____s are usually modeled as having diminishing marginal utility. The first individual purchase has high utility; the second has less.
a. Composite good
b. Good
c. Merit good
d. Pie method

43. In economics, economic output is divided into physical goods and intangible services. Consumption of _____ is assumed to produce utility. It is often used when referring to a _____ Tax.
a. Composite good
b. Private good
c. Manufactured goods
d. Goods and services

44. An _____, in economics, is the amount by which the real Gross domestic product exceeds potential GDP. The real GDP is also known as GDP 'adjusted for inflation', 'constant prices' GDP or 'constant dollar' GDP, because it measures the aggregate output in a country's income accounts in a given year, expressed in base-year prices. On the other hand, the potential GDP is the quantity of real GDP when a country's economy is at full-employment.
a. ACCRA Cost of Living Index
b. AD-IA Model
c. ACEA agreement
d. Inflationary gap

45. The _____, a unit of the United States Department of Labor, is the principal fact-finding agency for the U.S. government in the broad field of labor economics and statistics. The BLS is an independent national statistical agency that collects, processes, analyzes, and disseminates essential statistical data to the American public, the U.S. Congress, other Federal agencies, State and local governments, business, and labor representatives. The BLS also serves as a statistical resource to the Department of Labor.

Chapter 1. Introduction to Macroeconomics 9

a. Gross national product
b. Gross Regional Product
c. Gross world product
d. Bureau of Labor Statistics

46. Economists distinguish between various types of unemployment, including _____, frictional unemployment, structural unemployment and classical unemployment. Some additional types of unemployment that are occasionally mentioned are seasonal unemployment, hardcore unemployment, and hidden unemployment. Real-world unemployment may combine different types.

a. Types of unemployment
b. Cyclical unemployment
c. Structural unemployment
d. Seasonal unemployment

47. Economists distinguish between various types of unemployment, including cyclical unemployment, _____, structural unemployment and classical unemployment. Some additional types of unemployment that are occasionally mentioned are seasonal unemployment, hardcore unemployment, and hidden unemployment. Real-world unemployment may combine different types.

a. Seasonal unemployment
b. Structural unemployment
c. Types of unemployment
d. Frictional unemployment

48. Unemployment occurs when a person is available to work and seeking work but currently without work. The prevalence of unemployment is usually measured using the _____, which is defined as the percentage of those in the labor force who are unemployed. The _____ is also used in economic studies and economic indexes such as the United States' Conference Board's Index of Leading Indicators as a measure of the state of the macroeconomics.

a. ACEA agreement
b. Unemployment rate
c. ACCRA Cost of Living Index
d. AD-IA Model

49. In economics, _____ is a rise in the general level of prices of goods and services in an economy over a period of time. When the general price level rises, each unit of currency buys fewer goods and services; consequently, _____ is also a decline in the real value of money--a loss of purchasing power in the medium of exchange which is also the monetary unit of account in the economy. A chief measure of general price-level _____ is the general _____ rate, which is the percentage change in a general price index (normally the Consumer Price Index) over time.

a. Opportunity cost
b. Inflation
c. Energy economics
d. Economic

50. In economics, the _____ is a measure of inflation, the rate of increase of a price index (for example, a consumer price index.)It is the percentage rate of change in price level over time. The rate of decrease in the purchasing power of money is approximately equal.

It's used to calculate the real interest rate, as well as real increases in wages, and official measurements of this rate act as input variables to COLA adjustments and Inflation derivatives prices.

a. Interest rate option
b. Inflation rate
c. Edgeworth paradox
d. Equity value

Chapter 1. Introduction to Macroeconomics

51. _____ was a global military conflict which involved a majority of the world's nations, including all of the great powers, organized into two opposing military alliances: the Allies and the Axis. The war involved the mobilization of over 100 million military personnel, making it the most widespread war in history. In a state of 'total war', the major participants placed their entire economic, industrial, and scientific capabilities at the service of the war effort, erasing the distinction between civilian and military resources.

   a. 100-year flood
   b. 1921 recession
   c. World War II
   d. 130-30 fund

52. Necessary _____s:

If x is a necessary _____ of y, then the presence of y necessarily implies the presence of x. The presence of x, however, does not imply that y will occur.

Sufficient _____s:

If x is a sufficient _____ of y, then the presence of x necessarily implies the presence of y.

   a. Political philosophy
   b. Cause
   c. Philosophy of economics
   d. Materialism

53. _____ is a broad label that refers to any individuals or households that use goods and services generated within the economy. The concept of a _____ is used in different contexts, so that the usage and significance of the term may vary.

Typically when business people and economists talk of _____s they are talking about person as _____, an aggregated commodity item with little individuality other than that expressed in the buy/not-buy decision.

   a. Consumer
   b. 1921 recession
   c. 100-year flood
   d. 130-30 fund

54. A _____ is a measure of the average price of consumer goods and services purchased by households. A _____ measures a price change for a constant market basket of goods and services from one period to the next within the same area (city, region, or nation.) It is a price index determined by measuring the price of a standard group of goods meant to represent the typical market basket of a typical urban consumer.

   a. Cost-of-living index
   b. Consumer price index
   c. CPI
   d. Lipstick index

55. A _____ is a normalized average (typically a weighted average) of prices for a given class of goods or services in a given region, during a given interval of time. It is a statistic designed to help to compare how these prices, taken as a whole, differ between time periods or geographical locations.

Price indices have several potential uses.

Chapter 1. Introduction to Macroeconomics

a. Two-part tariff
b. Product sabotage
c. Transactional Net Margin Method
d. Price index

56. In economics, a _____ is a person of legal employment age who is not actively seeking employment. This is usually due to the fact that an individual has given up looking or has had no success in finding a job, hence the term 'discouraged.' Their belief may derive from a variety of factors including: a shortage of jobs in their locality or line of work; perceived discrimination for reasons such as age, race, sex and religion; a lack of necessary skills, training or experience; or, a chronic illness or disability. Some _____s, however, are voluntarily unemployed such as stay-at-home parents, pregnant mothers, and will beneficiaries.

a. Hedonimetry
b. Demand side economics
c. Relative income hypothesis
d. Discouraged worker

57. In economics, _____ is inflation that is very high or 'out of control', a condition in which prices increase rapidly as a currency loses its value. Definitions used by the media vary from a cumulative inflation rate over three years approaching 100% to 'inflation exceeding 50% a month.' In informal usage the term is often applied to much lower rates. As a rule of thumb, normal inflation is reported per year, but _____ is often reported for much shorter intervals, often per month.

a. 100-year flood
b. 130-30 fund
c. 1921 recession
d. Hyperinflation

58. In economics, a _____ is a monetary-policy rule that stipulates how much the central bank would or should change the nominal interest rate in response to divergences of actual inflation rates from target inflation rates and of actual Gross Domestic Product (GDP) from potential GDP. It was first proposed by the by U.S. economist John B. Taylor in 1993. The rule can be written as follows:

$$i_t = \pi_t + r_t^* + a_\pi(\pi_t - \pi_t^*) + a_y(y_t - \bar{y}_t).$$

In this equation, i_t is the target short-term nominal interest rate (e.g. the federal funds rate in the US), π_t is the rate of inflation as measured by the GDP deflator, π_t^* is the desired rate of inflation, r_t^* is the assumed equilibrium real interest rate, y_t is the logarithm of real GDP, and $\bar{y}_t$ is the logarithm of potential output, as determined by a linear trend.

a. Term Securities Lending Facility
b. Fed Funds Probability
c. Federal Reserve Banks
d. Taylor rule

12   *Chapter 1. Introduction to Macroeconomics*

59.   A _____ is:

- Rewrite _____, in generative grammar and computer science
- Standardization, a formal and widely-accepted statement, fact, definition, or qualification
- Operation, a determinate _____ for performing a mathematical operation and obtaining a certain result (Mathematics, Logic)
    - Unary operation
    - Binary operation
- _____ of inference, a function from sets of formulae to formulae (Mathematics, Logic)
- _____ of thumb, principle with broad application that is not intended to be strictly accurate or reliable for every situation. Also often simply referred to as a _____
- Moral, an atomic element of a moral code for guiding choices in human behavior
- Heuristic, a quantized '_____' which shows a tendency or probability for successful function
- A regulation, as in sports
- A Production _____, as in computer science
- Procedural law, a _____ set governing the application of laws to cases
    - A law, which may informally be called a '_____'
    - A court ruling, a decision by a court
- In the U.S. Government, a regulation mandated by Congress, but written or expanded upon by the Executive Branch.
- Norm (sociology), an informal but widely accepted _____, concept, truth, definition, or qualification (social norms, legal norms, coding norms)
- Norm (philosophy), a kind of sentence or a reason to act, feel or believe
- 'Rulership' is the concept of governance by a government:
    - Military _____, governance by a military body
    - Monastic _____, a collection of precepts that guides the life of monks or nuns in a religious order where the superior holds the place of Christ
- Slide _____

- '_____,' a song by Ayumi Hamasaki
- '_____,' a song by rapper Nas
- '_____s,' an album by the band The Whitest Boy Alive
- _____s: Pyaar Ka Superhit Formula, a 2003 Bollywood film
- ruler, an instrument for measuring lengths
- _____, a component of an astrolabe, circumferator or similar instrument
- The _____s, a bestselling self-help book
- _____ Project (Run Up-to-date Linux Everywhere), a project that aims to use up-to-date Linux software on old PCs
- _____ engine, a software system that helps managing business _____s
- Ja _____, a hip hop artist
    - R.U.L.E., a 2005 greatest hits album by rapper Ja _____
- '_____s,' a KMFDM song

a. Demand   b. Technocracy
c. Procter ' Gamble   d. Rule

60. In economics, _____ is the total demand for final goods and services in the economy (Y) at a given time and price level. It is the amount of goods and services in the economy that will be purchased at all possible price levels. This is the demand for the gross domestic product of a country when inventory levels are static.
- a. Aggregate demand
- b. Aggregation problem
- c. Aggregate expenditure
- d. Aggregate supply

61. In finance and economics _____ or nominal rate of interest refers to the rate of interest before adjustment for inflation (in contrast with the real interest rate); or, for interest rates 'as stated' without adjustment for the full effect of compounding (also referred to as the nominal annual rate.) An interest rate is called nominal if the frequency of compounding (e.g. a month) is not identical to the basic time unit (normally a year.)

The real interest rate includes compensation for the lender's lost value due to inflation, whereas the _____ excludes inflation.

- a. Fixed interest
- b. Nominal interest rate
- c. Risk-free interest rate
- d. London Interbank Offered Rate

62. _____ refers to a business or organization attempting to acquire goods or services to accomplish the goals of the enterprise. Though there are several organizations that attempt to set standards in the _____ process, processes can vary greatly between organizations. Typically the word '_____' is not used interchangeably with the word 'procurement', since procurement typically includes Expediting, Supplier Quality, and Traffic and Logistics (T'L) in addition to _____.
- a. Free port
- b. Purchasing
- c. 130-30 fund
- d. 100-year flood

63. _____ is the number of goods/services that can be purchased with a unit of currency. For example, if you had taken one dollar to a store in the 1950s, you would have been able to buy a greater number of items than you would today, indicating that you would have had a greater _____ in the 1950s. Currency can be either a commodity money, like gold or silver, or fiat currency like US dollars.
- a. Human Poverty Index
- b. Genuine progress indicator
- c. Compliance cost
- d. Purchasing power

64. The '_____' is approximately the nominal interest rate minus the inflation rate Since the inflation rate over the course of a loan is not known initially, volatility in inflation represents a risk to both the lender and the borrower.

In economics and finance, an individual who lends money for repayment at a later point in time expects to be compensated for the time value of money, or not having the use of that money while it is lent.

- a. Cost-push inflation
- b. Real interest rate
- c. Reflation
- d. Core inflation

Chapter 1. Introduction to Macroeconomics

65. Economics:

- _____, the desire to own something and the ability to pay for it
- _____ curve, a graphic representation of a _____ schedule
- _____ deposit, the money in checking accounts
- _____ pull theory, the theory that inflation occurs when _____ for goods and services exceeds existing supplies
- _____ schedule, a table that lists the quantity of a good a person will buy it each different price
- _____ side economics, the school of economics at believes government spending and tax cuts open economy by raising _____

   a. Production   b. Variability
   c. Demand   d. McKesson ' Robbins scandal

66. _____ is a fee paid on borrowed assets. It is the price paid for the use of borrowed money, or, money earned by deposited funds. Assets that are sometimes lent with _____ include money, shares, consumer goods through hire purchase, major assets such as aircraft, and even entire factories in finance lease arrangements.

   a. Asset protection   b. Insolvency
   c. Internal debt   d. Interest

67. An _____ is the price a borrower pays for the use of money they do not own, for instance a small company might borrow from a bank to kick start their business, and the return a lender receives for deferring the use of funds, by lending it to the borrower. _____s are normally expressed as a percentage rate over the period of one year.

_____s targets are also a vital tool of monetary policy and are used to control variables like investment, inflation, and unemployment.

   a. Arrow-Debreu model   b. Enterprise value
   c. ACCRA Cost of Living Index   d. Interest rate

68. _____ is an American economist and was the Chairman of the Federal Reserve of the United States from 1987 to 2006. He currently works as a private advisor and providing consulting for firms through his company, Greenspan Associates LLC.

First appointed Federal Reserve chairman by President Ronald Reagan in August 1987, he was reappointed at successive four-year intervals until retiring on January 31, 2006 after the second-longest tenure in the position.

   a. Alan Greenspan   b. Adolph Fischer
   c. Adolf Hitler   d. Adam Smith

69. A United States Treasury security is a government debt issued by the United States Department of the Treasury through the Bureau of the Public Debt. Treasury securities are the debt financing instruments of the United States Federal government, and they are often referred to simply as Treasuries. There are four types of marketable treasury securities: _____, Treasury notes, Treasury bonds, and Treasury Inflation Protected Securities (TIPS).

a. Treasury bills
b. Debt to Assets
c. Lawcards
d. Labour battalions

70. _____ is an assumption used in many contemporary macroeconomic models, and also in other areas of contemporary economics and game theory and in other applications of rational choice theory.

Since most macroeconomic models today study decisions over many periods, the expectations of workers, consumers, and firms about future economic conditions are an essential part of the model. How to model these expectations has long been controversial, and it is well known that the macroeconomic predictions of the model may differ depending on the assumptions made about expectations

a. Potential output
b. Rational expectations
c. Balanced-growth equilibrium
d. Minimum wage

71. A _____ is a public market for the trading of company stock and derivatives at an agreed price; these are securities listed on a stock exchange as well as those only traded privately.

The size of the world _____ was estimated at about $36.6 trillion US at the beginning of October 2008 . The total world derivatives market has been estimated at about $791 trillion face or nominal value, 11 times the size of the entire world economy.

a. Adolf Hitler
b. Adolph Fischer
c. Adam Smith
d. Stock market

72. A _____ is a type of economic bubble taking place in stock markets when price of stocks rise and become overvalued by any measure of stock valuation.

The existence of _____s is at odds with the assumptions of efficient market theory which assumes rational investor behaviour. Behavioral finance theory attribute _____s to cognitive biases that lead to groupthink and herd behavior.

a. Scrip issue
b. Fill or kill
c. Growth investing
d. Stock market bubble

73. In finance, _____ refers to quote and trade related-data associated with equity, fixed-income, financial derivatives, currency, and other investment instruments. The term _____ traditionally refers to numerical price data, reported from trading venues, such as stock exchanges. The price data is attached to a ticker symbol and additional data about the trade.

a. Payment for order flow
b. Market anomaly
c. Speculation
d. Market data

74. A _____ is a method of measuring a section of the stock market. Many indices are cited by news or financial services firms and are used to benchmark the performance of portfolios such as mutual funds.

Stock market indices may be classed in many ways.

a. Stock market bubble
b. Stock market index
c. Scrip issue
d. Lock up period

75. _____ is a term used in accounting relating to the increase in value of an asset. In this sense it is the reverse of depreciation, which measures the fall in value of assets over their normal life-time.

_____ is a rise of a currency in a floating exchange rate.

a. ACEA agreement
b. AD-IA Model
c. ACCRA Cost of Living Index
d. Appreciation

76. The _____ of monetary management established the rules for commercial and financial relations among the world's major industrial states in the mid 20th Century. The _____ was the first example of a fully negotiated monetary order intended to govern monetary relations among independent nation-states.

Preparing to rebuild the international economic system as World War II was still raging, 730 delegates from all 44 Allied nations gathered at the Mount Washington Hotel in Bretton Woods, New Hampshire, United States, for the United Nations Monetary and Financial Conference.

a. 130-30 fund
b. 100-year flood
c. 1921 recession
d. Bretton Woods system

77. _____ is a term used in accounting, economics and finance to spread the cost of an asset over the span of several years.

In simple words we can say that _____ is the reduction in the value of an asset due to usage, passage of time, wear and tear, technological outdating or obsolescence, depletion, inadequacy, rot, rust, decay or other such factors.

In accounting, _____ is a term used to describe any method of attributing the historical or purchase cost of an asset across its useful life, roughly corresponding to normal wear and tear.

a. Net income per employee
b. Salvage value
c. Depreciation
d. Historical cost

78. _____ is a specific term used in companies' financial reporting from the company-whole point of view. Because that use excludes the effects of changing ownership interest, an economic measure of _____ is necessary for financial analysis from the shareholders' point of view

_____ is defined by the Financial Accounting Standards Board, or FASB, as e;the change in equity [net assets] of a business enterprise during a period from transactions and other events and circumstances from nonowner sources. It includes all changes in equity during a period except those resulting from investments by owners and distributions to owners.e;

_____ is the sum of net income and other items that must bypass the income statement because they have not been realized, including items like an unrealized holding gain or loss from available for sale securities and foreign currency translation gains or losses.

a. Real income
b. Windfall gain
c. Comprehensive income
d. Net national income

79. _____ are the earnings returned on the initial investment amount.

In the US, the Financial Accounting Standards Board (FASB) requires companies' income statements to report _____ for each of the major categories of the income statement: continuing operations, discontinued operations, extraordinary items, and net income.

The _____ formula does not include preferred dividends for categories outside of continued operations and net income.

a. Earnings per share
b. Asset turnover
c. AlphaIC
d. Operating leverage

80. In economics, an _____ is any good or commodity, transported from one country to another country in a legitimate fashion, typically for use in trade. _____ goods or services are provided to foreign consumers by domestic producers. _____ is an important part of international trade.

a. ACEA agreement
b. AD-IA Model
c. ACCRA Cost of Living Index
d. Export

81. A _____, sometimes called a pegged exchange rate, is a type of exchange rate regime wherein a currency's value is matched to the value of another single currency or to a basket of other currencies such as gold.

A _____ is usually used to stabilize the value of a currency, vis-a-vis the currency it is pegged to. This facilitates trade and investments between the two countries, and is especially useful for small economies where external trade forms a large part of their GDP.

a. Monetary economics
b. Law of supply
c. Fixed exchange rate
d. Leading indicators

82. A _____ or a flexible exchange rate is a type of exchange rate regime wherein a currency's value is allowed to fluctuate according to the foreign exchange market. A currency that uses a _____ is known as a floating currency. The opposite of a _____ is a fixed exchange rate.

a. Foreign exchange market
b. Floating exchange rate
c. Trade Weighted US dollar Index
d. Floating currency

83. In economics, an _____ is any good (e.g. a commodity) or service brought into one country from another country in a legitimate fashion, typically for use in trade. It is a good that is brought in from another country for sale. _____ goods or services are provided to domestic consumers by foreign producers. An _____ in the receiving country is an export to the sending country.

a. Incoterms
b. Economic integration
c. Import quota
d. Import

84. _____ is exchange of capital, goods, and services across international borders or territories. In most countries, it represents a significant share of gross domestic product (GDP.) While _____ has been present throughout much of history , its economic, social, and political importance has been on the rise in recent centuries.
   a. International trade
   b. Import license
   c. Intra-industry trade
   d. Incoterms

85. '_____' is a phrase used by former Federal Reserve Board Chairman Alan Greenspan in a speech given at the American Enterprise Institute during the stock market boom of the 1990s. The phrase was interpreted by financial pundits as a typical extraordinary economy.

Greenspan's comment was made on December 5, 1996 (emphasis added in excerpt):

The presence of the short comment--not repeated by Greenspan since--within a rather dry and complex speech would not normally have been so memorable; however, it was followed by immediate slumps in stock markets worldwide, provoking a strong reaction in financial circles and making its way into colloquial speech.

   a. Irrational exuberance
   b. ACCRA Cost of Living Index
   c. AD-IA Model
   d. ACEA agreement

86. _____ is a concept found in moral, political, and bioethical philosophy. Within these contexts, it refers to the capacity of a rational individual to make an informed, un-coerced decision. In moral and political philosophy, _____ is often used as the basis for determining moral responsibility for one's actions.
   a. ACEA agreement
   b. ACCRA Cost of Living Index
   c. Autonomy
   d. AD-IA Model

87. The _____ is the central banking system of the United States. Created in 1913 by the enactment of the Federal Reserve Act (signed by Woodrow Wilson), it is a quasi-public and quasi-private (government entity with private components) banking system that comprises (1) the presidentially appointed Board of Governors of the _____ in Washington, D.C.; (2) the Federal Open Market Committee; (3) twelve regional Federal Reserve Banks located in major cities throughout the nation acting as fiscal agents for the U.S. Treasury, each with its own nine-member board of directors; (4) numerous other private U.S. member banks, which subscribe to required amounts of non-transferable stock in their regional Federal Reserve Banks; and (5) various advisory councils. Since February 2006, Ben Bernanke has served as the Chairman of the Board of Governors of the _____.
   a. Monetary Policy Report to the Congress
   b. Term auction facility
   c. Federal Reserve System Open Market Account
   d. Federal Reserve System

88. To _____ is to impose a financial charge or other levy upon a taxpayer by a state or the functional equivalent of a state.

_____es are also imposed by many subnational entities. _____es consist of direct _____ or indirect _____, and may be paid in money or as its labour equivalent (often but not always unpaid.)

Chapter 1. Introduction to Macroeconomics 19

a. 100-year flood
b. 1921 recession
c. Tax
d. 130-30 fund

89. A _____ is a reduction in taxes. Economic stimulus via _____s, along with interest rate intervention and deficit spending, are one of the central tenets of Keynesian economics.

The immediate effects of a _____ are, generally, a decrease in the real income of the government and an increase in the real income of those whose tax rate has been lowered.

a. Direct taxes
b. Tax cut
c. Withholding tax
d. Popiwek

90. A _____, reserve bank, or monetary authority is the entity responsible for the monetary policy of a country or of a group of member states. It is a bank that can lend money to other banks in times of need. Its primary responsibility is to maintain the stability of the national currency and money supply, but more active duties include controlling subsidized-loan interest rates, and acting as a lender of last resort to the banking sector during times of financial crisis (private banks often being integral to the national financial system.)

a. 100-year flood
b. 130-30 fund
c. Central Bank
d. 1921 recession

91. The _____ is the official currency of 16 of the 27 member states of the European Union (EU.) The states, known collectively as the Eurozone, are Austria, Belgium, Cyprus, Finland, France, Germany, Greece, Ireland, Italy, Luxembourg, Malta, the Netherlands, Portugal, Slovakia, Slovenia, and Spain. The currency is also used in a further five European countries, with and without formal agreements and is consequently used daily by some 327 million Europeans.

a. IRS Code 3401
b. Equity capital market
c. Import and Export Price Indices
d. Euro

92. The _____ is one of the world's most important central banks, responsible for monetary policy covering the 16 member States of the Eurozone. It was established by the European Union (EU) in 1998 with its headquarters in Frankfurt, Germany.

The predecessor to the _____ was the European Monetary Institute.

a. ACEA agreement
b. ACCRA Cost of Living Index
c. AD-IA Model
d. European Central Bank

93. The _____ was an evolution of developed countries from an industrial/manufacturing-based wealth producing economy into a service sector asset based economy, brought about by globalization and currency manipulation by governments and their central banks. Some analysts claimed that this change in the economic structure of the United States had created a state of permanent steady growth, low unemployment, and immunity to boom and bust macroeconomic cycles. They believed that the change rendered obsolete many business practices.

a. New economy
b. 130-30 fund
c. 1921 recession
d. 100-year flood

94. _____ in economics refers to metrics and measures of output from production processes, per unit of input. Labor _____, for example, is typically measured as a ratio of output per labor-hour, an input. _____ may be conceived of as a metrics of the technical or engineering efficiency of production.

   a. Fordism
   c. Productivity
   b. Production-possibility frontier
   d. Piece work

95. The term _____ is used to describe a nation's social or business activity in the process of rapid growth and industrialization. Currently, there are approximately 28 _____ in the world, with the economies of China and India considered to be two of the largest. According to The Economist many people find the term dated, but a new term has yet to gain much traction.

   a. Occupational welfare
   c. Asymmetric price transmission
   b. Affinity diagram
   d. Emerging markets

96. _____ is money accepted for exchange of goods in an economy. The prevalence of one money over another arises, usually, when a government designates through decrees that the government shall accept only particular notes and coins in payment for taxes. Typically, money of _____ consists of stamped coins and minted paper bills.

   a. Security thread
   c. Currency
   b. Totnes pound
   d. Local currency

97. A _____ is a monetary authority which is required to maintain a fixed exchange rate with a foreign currency. This policy objective requires the conventional objectives of a central bank to be subordinated to the exchange rate target.

The main qualities of an orthodox _____ are:

- A _____'s foreign currency reserves must be sufficient to ensure that all holders of its notes and coins (and all banks creditor of a Reserve Account at the _____) can convert them into the reserve currency (usually 110-115% of the monetary base M0.)
- A _____ maintains absolute, unlimited convertibility between its notes and coins and the currency against which they are pegged (the anchor currency), at a fixed rate of exchange, with no restrictions on current-account or capital-account transactions.
- A _____ only earns profit from interests on foreign reserves (less the expense of note-issuing), and does not engage in forward-exchange transactions. These foreign reserves exist (1) because local notes have been issued in exchange, or (2) because commercial banks must by regulation deposit a minimum reserve at the _____. (1) generates a seignorage revenue. (2) is the revenue on minimum reserves (revenue of investment activities less cost of minimum reserves remuneration)
- A _____ has no discretionary powers to effect monetary policy and does not lend to the government. Governments cannot print money, and can only tax or borrow to meet their spending commitments.
- A _____ does not act as a lender of last resort to commercial banks, and does not regulate reserve requirements.
- A _____ does not attempt to manipulate interest rates by establishing a discount rate like a central bank. The peg with the foreign currency tends to keep interest rates and inflation very closely aligned to those in the country against whose currency the peg is fixed.

The _____ in question will no longer issue fiat money but instead will only issue one unit of local currency for each unit (or decided amount) of foreign currency it has in its vault (often a hard currency such as the U.S. dollar or the euro.) The surplus on the balance of payments of that country is reflected by higher deposits local banks hold at the central bank as well as (initially) higher deposits of the (net) exporting firms at their local banks.

 a. Currency board
 b. Currency competition
 c. Reserve currency
 d. Petrodollar

98. The term _____ is applied broadly to a variety of situations in which some financial institutions or assets suddenly lose a large part of their value. In the 19th and early 20th centuries, many financial crises were associated with banking panics, and many recessions coincided with these panics. Other situations that are often called financial crises include stock market crashes and the bursting of other financial bubbles, currency crises, and sovereign defaults.

 a. Co-operative economics
 b. Macroeconomics
 c. Financial crisis
 d. Market failure

Chapter 2. Measuring the Macroeconomy

1. _____s is the social science that studies the production, distribution, and consumption of goods and services. The term _____s comes from the Ancient Greek οἰκονομία from οἶκος (oikos, 'house') + νόμος (nomos, 'custom' or 'law'), hence 'rules of the house(hold)'. Current _____ models developed out of the broader field of political economy in the late 19th century, owing to a desire to use an empirical approach more akin to the physical sciences.
   - a. Opportunity cost
   - b. Energy economics
   - c. Inflation
   - d. Economic

2. The _____ or gross domestic income (GDI), a basic measure of an economy's economic performance, is the market value of all final goods and services produced within the borders of a nation in a year. _____ can be defined in three ways, all of which are conceptually identical. First, it is equal to the total expenditures for all final goods and services produced within the country in a stipulated period of time (usually a 365-day year.)
   - a. Countercyclical
   - b. Gross domestic product
   - c. Market structure
   - d. Monopolistic competition

3. In economics, _____ is a rise in the general level of prices of goods and services in an economy over a period of time. When the general price level rises, each unit of currency buys fewer goods and services; consequently, _____ is also a decline in the real value of money--a loss of purchasing power in the medium of exchange which is also the monetary unit of account in the economy. A chief measure of general price-level _____ is the general _____ rate, which is the percentage change in a general price index (normally the Consumer Price Index) over time.
   - a. Inflation
   - b. Economic
   - c. Energy economics
   - d. Opportunity cost

4. In economics, the _____ is a measure of inflation, the rate of increase of a price index (for example, a consumer price index.)It is the percentage rate of change in price level over time. The rate of decrease in the purchasing power of money is approximately equal.

It's used to calculate the real interest rate, as well as real increases in wages, and official measurements of this rate act as input variables to COLA adjustments and Inflation derivatives prices.

   - a. Edgeworth paradox
   - b. Equity value
   - c. Interest rate option
   - d. Inflation rate

5. The _____ says that it is naïve to try to predict the effects of a change in economic policy entirely on the basis of relationships observed in historical data, especially highly aggregated historical data.

The basic idea pre-dates Lucas's contribution, but in a 1976 paper he drove home the point that this simple notion invalidated policy advice based on conclusions drawn from estimated system of equation models. Because the parameters of those models were not structural - that is, not policy-invariant - they would necessarily change whenever policy - the rules of the game - was changed.

   - a. Peak-load pricing
   - b. Demand management
   - c. Dahrendorf hypothesis
   - d. Lucas critique

6. An _____, in economics, is the amount by which the real Gross domestic product exceeds potential GDP. The real GDP is also known as GDP 'adjusted for inflation', 'constant prices' GDP or 'constant dollar' GDP, because it measures the aggregate output in a country's income accounts in a given year, expressed in base-year prices. On the other hand, the potential GDP is the quantity of real GDP when a country's economy is at full-employment.

a. ACEA agreement
b. Inflationary gap
c. ACCRA Cost of Living Index
d. AD-IA Model

7. Unemployment occurs when a person is available to work and seeking work but currently without work. The prevalence of unemployment is usually measured using the _____, which is defined as the percentage of those in the labor force who are unemployed. The _____ is also used in economic studies and economic indexes such as the United States' Conference Board's Index of Leading Indicators as a measure of the state of the macroeconomics.

a. ACEA agreement
b. AD-IA Model
c. ACCRA Cost of Living Index
d. Unemployment rate

8. In economics, _____ is the total demand for final goods and services in the economy (Y) at a given time and price level. It is the amount of goods and services in the economy that will be purchased at all possible price levels. This is the demand for the gross domestic product of a country when inventory levels are static.

a. Aggregation problem
b. Aggregate supply
c. Aggregate demand
d. Aggregate expenditure

9. Necessary _____s:

If x is a necessary _____ of y, then the presence of y necessarily implies the presence of x. The presence of x, however, does not imply that y will occur.

Sufficient _____s:

If x is a sufficient _____ of y, then the presence of x necessarily implies the presence of y.

a. Philosophy of economics
b. Materialism
c. Political philosophy
d. Cause

10. Economics:

- _____, the desire to own something and the ability to pay for it
- _____ curve, a graphic representation of a _____ schedule
- _____ deposit, the money in checking accounts
- _____ pull theory, the theory that inflation occurs when _____ for goods and services exceeds existing supplies
- _____ schedule, a table that lists the quantity of a good a person will buy it each different price
- _____ side economics, the school of economics at believes government spending and tax cuts open economy by raising _____

a. McKesson ' Robbins scandal
b. Variability
c. Production
d. Demand

11. In finance, the _____s between two currencies specifies how much one currency is worth in terms of the other. It is the value of a foreign natione;s currency in terms of the home natione;s currency. For example an _____ of 102 Japanese yen to the United States dollar means that JPY 102 is worth the same as USD 1.

Chapter 2. Measuring the Macroeconomy

    a. ACEA agreement
    b. Interbank market
    c. Exchange rate
    d. ACCRA Cost of Living Index

12. In economics, an _____ is any good or commodity, transported from one country to another country in a legitimate fashion, typically for use in trade. _____ goods or services are provided to foreign consumers by domestic producers. _____ is an important part of international trade.
    a. ACEA agreement
    b. ACCRA Cost of Living Index
    c. Export
    d. AD-IA Model

13. The _____ is where currency trading takes place. It is where banks and other official institutions facilitate the buying and selling of foreign currencies. FX transactions typically involve one party purchasing a quantity of one currency in exchange for paying a quantity of another.
    a. Floating currency
    b. Covered interest arbitrage
    c. Currency swap
    d. Foreign exchange market

14. In economics, an _____ is any good (e.g. a commodity) or service brought into one country from another country in a legitimate fashion, typically for use in trade. It is a good that is brought in from another country for sale. _____ goods or services are provided to domestic consumers by foreign producers. An _____ in the receiving country is an export to the sending country.
    a. Incoterms
    b. Import quota
    c. Economic integration
    d. Import

15. _____ is exchange of capital, goods, and services across international borders or territories. In most countries, it represents a significant share of gross domestic product (GDP.) While _____ has been present throughout much of history, its economic, social, and political importance has been on the rise in recent centuries.
    a. Incoterms
    b. Import license
    c. Intra-industry trade
    d. International trade

16. _____ is a concept found in moral, political, and bioethical philosophy. Within these contexts, it refers to the capacity of a rational individual to make an informed, un-coerced decision. In moral and political philosophy, _____ is often used as the basis for determining moral responsibility for one's actions.
    a. AD-IA Model
    b. ACCRA Cost of Living Index
    c. ACEA agreement
    d. Autonomy

17. _____ is money accepted for exchange of goods in an economy. The prevalence of one money over another arises, usually, when a government designates through decrees that the government shall accept only particular notes and coins in payment for taxes. Typically, money of _____ consists of stamped coins and minted paper bills.
    a. Totnes pound
    b. Security thread
    c. Currency
    d. Local currency

18. _____ is a fee paid on borrowed assets. It is the price paid for the use of borrowed money, or, money earned by deposited funds. Assets that are sometimes lent with _____ include money, shares, consumer goods through hire purchase, major assets such as aircraft, and even entire factories in finance lease arrangements.
    a. Asset protection
    b. Internal debt
    c. Insolvency
    d. Interest

Chapter 2. Measuring the Macroeconomy

19. An _____ is the price a borrower pays for the use of money they do not own, for instance a small company might borrow from a bank to kick start their business, and the return a lender receives for deferring the use of funds, by lending it to the borrower. _____s are normally expressed as a percentage rate over the period of one year.

_____s targets are also a vital tool of monetary policy and are used to control variables like investment, inflation, and unemployment.

   a. ACCRA Cost of Living Index
   b. Interest rate
   c. Enterprise value
   d. Arrow-Debreu model

20. _____ is a common concept in economics, and gives rise to derived concepts such as consumer debt. Generally _____ is defined by opposition to production. But the precise definition can vary because different schools of economists define production quite differently.
   a. Federal Reserve Bank Notes
   b. Consumption
   c. Cash or share options
   d. Foreclosure data providers

21. A _____ is a public market for the trading of company stock and derivatives at an agreed price; these are securities listed on a stock exchange as well as those only traded privately.

The size of the world _____ was estimated at about $36.6 trillion US at the beginning of October 2008 . The total world derivatives market has been estimated at about $791 trillion face or nominal value, 11 times the size of the entire world economy.

   a. Adolf Hitler
   b. Adolph Fischer
   c. Adam Smith
   d. Stock market

22. _____ in economics and business is the result of an exchange and from that trade we assign a numerical monetary value to a good, service or asset. If Alice trades Bob 4 apples for an orange, the _____ of an orange is 4 apples. Inversely, the _____ of an apple is 1/4 oranges.
   a. Premium pricing
   b. Price
   c. Price book
   d. Price war

23. A _____ is a hypothetical measure of overall prices for some set of goods and services, in a given region during a given interval, normalized relative to some base set. Typically, a _____ is approximated with a price index.

The classical dichotomy is the assumption that there is a relatively clean distinction between overall increases or decreases in prices and underlying, e;reale; economic variables.

   a. Discretionary spending
   b. Discouraged worker
   c. Price level
   d. Price elasticity of supply

24. The _____ of monetary management established the rules for commercial and financial relations among the world's major industrial states in the mid 20th Century. The _____ was the first example of a fully negotiated monetary order intended to govern monetary relations among independent nation-states.

Preparing to rebuild the international economic system as World War II was still raging, 730 delegates from all 44 Allied nations gathered at the Mount Washington Hotel in Bretton Woods, New Hampshire, United States, for the United Nations Monetary and Financial Conference.

    a. 130-30 fund
    b. 100-year flood
    c. 1921 recession
    d. Bretton Woods system

25. A _____, sometimes called a pegged exchange rate, is a type of exchange rate regime wherein a currency's value is matched to the value of another single currency or to a basket of other currencies such as gold.

A _____ is usually used to stabilize the value of a currency, vis-a-vis the currency it is pegged to. This facilitates trade and investments between the two countries, and is especially useful for small economies where external trade forms a large part of their GDP.

    a. Law of supply
    b. Monetary economics
    c. Leading indicators
    d. Fixed exchange rate

26. A _____ or a flexible exchange rate is a type of exchange rate regime wherein a currency's value is allowed to fluctuate according to the foreign exchange market. A currency that uses a _____ is known as a floating currency. The opposite of a _____ is a fixed exchange rate.

    a. Floating exchange rate
    b. Floating currency
    c. Trade Weighted US dollar Index
    d. Foreign exchange market

27. An _____ is an economic data figure reflecting price or quantity compared with a standard or base value. The base usually equals 100 and the _____ is usually expressed as 100 times the ratio to the base value. For example, if a commodity costs twice as much in 1970 as it did in 1960, its _____ would be 200 relative to 1960.

    a. ACCRA Cost of Living Index
    b. Index number
    c. Economic depreciation
    d. International economics

28. In finance, a _____ is a debt security, in which the authorized issuer owes the holders a debt and, depending on the terms of the _____, is obliged to pay interest (the coupon) and/or to repay the principal at a later date, termed maturity. A _____ is a formal contract to repay borrowed money with interest at fixed intervals.

Thus a _____ is like a loan: the issuer is the borrower (debtor), the holder is the lender (creditor), and the coupon is the interest.

    a. Zero-coupon
    b. Bond
    c. Prize Bond
    d. Callable

29. _____s are payments made by a corporation to its shareholders. It is the portion of corporate profits paid out to stockholders. When a corporation earns a profit or surplus, that money can be put to two uses: it can either be re-invested in the business (called retained earnings), or it can be paid to the shareholders as a _____.

    a. Dividend
    b. Dividend puzzle
    c. Dividend yield
    d. Dividend cover

Chapter 2. Measuring the Macroeconomy   27

30. _____ is a life of security. It may also refer to the final payment date of a loan or other financial instrument, at which point all remaining interest and principal is due to be paid.

1, 3, 6 months _____ band can be calculated by using 30-day per month periods.

- a. Future-oriented
- c. Future value
- b. Refinancing risk
- d. Maturity

31. In finance, _____ rate of profit or sometimes just return, is the ratio of money gained or lost on an investment relative to the amount of money invested. The amount of money gained or lost may be referred to as interest, profit/loss, gain/loss, or net income/loss. The money invested may be referred to as the asset, capital, principal, or the cost basis of the investment.
- a. Cost accrual ratio
- c. Sortino ratio
- b. Current ratio
- d. Rate of return

32. A mutual _____ or stockholder is an individual or company (including a corporation) that legally owns one or more shares of stock in a joint stock company. A company's _____s collectively own that company. Thus, the typical goal of such companies is to enhance _____ value.
- a. Relative valuation
- c. Shareholder
- b. Prime Standard
- d. Profit warning

33. A _____ is a type of economic bubble taking place in stock markets when price of stocks rise and become overvalued by any measure of stock valuation.

The existence of _____s is at odds with the assumptions of efficient market theory which assumes rational investor behaviour. Behavioral finance theory attribute _____s to cognitive biases that lead to groupthink and herd behavior.

- a. Scrip issue
- c. Growth investing
- b. Stock market bubble
- d. Fill or kill

34. A _____ is a method of measuring a section of the stock market. Many indices are cited by news or financial services firms and are used to benchmark the performance of portfolios such as mutual funds.

Stock market indices may be classed in many ways.

- a. Scrip issue
- c. Lock up period
- b. Stock market bubble
- d. Stock market index

35. _____ is a specific term used in companies' financial reporting from the company-whole point of view. Because that use excludes the effects of changing ownership interest, an economic measure of _____ is necessary for financial analysis from the shareholders' point of view

28   *Chapter 2. Measuring the Macroeconomy*

_____ is defined by the Financial Accounting Standards Board, or FASB, as e;the change in equity [net assets] of a business enterprise during a period from transactions and other events and circumstances from nonowner sources. It includes all changes in equity during a period except those resulting from investments by owners and distributions to owners.e;

_____ is the sum of net income and other items that must bypass the income statement because they have not been realized, including items like an unrealized holding gain or loss from available for sale securities and foreign currency translation gains or losses.

   a. Windfall gain   b. Comprehensive income
   c. Real income   d. Net national income

36.   _____ is a branch of applied statistics focusing on the collection, processing, compilation and dissemination of statistics concerning the economy of a region, a country or a group of countries. _____ is also referred as a subtopic of official statistics, since most of the _____ are produced by official organizations (e.g. statistical institutes, intergovernmental organizations such as United Nations, European Union or OECD, central banks, ministries, etc.). _____ provide the empirical data needed in economic research (econometrics) and they are the basis for decision and economic policy making.
   a. Event study   b. ACCRA Cost of Living Index
   c. Indirect least squares   d. Economic statistics

37.   A _____ is the minimum difference a person requires to be willing to take an uncertain bet, between the expected value of the bet and the certain value that he is indifferent to.

The certainty equivalent is the guaranteed payoff at which a person is 'indifferent' between accepting the guaranteed payoff and a higher but uncertain payoff. (It is the amount of the higher payout minus the _____.)

   a. Ruin theory   b. Risk premium
   c. Linear model   d. Workers compensation

38.   _____ is the a method of technical and economic research of the systems for purpose to optimize a parity between system's consumer functions or properties and expenses to achieve those functions or properties.

This methodology for continuous perfection of production, industrial technologies, organizational structures was developed by Juryj Sobolev in 1948 at the 'Perm telephone factory'

- 1948 Juryj Sobolev - the first success in application of a method analysis at the 'Perm telephone factory' .
- 1949 - the first application for the invention as result of use of the new method.

Today in economically developed countries practically each enterprise or the company use methodology of the kind of functional-cost analysis as a practice of the quality management, most full satisfying to principles of standards of series ISO 9000.

- Interest of consumer not in products itself, but the advantage which it will receive from its usage.
- The consumer aspires to reduce his expenses
- Functions needed by consumer can be executed in the various ways, and, hence, with various efficiency and expenses. Among possible alternatives of realization of functions exist such in which the parity of quality and the price is the optimal for the consumer.

The goal of _____ is achievement of the highest consumer satisfaction of production at simultaneous decrease in all kinds of industrial expenses Classical _____ has three English synonyms - Value Engineering, Value Management, Value Analysis.

a. Staple financing
c. Willingness to pay
b. Function cost analysis
d. Monopoly wage

39. The _____ is an expected return that the provider of capital plans to earn on their investment.

Capital (money) used for funding a business should earn returns for the capital providers who risk their capital. For an investment to be worthwhile, the expected return on capital must be greater than the _____.

a. Capital intensive
c. Modigliani-Miller theorem
b. Cost of capital
d. Capital expenditure

40. In finance and economics _____ or nominal rate of interest refers to the rate of interest before adjustment for inflation (in contrast with the real interest rate); or, for interest rates 'as stated' without adjustment for the full effect of compounding (also referred to as the nominal annual rate.) An interest rate is called nominal if the frequency of compounding (e.g. a month) is not identical to the basic time unit (normally a year.)

The real interest rate includes compensation for the lender's lost value due to inflation, whereas the _____ excludes inflation.

a. Nominal interest rate
c. Fixed interest
b. Risk-free interest rate
d. London Interbank Offered Rate

41. The '_____' is approximately the nominal interest rate minus the inflation rate Since the inflation rate over the course of a loan is not known initially, volatility in inflation represents a risk to both the lender and the borrower.

In economics and finance, an individual who lends money for repayment at a later point in time expects to be compensated for the time value of money, or not having the use of that money while it is lent.

Chapter 2. Measuring the Macroeconomy

a. Reflation
b. Core inflation
c. Cost-push inflation
d. Real interest rate

42. The term _____ or commodity bundle refers to a fixed list of items used specifically to track the progress of inflation in an economy or specific market.

The most common type of _____ is the basket of consumer goods, used to define the Consumer Price Index (CPI.) Other types of baskets are used to define

- Producer Price Index (PPI), previously known as Wholesale Price Index (WPI)
- various commodity price indices

The term _____ analysis in the retail business refers to research that provides the retailer with information to understand the purchase behaviour of a buyer. This information will enable the retailer to understand the buyer's needs and rewrite the store's layout accordingly, develop cross-promotional programs, or even capture new buyers (much like the cross-selling concept.)

a. Market basket
b. Category Development Index
c. Robin Hood index
d. Cost-weighted activity index

43. _____ refers to a business or organization attempting to acquire goods or services to accomplish the goals of the enterprise. Though there are several organizations that attempt to set standards in the _____ process, processes can vary greatly between organizations. Typically the word '_____' is not used interchangeably with the word 'procurement', since procurement typically includes Expediting, Supplier Quality, and Traffic and Logistics (T'L) in addition to _____.

a. Purchasing
b. Free port
c. 130-30 fund
d. 100-year flood

44. _____ is the number of goods/services that can be purchased with a unit of currency. For example, if you had taken one dollar to a store in the 1950s, you would have been able to buy a greater number of items than you would today, indicating that you would have had a greater _____ in the 1950s. Currency can be either a commodity money, like gold or silver, or fiat currency like US dollars.

a. Purchasing power
b. Genuine progress indicator
c. Human Poverty Index
d. Compliance cost

45. A _____ is an object whose consumption increases the utility of the consumer, for which the quantity demanded exceeds the quantity supplied at zero price. _____s are usually modeled as having diminishing marginal utility. The first individual purchase has high utility; the second has less.

a. Pie method
b. Merit good
c. Composite good
d. Good

46. In economics, economic output is divided into physical goods and intangible services. Consumption of _____ is assumed to produce utility. It is often used when referring to a _____ Tax.

a. Private good
b. Composite good
c. Manufactured goods
d. Goods and services

Chapter 2. Measuring the Macroeconomy

47. The _____, a unit of the United States Department of Labor, is the principal fact-finding agency for the U.S. government in the broad field of labor economics and statistics. The BLS is an independent national statistical agency that collects, processes, analyzes, and disseminates essential statistical data to the American public, the U.S. Congress, other Federal agencies, State and local governments, business, and labor representatives. The BLS also serves as a statistical resource to the Department of Labor.

a. Gross world product
b. Gross national product
c. Gross Regional Product
d. Bureau of Labor Statistics

48. _____ is a broad label that refers to any individuals or households that use goods and services generated within the economy. The concept of a _____ is used in different contexts, so that the usage and significance of the term may vary.

Typically when business people and economists talk of _____s they are talking about person as _____, an aggregated commodity item with little individuality other than that expressed in the buy/not-buy decision.

a. 130-30 fund
b. Consumer
c. 1921 recession
d. 100-year flood

49. A _____ is a measure of the average price of consumer goods and services purchased by households. A _____ measures a price change for a constant market basket of goods and services from one period to the next within the same area (city, region, or nation.) It is a price index determined by measuring the price of a standard group of goods meant to represent the typical market basket of a typical urban consumer.

a. Cost-of-living index
b. CPI
c. Lipstick index
d. Consumer price index

50. A _____ is a normalized average (typically a weighted average) of prices for a given class of goods or services in a given region, during a given interval of time. It is a statistic designed to help to compare how these prices, taken as a whole, differ between time periods or geographical locations.

Price indices have several potential uses.

a. Product sabotage
b. Two-part tariff
c. Transactional Net Margin Method
d. Price index

51. A _____ measures average changes in prices received by domestic producers for their output. It is one of several price indices

Its importance is being undermined by the steady decline in manufactured goods as a share of spending.

A number of countries that now report a _____ previously reported a Wholesale Price Index.

a. Visible balance
b. Gross national product
c. Producer price index
d. Hemline index

Chapter 2. Measuring the Macroeconomy

52. In statistics, a _____ is a value that allows data to be measured over time in terms of some base period ussually through a price index in order to distinguish between changes in the money value of GNP which result from a change in prices and those which result from a change in physical output. It is the measure of the price level for some quantity. A _____ serves as a price index in which the effects of inflation are nulled.
   a. Contingent employment
   b. Blanket order
   c. Deflator
   d. Market microstructure

53. _____ describes a bias in gay economics index numbers arising from tendency to purchase inexpensive substitutes for expensive items when prices change.

   _____ occurs when two or more items experience a change of price relative to each other. Consumers will consume more of the now comparatively inexpensive good and less of the now relatively more expensive good.

   a. State of World Liberty Index
   b. Constant dollars
   c. Market basket
   d. Substitution bias

54. _____ is a term used to described a tendency or preference towards a particular perspective, ideology or result, especially when the tendency interferes with the ability to be impartial, unprejudiced, or objective. The term _____ed is used to describe an action, judgment, or other outcome influenced by a prejudged perspective. It is also used to refer to a person or body of people whose actions or judgments exhibit _____.
   a. Bias
   b. 100-year flood
   c. 1921 recession
   d. 130-30 fund

55. The _____ was a worldwide economic downturn starting in most places in 1929 and ending at different times in the 1930s or early 1940s for different countries. It was the largest and most important economic depression in the 20th century, and is used in the 21st century as an example of how far the world's economy can fall. The _____ originated in the United States; historians most often use as a starting date the stock market crash on October 29, 1929, known as Black Tuesday.
   a. Great Depression
   b. Wall Street Crash of 1929
   c. Jarrow March
   d. British Empire Economic Conference

56. _____, 1st Baron Keynes was a renowned economist from Britain whose many ideas on economic and political theories as well as on many governments' monetary policies influenced America. He advocated a government that played an active role in the lives of people regarding business, economy, etc. In this role, the government would use fiscal measures to reduce the consequences of recessions, economic depressions and booms.
   a. John Maynard Keynes
   b. Adolph Fischer
   c. Adam Smith
   d. Adolf Hitler

57. _____ refers to the actions that governments take in the economic field. It covers the systems for setting interest rates and government deficit as well as the labour market, national ownership, and many other areas of government.

Such policies are often influenced by international institutions like the International Monetary Fund or World Bank as well as political beliefs and the consequent policies of parties.

a. ACEA agreement	b. Economic policy
c. AD-IA Model	d. ACCRA Cost of Living Index

58. _____ and Keynesian Theory) is a macroeconomic theory based on the ideas of 20th-century British economist John Maynard Keynes. _____ argues that private sector decisions sometimes lead to inefficient macroeconomic outcomes and therefore advocates active policy responses by the public sector, including monetary policy actions by the central bank and fiscal policy actions by the government to stabilize output over the business cycle.

The theories forming the basis of _____ were first presented in The General Theory of Employment, Interest and Money, published in 1936.

a. Market failure	b. Rational choice theory
c. Deflation	d. Keynesian economics

59. In economics, the people in the _____ are the suppliers of labor. The _____ is all the nonmilitary people who are employed or unemployed. In 2005, the worldwide _____ was over 3 billion people.

a. Distributed workforce	b. Grenelle agreements
c. Departmentalization	d. Labor force

60. _____ data refers to selected population characteristics as used in government, marketing or opinion research, or the _____ profiles used in such research. Note the distinction from the term 'demography' Commonly-used _____s include race, age, income, disabilities, mobility (in terms of travel time to work or number of vehicles available), educational attainment, home ownership, employment status, and even location.

a. Demographic warfare	b. Generation Z
c. NEET	d. Demographic

61. In economics, a _____ is a person of legal employment age who is not actively seeking employment. This is usually due to the fact that an individual has given up looking or has had no success in finding a job, hence the term 'discouraged.' Their belief may derive from a variety of factors including: a shortage of jobs in their locality or line of work; perceived discrimination for reasons such as age, race, sex and religion; a lack of necessary skills, training or experience; or, a chronic illness or disability. Some _____s, however, are voluntarily unemployed such as stay-at-home parents, pregnant mothers, and will beneficiaries.

a. Demand side economics	b. Hedonimetry
c. Discouraged worker	d. Relative income hypothesis

62. The _____ is the central banking system of the United States. Created in 1913 by the enactment of the Federal Reserve Act (signed by Woodrow Wilson), it is a quasi-public and quasi-private (government entity with private components) banking system that comprises (1) the presidentially appointed Board of Governors of the _____ in Washington, D.C.; (2) the Federal Open Market Committee; (3) twelve regional Federal Reserve Banks located in major cities throughout the nation acting as fiscal agents for the U.S. Treasury, each with its own nine-member board of directors; (4) numerous other private U.S. member banks, which subscribe to required amounts of non-transferable stock in their regional Federal Reserve Banks; and (5) various advisory councils. Since February 2006, Ben Bernanke has served as the Chairman of the Board of Governors of the _____.

a. Monetary Policy Report to the Congress	b. Term auction facility
c. Federal Reserve System	d. Federal Reserve System Open Market Account

63. _____ in a strict sense are only the foreign currency deposits and bonds held by central banks and monetary authorities. However, the term in popular usage commonly includes foreign exchange and gold, SDRs and IMF reserve positions. This broader figure is more readily available, but it is more accurately termed official international reserves or international reserves.
   a. Foreign exchange trading
   b. Foreign exchange reserves
   c. Foreign exchange market
   d. Currency swap

64. The _____ is a concept of economic activity developed in particular by Milton Friedman and Edmund Phelps in the 1960s, both recipients of the Nobel prize in economics. In both cases, the development of the concept is cited as a main motivation behind the prize. It represents the hypothetical unemployment rate consistent with aggregate production being at the 'long-run' level.
   a. Real Business Cycle Theory
   b. Romer Model
   c. Robertson lag
   d. Natural rate of unemployment

65. In economics, the _____ is a historical inverse relation between the rate of unemployment and the rate of inflation in an economy. Stated simply, the lower the unemployment in an economy, the higher the rate of increase in nominal wages in the economy. Rate of Change of Wages against Unemployment, United Kingdom 1913-1948 from Phillips (1958)

William Phillips, a New Zealand born economist, wrote a paper in 1958 titled The Relationship between Unemployment and the Rate of Change of Money Wages in the United Kingdom 1861-1957, which was published in the quarterly journal Economica.

   a. Lorenz curve
   b. Demand curve
   c. Cost curve
   d. Phillips curve

66. In economics, _____ is the total supply of goods and services produced by a national economy during a specific time period. It is the total amount of goods and services in the economy available at all possible price levels.
   a. Aggregation problem
   b. Aggregate demand
   c. Aggregate expenditure
   d. Aggregate supply

67. In finance, the _____ of a financial asset measures the sensitivity of the asset's price to interest rate movements. There are various definitions of _____ and derived quantities, discussed below. If not otherwise specified, '_____' generally means the Macaulay _____, as defined below.
   a. Time value of money
   b. 100-year flood
   c. Duration
   d. Newtonian time

68. In economics, _____ refers to the highest level of real Gross Domestic Product output that can be sustained over the long term. The existence of a limit is due to natural and institutional constraints. If actual GDP rises and stays above _____, then (in the absence of wage and price controls) inflation tends to increase as demand exceeds supply.
   a. Potential output
   b. Monetary conditions index
   c. Monetary policy reaction function
   d. Fundamental psychological law

69. In mathematics, a _____ is a constant multiplicative factor of a certain object. For example, in the expression $9x^2$, the _____ of x^2 is 9.

The object can be such things as a variable, a vector, a function, etc.

Chapter 2. Measuring the Macroeconomy

a. 130-30 fund
b. 100-year flood
c. 1921 recession
d. Coefficient

70. _____, in microeconomics, are the cost advantages that a business obtains due to expansion. They are factors that cause a producere;s average cost per unit to fall as scale is increased. _____ is a long run concept and refers to reductions in unit cost as the size of a facility, or scale, increases.
  a. Economic production quantity
  b. Isoquant
  c. Underinvestment employment relationship
  d. Economies of scale

71. A variety of measures of national income and output are used in economics to estimate total economic activity in a country or region, including gross domestic product (GDP), _____ , and net national income (NNI.)

There are three main ways of calculating these numbers; the output approach, the income approach and the expenditure approach. In theory, the three must yield the same, because total expenditures on goods and services must equal the total income paid to the producers (GNI), and that must also equal the total value of the output of goods and services (_____.)

  a. Purchasing power parity
  b. Household final consumption expenditure
  c. Gross national product
  d. Gross world product

72. The _____ is 'the basic residential unit in which economic production, consumption, inheritance, child rearing, and shelter are organized and carried out'; [the _____] 'may or may not be synonomous with family'.

The _____ is the basic unit of analysis in many social, microeconomic and government models. The term refers to all individuals who live in the same dwelling.

  a. Household
  b. Family economics
  c. 100-year flood
  d. 130-30 fund

73. A variety of measures of _____ and output are used in economics to estimate total economic activity in a country or region, including gross domestic product (GDP), gross national product (GNP), and net _____

There are three main ways of calculating these numbers; the output approach, the income approach and the expenditure approach. In theory, the three must yield the same, because total expenditures on goods and services must equal the total income paid to the producers (Gnational income), and that must also equal the total value of the output of goods and services (GNP.)

  a. GNI per capita
  b. Volume index
  c. Gross world product
  d. National income

74. _____ use double-entry accounting to report the monetary value and sources of output produced in a country and the distribution of incomes that production generates. Data are available at the national and industry levels.

The NIPA summarizes national income on the left (debit, revenue) side and national product on the right (credit, expense) side of a two-column accounting report.

a. Current account
b. Gross private domestic investment
c. Net national product
d. National income and product accounts

75. The _____ equals the gross domestic product (GDP) minus depreciation on a country's capital goods.

_____ accounts for capital that has been consumed over the year in the form of housing, vehicle, or machinery deterioration. The depreciation accounted for is often referred to as capital consumption allowance and represents the amount needed in order to replace those depreciated assets.

    a. Cass criterion
    b. Net domestic product
    c. Carrying charge
    d. Commodity price shocks

76. _____ is the total market value of all final goods and services produced by citizens of an economy during a given period of time (gross national product or GNP) minus depreciation. The _____ can be similarly applied at a country's domestic output level. The net domestic product (NDP) is the equivalent application of _____ within macroeconomics, and NDP is equal to gross domestic product (GDP) minus depreciation: NDP = GDP - depreciation.

    a. Current account
    b. Compensation of employees
    c. Gross private domestic investment
    d. Net national product

77. In microeconomics, _____ is quite simply the conversion of inputs into outputs. It is an economic process that uses resources to create a good or service that is suitable for exchange. This can include manufacturing, storing, shipping, and packaging.

    a. Production
    b. Solved
    c. MET
    d. Red Guards

78. In economics, the term _____ of income or _____ refers to a simple economic model which describes the reciprocal circulation of income between producers and consumers. In the _____ model, the inter-dependent entities of producer and consumer are referred to as 'firms' and 'households' respectively and provide each other with factors in order to facilitate the flow of income. Firms provide consumers with goods and services in exchange for consumer expenditure and 'factors of production' from households.

    a. 1921 recession
    b. Circular flow
    c. 130-30 fund
    d. 100-year flood

79. _____ is a macroeconomic measure of the size of an economy adjusted for price changes and inflation. It measures in constant prices the output of final goods and services and incomes within an economy. The formula for its definition is [(Nominal GDP)/(GDP deflator)] x 100, however, it is not calculated in this way.

    a. TED spread
    b. Bureau of Labor Statistics
    c. Gross world product
    d. Real Gross Domestic Product

80. _____ is the price at which an asset would trade in a competitive Walrasian auction setting. _____ is often used interchangeably with open _____, fair value or fair _____, although these terms have distinct definitions in different standards, and may differ in some circumstances.

International Valuation Standards defines _____ as 'the estimated amount for which a property should exchange on the date of valuation between a willing buyer and a willing seller in an arm's-length transaction after proper marketing wherein the parties had each acted knowledgeably, prudently, and without compulsion.'

_____ is a concept distinct from market price, which is 'the price at which one can transact', while _____ is 'the true underlying value' according to theoretical standards.

a. Personal financial management
b. Market value
c. Netting
d. Secured loan

81. In economics, the _____ functional form of production functions is widely used to represent the relationship of an output to inputs. It was proposed by Knut Wicksell (1851-1926), and tested against statistical evidence by Charles Cobb and Paul Douglas in 1900-1928.

For production, the function is

$$Y = AL^{\alpha}K^{\beta},$$

where:

- Y = total production (the monetary value of all goods produced in a year)
- L = labor input
- K = capital input
- A = total factor productivity
- α and β are the output elasticities of labor and capital, respectively. These values are constants determined by available technology.

Output elasticity measures the responsiveness of output to a change in levels of either labor or capital used in production, ceteris paribus. For example if α = 0.15, a 1% increase in labor would lead to approximately a 0.15% increase in output.

a. Growth accounting
b. Social savings
c. Demand-pull theory
d. Cobb-Douglas

82. _____ in economics refers to metrics and measures of output from production processes, per unit of input. Labor _____, for example, is typically measured as a ratio of output per labor-hour, an input. _____ may be conceived of as a metrics of the technical or engineering efficiency of production.

a. Piece work
b. Productivity
c. Fordism
d. Production-possibility frontier

83. In economics, a _____ is a function that specifies the output of a firm, an industry, or an entire economy for all combinations of inputs. A meta-_____ compares the practice of the existing entities converting inputs X into output y to determine the most efficient practice _____ of the existing entities, whether the most efficient feasible practice production or the most efficient actual practice production. In either case, the maximum output of a technologically-determined production process is a mathematical function of input factors of production.

a. Post-Fordism
b. Constant elasticity of substitution
c. Production function
d. Short-run

84. A _____ is an expression that compares quantities relative to each other. The most common examples involve two quantities, but any number of quantities can be compared. _____s are represented mathematically by separating each quantity with a colon, for example the _____ 2:3, which is read as the _____ 'two to three'.
   a. Y-intercept
   b. 130-30 fund
   c. 100-year flood
   d. Ratio

85. _____ or producer goods are goods used as inputs in the production of other goods, such as partly finished goods. They are goods used in production of final goods. A firm may make then use _____, or make then sell, or buy then use them.
   a. Economic forecasting
   b. Inflation adjustment
   c. Income distribution
   d. Intermediate goods

86. _____ refers to the additional value of a commodity over the cost of commodities used to produce it from the previous stage of production. An example is the price of gasoline at the pump over the price of the oil in it. In national accounts used in macroeconomics, it refers to the contribution of the factors of production, i.e., land, labor, and capital goods, to raising the value of a product and corresponds to the incomes received by the owners of these factors.
   a. Value added
   b. Full employment
   c. Solow residual
   d. Hodrick-Prescott filter

87. _____ is a term used in accounting, economics and finance to spread the cost of an asset over the span of several years.

In simple words we can say that _____ is the reduction in the value of an asset due to usage, passage of time, wear and tear, technological outdating or obsolescence, depletion, inadequacy, rot, rust, decay or other such factors.

In accounting, _____ is a term used to describe any method of attributing the historical or purchase cost of an asset across its useful life, roughly corresponding to normal wear and tear.

   a. Net income per employee
   b. Depreciation
   c. Salvage value
   d. Historical cost

88. In economics, _____ refers to an activity of spending which increases the availability of fixed capital goods or means of production. It is the total spending on new fixed investment minus replacement investment, which simply replaces depreciated capital goods.
   a. Lehman Formula
   b. Greenfield investment
   c. Tangible investments
   d. Net investment

89. A _____ product is a product designed for cheapness and short-term convenience rather than medium to long-term durability, with most products only intended for single use. The term is also sometimes used for products that may last several months (ex. _____ air filters) to distinguish from similar products that last indefinitely (ex.
   a. 1921 recession
   b. 100-year flood
   c. 130-30 fund
   d. Disposable

90. _____ is gross income minus income tax on that income.

Discretionary income is income after subtracting taxes and normal expenses (such as rent or mortgage, utilities, insurance, medical, transportation, property maintenance, child support, inflation, food and sundries, 'c.) to maintain a certain standard of living.

- a. Stamp Act
- b. Disposable personal income
- c. Taxation as theft
- d. Disposable income

91. Economic _____ is defined as an excess distribution to any factor in a production process above that which is required to induce the factor into the process or any excess above that which is necessary to keep the factor in its current use..

Classical Factor _____ is primarily concerned with the fee paid for the use of fixed (e.g. natural) resources. The classical definition is expressed as any excess payment above that required to induce or provide for production.

- a. 1921 recession
- b. 100-year flood
- c. 130-30 fund
- d. Rent

92. An autarky is an economy that is self-sufficient and does not take part in international trade, or severely limits trade with the outside world. Likewise the term refers to an ecosystem not affected by influences from the outside, which relies entirely on its own resources. In the economic meaning, it is also referred to as a _____.

- a. Network Economy
- b. Transition economy
- c. Digital economy
- d. Closed economy

93. _____s (economically referred to as land or raw materials) occur naturally within environments that exist relatively undisturbed by mankind, in a natural form. A _____'s is often characterized by amounts of biodiversity existent in various ecosystems.

Mining, petroleum extraction, fishing, hunting, and forestry are generally considered natural-resource industries.

- a. Natural resource
- b. 130-30 fund
- c. 100-year flood
- d. 1921 recession

Chapter 3. Thinking Like an Economist

1. _____s is the social science that studies the production, distribution, and consumption of goods and services. The term _____s comes from the Ancient Greek οἰκονομία from οἶκος (oikos, 'house') + νόμος (nomos, 'custom' or 'law'), hence 'rules of the house(hold)'. Current _____ models developed out of the broader field of political economy in the late 19th century, owing to a desire to use an empirical approach more akin to the physical sciences.

   a. Opportunity cost
   b. Inflation
   c. Energy economics
   d. Economic

2. The _____ says that it is naïve to try to predict the effects of a change in economic policy entirely on the basis of relationships observed in historical data, especially highly aggregated historical data.

   The basic idea pre-dates Lucas's contribution, but in a 1976 paper he drove home the point that this simple notion invalidated policy advice based on conclusions drawn from estimated system of equation models. Because the parameters of those models were not structural - that is, not policy-invariant - they would necessarily change whenever policy - the rules of the game - was changed.

   a. Dahrendorf hypothesis
   b. Demand management
   c. Peak-load pricing
   d. Lucas critique

3. _____ has several particular meanings:

   - in mathematics
     - _____ function
     - Euler _____
     - _____
     - _____ subgroup
     - method of _____s (partial differential equations)
   - in physics and engineering
     - any _____ curve that shows the relationship between certain input- and output parameters, e.g.
     - an I-V or current-voltage _____ is the current in a circuit as a function of the applied voltage
     - Receiver-Operator _____
   - in fiction
     - in Dungeons ' Dragons, _____ is another name for ability score

   a. Technocracy
   b. Demand
   c. Russian financial crisis
   d. Characteristic

4. _____ refers to the actions that governments take in the economic field. It covers the systems for setting interest rates and government deficit as well as the labour market, national ownership, and many other areas of government.

   Such policies are often influenced by international institutions like the International Monetary Fund or World Bank as well as political beliefs and the consequent policies of parties.

   a. ACCRA Cost of Living Index
   b. ACEA agreement
   c. Economic policy
   d. AD-IA Model

Chapter 3. Thinking Like an Economist

5. The term _____ refers to economy-wide fluctuations in production or economic activity over several months or years. These fluctuations occur around a long-term growth trend, and typically involve shifts over time between periods of relatively rapid economic growth (expansion or boom), and periods of relative stagnation or decline (contraction or recession.)

These fluctuations are often measured using the growth rate of real gross domestic product.

 a. Business cycle
 b. Nominal value
 c. Tobit model
 d. Consumer theory

6. _____ is a broad label that refers to any individuals or households that use goods and services generated within the economy. The concept of a _____ is used in different contexts, so that the usage and significance of the term may vary.

Typically when business people and economists talk of _____s they are talking about person as _____, an aggregated commodity item with little individuality other than that expressed in the buy/not-buy decision.

 a. 1921 recession
 b. 100-year flood
 c. 130-30 fund
 d. Consumer

7. _____ is the degree of optimism that consumers feel about the overall state of the economy and their personal financial situation. How confident people feel about stability of their incomes determines their spending activity and therefore serves as one of the key indicators for the overall shape of the economy. In essence, if _____ is higher, consumers are making more purchases, boosting the economic expansion.

 a. Consumer confidence
 b. Rule Developing Experimentation
 c. Communal marketing
 d. Consumer behavior

8. The _____ was a worldwide economic downturn starting in most places in 1929 and ending at different times in the 1930s or early 1940s for different countries. It was the largest and most important economic depression in the 20th century, and is used in the 21st century as an example of how far the world's economy can fall. The _____ originated in the United States; historians most often use as a starting date the stock market crash on October 29, 1929, known as Black Tuesday.

 a. Jarrow March
 b. British Empire Economic Conference
 c. Great Depression
 d. Wall Street Crash of 1929

9. _____ is an assumption used in many contemporary macroeconomic models, and also in other areas of contemporary economics and game theory and in other applications of rational choice theory.

Since most macroeconomic models today study decisions over many periods, the expectations of workers, consumers, and firms about future economic conditions are an essential part of the model. How to model these expectations has long been controversial, and it is well known that the macroeconomic predictions of the model may differ depending on the assumptions made about expectations

a. Potential output
b. Balanced-growth equilibrium
c. Minimum wage
d. Rational expectations

10. A _____ is a public market for the trading of company stock and derivatives at an agreed price; these are securities listed on a stock exchange as well as those only traded privately.

The size of the world _____ was estimated at about $36.6 trillion US at the beginning of October 2008 . The total world derivatives market has been estimated at about $791 trillion face or nominal value, 11 times the size of the entire world economy.

a. Adam Smith
b. Stock market
c. Adolph Fischer
d. Adolf Hitler

11. A _____ is a type of economic bubble taking place in stock markets when price of stocks rise and become overvalued by any measure of stock valuation.

The existence of _____s is at odds with the assumptions of efficient market theory which assumes rational investor behaviour. Behavioral finance theory attribute _____s to cognitive biases that lead to groupthink and herd behavior.

a. Scrip issue
b. Growth investing
c. Fill or kill
d. Stock market bubble

12. _____ and Keynesian Theory) is a macroeconomic theory based on the ideas of 20th-century British economist John Maynard Keynes. _____ argues that private sector decisions sometimes lead to inefficient macroeconomic outcomes and therefore advocates active policy responses by the public sector, including monetary policy actions by the central bank and fiscal policy actions by the government to stabilize output over the business cycle.

The theories forming the basis of _____ were first presented in The General Theory of Employment, Interest and Money, published in 1936.

a. Deflation
b. Keynesian economics
c. Market failure
d. Rational choice theory

13. A _____, reserve bank, or monetary authority is the entity responsible for the monetary policy of a country or of a group of member states. It is a bank that can lend money to other banks in times of need. Its primary responsibility is to maintain the stability of the national currency and money supply, but more active duties include controlling subsidized-loan interest rates, and acting as a lender of last resort to the banking sector during times of financial crisis (private banks often being integral to the national financial system.)

a. Central bank
b. 1921 recession
c. 100-year flood
d. 130-30 fund

14. In economics, the _____ is a historical inverse relation between the rate of unemployment and the rate of inflation in an economy. Stated simply, the lower the unemployment in an economy, the higher the rate of increase in nominal wages in the economy. Rate of Change of Wages against Unemployment, United Kingdom 1913-1948 from Phillips (1958)

William Phillips, a New Zealand born economist, wrote a paper in 1958 titled The Relationship between Unemployment and the Rate of Change of Money Wages in the United Kingdom 1861-1957, which was published in the quarterly journal Economica.

- a. Cost curve
- b. Lorenz curve
- c. Phillips curve
- d. Demand curve

15. In economics, the term _____ of income or _____ refers to a simple economic model which describes the reciprocal circulation of income between producers and consumers. In the _____ model, the inter-dependent entities of producer and consumer are referred to as 'firms' and 'households' respectively and provide each other with factors in order to facilitate the flow of income. Firms provide consumers with goods and services in exchange for consumer expenditure and 'factors of production' from households.
    - a. 1921 recession
    - b. Circular flow
    - c. 100-year flood
    - d. 130-30 fund

16. _____, 1st Baron Keynes was a renowned economist from Britain whose many ideas on economic and political theories as well as on many governments' monetary policies influenced America. He advocated a government that played an active role in the lives of people regarding business, economy, etc. In this role, the government would use fiscal measures to reduce the consequences of recessions, economic depressions and booms.
    - a. John Maynard Keynes
    - b. Adolph Fischer
    - c. Adam Smith
    - d. Adolf Hitler

17. _____ is a branch of economics that deals with the performance, structure, and behavior of a national or regional economy as a whole. Along with microeconomics, _____ is one of the two most general fields in economics. It is the study of the behavior and decision-making of entire economies.
    - a. Tobit model
    - b. Nominal value
    - c. New Trade Theory
    - d. Macroeconomics

18. _____ refers to a business or organization attempting to acquire goods or services to accomplish the goals of the enterprise. Though there are several organizations that attempt to set standards in the _____ process, processes can vary greatly between organizations. Typically the word '_____' is not used interchangeably with the word 'procurement', since procurement typically includes Expediting, Supplier Quality, and Traffic and Logistics (T'L) in addition to _____.
    - a. Purchasing
    - b. 100-year flood
    - c. 130-30 fund
    - d. Free port

19. _____ is the number of goods/services that can be purchased with a unit of currency. For example, if you had taken one dollar to a store in the 1950s, you would have been able to buy a greater number of items than you would today, indicating that you would have had a greater _____ in the 1950s. Currency can be either a commodity money, like gold or silver, or fiat currency like US dollars.
    - a. Compliance cost
    - b. Purchasing power
    - c. Genuine progress indicator
    - d. Human Poverty Index

20. In economics, _____ is the total demand for final goods and services in the economy (Y) at a given time and price level. It is the amount of goods and services in the economy that will be purchased at all possible price levels. This is the demand for the gross domestic product of a country when inventory levels are static.

a. Aggregate demand
b. Aggregation problem
c. Aggregate supply
d. Aggregate expenditure

21. In economics, the _____ is a subset of the domestic economy excluding the economic activities of general government, private households, and nonprofit organizations serving individuals. In the United States the _____ accounted for about 78 percent of the value of gross domestic product (GDP) in 2000. .
   a. Happiness economics
   b. Social savings
   c. Reaganomics
   d. Business sector

22. In economics, a _____ is a mechanism that allows people to easily buy and sell (trade) financial securities (such as stocks and bonds), commodities (such as precious metals or agricultural goods), and other fungible items of value at low transaction costs and at prices that reflect the efficient-market hypothesis.

_____s have evolved significantly over several hundred years and are undergoing constant innovation to improve liquidity.

Both general markets (where many commodities are traded) and specialized markets (where only one commodity is traded) exist.

   a. Financial market
   b. Noise trader
   c. Market anomaly
   d. Convertible arbitrage

23. The _____ is 'the basic residential unit in which economic production, consumption, inheritance, child rearing, and shelter are organized and carried out'; [the _____] 'may or may not be synonomous with family'.

The _____ is the basic unit of analysis in many social, microeconomic and government models. The term refers to all individuals who live in the same dwelling.

   a. Family economics
   b. Household
   c. 130-30 fund
   d. 100-year flood

24. A _____ occurs when an entity spends more money than it takes in. The opposite of a _____ is a budget surplus. Debt is essentially an accumulated flow of deficits.
   a. Lump-sum tax
   b. Public Financial Management
   c. Funding body
   d. Budget deficit

Chapter 3. Thinking Like an Economist   45

25. Economics:

- _____ ,the desire to own something and the ability to pay for it
- _____ curve,a graphic representation of a _____ schedule
- _____ deposit, the money in checking accounts
- _____ pull theory,the theory that inflation occurs when _____ for goods and services exceeds existing supplies
- _____ schedule,a table that lists the quantity of a good a person will buy it each different price
- _____ side economics,the school of economics at believes government spending and tax cuts open economy by raising _____

a. McKesson ' Robbins scandal   b. Production
c. Variability   d. Demand

26. A _____ is a legal document that is often passed by the legislature, and approved by the chief executive-or president. For example, only certain types of revenue may be imposed and collected. Property tax is frequently the basis for municipal and county revenues, while sales tax and/or income tax are the basis for state revenues, and income tax and corporate tax are the basis for national revenues.

a. Structural deficit   b. Lump-sum tax
c. Right-financing   d. Government budget

27. To _____ is to impose a financial charge or other levy upon a taxpayer by a state or the functional equivalent of a state.

_____ es are also imposed by many subnational entities. _____ es consist of direct _____ or indirect _____ , and may be paid in money or as its labour equivalent (often but not always unpaid.)

a. 100-year flood   b. Tax
c. 130-30 fund   d. 1921 recession

28. To tax is to impose a financial charge or other levy upon a taxpayer by a state or the functional equivalent of a state.

_____ are also imposed by many subnational entities. _____ consist of direct tax or indirect tax, and may be paid in money or as its labour equivalent (often but not always unpaid.)

a. 100-year flood   b. 1921 recession
c. 130-30 fund   d. Taxes

29. _____ is a common concept in economics, and gives rise to derived concepts such as consumer debt. Generally _____ is defined by opposition to production. But the precise definition can vary because different schools of economists define production quite differently.

a. Cash or share options   b. Foreclosure data providers
c. Federal Reserve Bank Notes   d. Consumption

30. The _____ or gross domestic income (GDI), a basic measure of an economy's economic performance, is the market value of all final goods and services produced within the borders of a nation in a year. _____ can be defined in three ways, all of which are conceptually identical. First, it is equal to the total expenditures for all final goods and services produced within the country in a stipulated period of time (usually a 365-day year.)
   a. Gross domestic product
   b. Countercyclical
   c. Market structure
   d. Monopolistic competition

31. A variety of measures of _____ and output are used in economics to estimate total economic activity in a country or region, including gross domestic product (GDP), gross national product (GNP), and net _____

There are three main ways of calculating these numbers; the output approach, the income approach and the expenditure approach. In theory, the three must yield the same, because total expenditures on goods and services must equal the total income paid to the producers (Gnational income), and that must also equal the total value of the output of goods and services (GNP.)

   a. National income
   b. Gross world product
   c. GNI per capita
   d. Volume index

32. _____ use double-entry accounting to report the monetary value and sources of output produced in a country and the distribution of incomes that production generates. Data are available at the national and industry levels.

The NIPA summarizes national income on the left (debit, revenue) side and national product on the right (credit, expense) side of a two-column accounting report.

   a. Net national product
   b. Current account
   c. Gross private domestic investment
   d. National income and product accounts

33. In microeconomics, _____ is quite simply the conversion of inputs into outputs. It is an economic process that uses resources to create a good or service that is suitable for exchange. This can include manufacturing, storing, shipping, and packaging.
   a. Solved
   b. Red Guards
   c. MET
   d. Production

34. An _____, in economics, is the amount by which the real Gross domestic product exceeds potential GDP. The real GDP is also known as GDP 'adjusted for inflation', 'constant prices' GDP or 'constant dollar' GDP, because it measures the aggregate output in a country's income accounts in a given year, expressed in base-year prices. On the other hand, the potential GDP is the quantity of real GDP when a country's economy is at full-employment.
   a. ACCRA Cost of Living Index
   b. ACEA agreement
   c. AD-IA Model
   d. Inflationary gap

35. In statistics, a _____ is a value that allows data to be measured over time in terms of some base period usually through a price index in order to distinguish between changes in the money value of GNP which result from a change in prices and those which result from a change in physical output. It is the measure of the price level for some quantity. A _____ serves as a price index in which the effects of inflation are nulled.

a. Blanket order
b. Contingent employment
c. Deflator
d. Market microstructure

36. A _____ is an object whose consumption increases the utility of the consumer, for which the quantity demanded exceeds the quantity supplied at zero price. _____s are usually modeled as having diminishing marginal utility. The first individual purchase has high utility; the second has less.
a. Pie method
b. Good
c. Merit good
d. Composite good

37. In finance, the _____ is the global financial market for short-term borrowing and lending. It provides short-term liquidity funding for the global financial system. The _____ is where short-term obligations such as Treasury bills, commercial paper and bankers' acceptances are bought and sold.
a. Deferred compensation
b. Money market
c. Consignment stock
d. T-Model

38. _____ is long-term and chronic unemployment arising from imbalances between the skills and other characteristics of workers in the market and the needs of employers. It involves a mismatch between workers looking for jobs and the vacancies available often despite the number of vacancies being similar to the number of unemployed people. In this case, the unemployed workers lack the specific skills required for the jobs, or are located in a different geographical region to the vacant jobs.
a. Seasonal unemployment
b. Structural unemployment
c. Types of unemployment
d. Frictional unemployment

39. In economics, a model is a theoretical construct that represents economic processes by a set of variables and a set of logical and/or quantitative relationships between them. The _____ is a simplified framework designed to illustrate complex processes, often but not always using mathematical techniques. Frequently, _____s use structural parameters.
a. ACEA agreement
b. AD-IA Model
c. ACCRA Cost of Living Index
d. Economic model

40. In economics, a _____ is a function that specifies the output of a firm, an industry, or an entire economy for all combinations of inputs. A meta-_____ compares the practice of the existing entities converting inputs X into output y to determine the most efficient practice _____ of the existing entities, whether the most efficient feasible practice production or the most efficient actual practice production. In either case, the maximum output of a technologically-determined production process is a mathematical function of input factors of production.
a. Post-Fordism
b. Constant elasticity of substitution
c. Short-run
d. Production function

41. _____ or economic opportunity loss is the value of the next best alternative foregone as the result of making a decision. _____ analysis is an important part of a company's decision-making processes but is not treated as an actual cost in any financial statement. The next best thing that a person can engage in is referred to as the _____ of doing the best thing and ignoring the next best thing to be done.
a. Economic ideology
b. Industrial organization
c. Economic
d. Opportunity cost

48   *Chapter 3. Thinking Like an Economist*

42. Economists use the term _____ to refer to the typical decision-maker of a certain type (for example, the typical consumer, or the typical firm.)

More technically, an economic model is said to have a _____ if all agents of the same type are identical. Also, economists sometimes say a model has a _____ when agents differ, but act in such a way that the sum of their choices is mathematically equivalent to the decision of one individual or many identical individuals.

- a. Harrod-Domar model
- b. Representative agent
- c. Rostovian take-off model
- d. Classical general equilibrium model

43. _____ was a survey conducted by the U.S. Department of Justice to gauge the prevalence of alcohol and illegal drug use among prior arrestees. It was a reformulation of the prior Drug Use Forecasting (DUF) program, focused on five drugs in particular: cocaine, marijuana, methamphetamine, opiates, and PCP.

Participants were randomly selected from arrest records in major metropolitan areas; because no personally identifying information is taken from each record chosen, the resulting data can be correlated to arrest rates, but not to the total population of persons charged.

- a. ACCRA Cost of Living Index
- b. AD-IA Model
- c. ACEA agreement
- d. Arrestee Drug Abuse Monitoring

44. In economics, _____ means that people form their expectations about what will happen in the future based on what has happened in the past. For example, if inflation has been higher than expected in the past, people would revise expectations for the future.

One simple version of _____ is stated in the following equation, where p^e is the next year's rate of inflation that is currently expected; p^e_{-1} is this year's rate of inflation that was expected last year; and p is this year's actual rate of inflation:

$$p^e = p^e_{-1} + \lambda(p_{-1} - p^e_{-1})$$

With λ is between 0 and 1, this says that current expectations of future inflation reflect past expectations and an 'error-adjustment' term, in which current expectations are raised (or lowered) according to the gap between actual inflation and previous expectations.

- a. AD-IA Model
- b. Investment-specific technological progress
- c. Adaptive expectations
- d. Economic interdependence

45. In economics, _____ refers to how the marginal contribution of a factor of production usually decreases as more of the factor is used. According to this relationship, in a production system with fixed and variable inputs, beyond some point, each additional unit of the variable input yields smaller and smaller increases in output. Conversely, producing one more unit of output costs more and more in variable inputs.

Chapter 3. Thinking Like an Economist 49

a. Patent troll
b. Diminishing returns
c. Community property
d. Derivatives law

46. A _____ is:

- Rewrite _____, in generative grammar and computer science
- Standardization, a formal and widely-accepted statement, fact, definition, or qualification
- Operation, a determinate _____ for performing a mathematical operation and obtaining a certain result (Mathematics, Logic)
  - Unary operation
  - Binary operation
- _____ of inference, a function from sets of formulae to formulae (Mathematics, Logic)
- _____ of thumb, principle with broad application that is not intended to be strictly accurate or reliable for every situation. Also often simply referred to as a _____
- Moral, an atomic element of a moral code for guiding choices in human behavior
- Heuristic, a quantized '_____' which shows a tendency or probability for successful function
- A regulation, as in sports
- A Production _____, as in computer science
- Procedural law, a _____ set governing the application of laws to cases
  - A law, which may informally be called a '_____'
  - A court ruling, a decision by a court
- In the U.S. Government, a regulation mandated by Congress, but written or expanded upon by the Executive Branch.
- Norm (sociology), an informal but widely accepted _____, concept, truth, definition, or qualification (social norms, legal norms, coding norms)
- Norm (philosophy), a kind of sentence or a reason to act, feel or believe
- 'Rulership' is the concept of governance by a government:
  - Military _____, governance by a military body
  - Monastic _____, a collection of precepts that guides the life of monks or nuns in a religious order where the superior holds the place of Christ
- Slide _____

- '_____,' a song by Ayumi Hamasaki
- '_____,' a song by rapper Nas
- '_____s,' an album by the band The Whitest Boy Alive
- _____s: Pyaar Ka Superhit Formula, a 2003 Bollywood film
- ruler, an instrument for measuring lengths
- _____, a component of an astrolabe, circumferator or similar instrument
- The _____s, a bestselling self-help book
- _____ Project (Run Up-to-date Linux Everywhere), a project that aims to use up-to-date Linux software on old PCs
- _____ engine, a software system that helps managing business _____s
- Ja _____, a hip hop artist
  - R.U.L.E., a 2005 greatest hits album by rapper Ja _____
- '_____s,' a KMFDM song

a. Demand	b. Technocracy
c. Procter ' Gamble	d. Rule

47. In economics, the _____ functional form of production functions is widely used to represent the relationship of an output to inputs. It was proposed by Knut Wicksell (1851-1926), and tested against statistical evidence by Charles Cobb and Paul Douglas in 1900-1928.

For production, the function is

$$Y = AL^{\alpha}K^{\beta},$$

where:

- Y = total production (the monetary value of all goods produced in a year)
- L = labor input
- K = capital input
- A = total factor productivity
- α and β are the output elasticities of labor and capital, respectively. These values are constants determined by available technology.

Output elasticity measures the responsiveness of output to a change in levels of either labor or capital used in production, ceteris paribus. For example if $\alpha = 0.15$, a 1% increase in labor would lead to approximately a 0.15% increase in output.

a. Demand-pull theory	b. Cobb-Douglas
c. Social savings	d. Growth accounting

48. A _____ is an expression that compares quantities relative to each other. The most common examples involve two quantities, but any number of quantities can be compared. _____s are represented mathematically by separating each quantity with a colon, for example the _____ 2:3, which is read as the _____ 'two to three'.

a. Y-intercept	b. 100-year flood
c. 130-30 fund	d. Ratio

49. _____ is the a method of technical and economic research of the systems for purpose to optimize a parity between system's consumer functions or properties and expenses to achieve those functions or properties.

This methodology for continuous perfection of production, industrial technologies, organizational structures was developed by Juryj Sobolev in 1948 at the 'Perm telephone factory'

- 1948 Juryj Sobolev - the first success in application of a method analysis at the 'Perm telephone factory' .
- 1949 - the first application for the invention as result of use of the new method.

Chapter 3. Thinking Like an Economist　　　　　　　　　　　　　　　　　　　　　　　　　　　　51

Today in economically developed countries practically each enterprise or the company use methodology of the kind of functional-cost analysis as a practice of the quality management, most full satisfying to principles of standards of series ISO 9000.

- Interest of consumer not in products itself, but the advantage which it will receive from its usage.
- The consumer aspires to reduce his expenses
- Functions needed by consumer can be executed in the various ways, and, hence, with various efficiency and expenses. Among possible alternatives of realization of functions exist such in which the parity of quality and the price is the optimal for the consumer.

The goal of _____ is achievement of the highest consumer satisfaction of production at simultaneous decrease in all kinds of industrial expenses Classical _____ has three English synonyms - Value Engineering, Value Management, Value Analysis.

a. Monopoly wage
c. Staple financing
b. Function cost analysis
d. Willingness to pay

50.　In the standard exogenous growth model the type of equilibrium studied is a _____. In the _____ the capital intensity of the economy--its capital stock divided by its total output--is constant. However, other variables like the capital stock, real GDP, and output per worker are growing.

a. Monetary conditions index
c. Marginal propensity to consume
b. War economy
d. Balanced-growth equilibrium

51.　_____ is a term used in accounting, economics and finance to spread the cost of an asset over the span of several years.

In simple words we can say that _____ is the reduction in the value of an asset due to usage, passage of time, wear and tear, technological outdating or obsolescence, depletion, inadequacy, rot, rust, decay or other such factors.

In accounting, _____ is a term used to describe any method of attributing the historical or purchase cost of an asset across its useful life, roughly corresponding to normal wear and tear.

a. Net income per employee
c. Depreciation
b. Salvage value
d. Historical cost

Chapter 4. The Theory of Economic Growth

1. The _____ or gross domestic income (GDI), a basic measure of an economy's economic performance, is the market value of all final goods and services produced within the borders of a nation in a year. _____ can be defined in three ways, all of which are conceptually identical. First, it is equal to the total expenditures for all final goods and services produced within the country in a stipulated period of time (usually a 365-day year.)
    a. Gross Domestic Product
    b. Monopolistic competition
    c. Market structure
    d. Countercyclical

2. In economic models, the _____ time frame assumes no fixed factors of production. Firms can enter or leave the marketplace, and the cost (and availability) of land, labor, raw materials, and capital goods can be assumed to vary. In contrast, in the short-run time frame, certain factors are assumed to be fixed, because there is not sufficient time for them to change.
    a. Productivity world
    b. Price/performance ratio
    c. Diseconomies of scale
    d. Long-run

3. _____ is generally measured by standards such as real (i.e. inflation adjusted) income per person and poverty rate. Other measures such as access and quality of health care, income growth inequality and educational standards are also used. Examples are access to certain goods (such as number of refrigerators per 1000 people), or measures of health such as life expectancy.
    a. 130-30 fund
    b. Remuneration
    c. 100-year flood
    d. Standard of living

4. _____s is the social science that studies the production, distribution, and consumption of goods and services. The term _____s comes from the Ancient Greek οἰκονομία from οἶκος (oikos, 'house') + νόμος (nomos, 'custom' or 'law'), hence 'rules of the house(hold)'. Current _____ models developed out of the broader field of political economy in the late 19th century, owing to a desire to use an empirical approach more akin to the physical sciences.
    a. Inflation
    b. Energy economics
    c. Opportunity cost
    d. Economic

5. _____ is the increase in the amount of the goods and services produced by an economy over time. It is conventionally measured as the percent rate of increase in real gross domestic product, or real GDP. Growth is usually calculated in real terms, i.e. inflation-adjusted terms, in order to net out the effect of inflation on the price of the goods and services produced.
    a. ACEA agreement
    b. ACCRA Cost of Living Index
    c. AD-IA Model
    d. Economic growth

6. In economics, the people in the _____ are the suppliers of labor. The _____ is all the nonmilitary people who are employed or unemployed. In 2005, the worldwide _____ was over 3 billion people.
    a. Distributed workforce
    b. Departmentalization
    c. Grenelle agreements
    d. Labor force

7. _____ is a misspelled phrase from Latin 'pro capite' phrase meaning per head with pro meaning 'per' or 'for each' and capite meaning 'head.' Both words together equate to the phrase 'for each head.'

It is usually used in the field of statistics to indicate the average per person for any given concern, such as income, crime rate, etc.

It is also used in wills to indicate that each of the named beneficiaries should receive, by devise or bequest, equal shares of the estate. This is in contrast to a per stirpes division, in which each branch of the inheriting family inherits an equal share of the estate.

a. False positive rate
b. Sargan test
c. Per capita
d. Population statistics

8. In economics, the _____ functional form of production functions is widely used to represent the relationship of an output to inputs. It was proposed by Knut Wicksell (1851-1926), and tested against statistical evidence by Charles Cobb and Paul Douglas in 1900-1928.

For production, the function is

$Y = AL^{\alpha}K^{\beta}$,

where:

- Y = total production (the monetary value of all goods produced in a year)
- L = labor input
- K = capital input
- A = total factor productivity
- α and β are the output elasticities of labor and capital, respectively. These values are constants determined by available technology.

Output elasticity measures the responsiveness of output to a change in levels of either labor or capital used in production, ceteris paribus. For example if α = 0.15, a 1% increase in labor would lead to approximately a 0.15% increase in output.

a. Cobb-Douglas
b. Demand-pull theory
c. Social savings
d. Growth accounting

9. In microeconomics, _____ is quite simply the conversion of inputs into outputs. It is an economic process that uses resources to create a good or service that is suitable for exchange. This can include manufacturing, storing, shipping, and packaging.
a. Solved
b. MET
c. Production
d. Red Guards

10. In economics, a _____ is a function that specifies the output of a firm, an industry, or an entire economy for all combinations of inputs. A meta-_____ compares the practice of the existing entities converting inputs X into output y to determine the most efficient practice _____ of the existing entities, whether the most efficient feasible practice production or the most efficient actual practice production. In either case, the maximum output of a technologically-determined production process is a mathematical function of input factors of production.

a. Production function
b. Short-run
c. Constant elasticity of substitution
d. Post-Fordism

11. A _____ is an expression that compares quantities relative to each other. The most common examples involve two quantities, but any number of quantities can be compared. _____s are represented mathematically by separating each quantity with a colon, for example the _____ 2:3, which is read as the _____ 'two to three'.
   a. Ratio
   b. 100-year flood
   c. Y-intercept
   d. 130-30 fund

12. An _____, in economics, is the amount by which the real Gross domestic product exceeds potential GDP. The real GDP is also known as GDP 'adjusted for inflation', 'constant prices' GDP or 'constant dollar' GDP, because it measures the aggregate output in a country's income accounts in a given year, expressed in base-year prices. On the other hand, the potential GDP is the quantity of real GDP when a country's economy is at full-employment.
   a. Inflationary gap
   b. AD-IA Model
   c. ACEA agreement
   d. ACCRA Cost of Living Index

13. _____ is a common concept in economics, and gives rise to derived concepts such as consumer debt. Generally _____ is defined by opposition to production. But the precise definition can vary because different schools of economists define production quite differently.
   a. Foreclosure data providers
   b. Cash or share options
   c. Federal Reserve Bank Notes
   d. Consumption

14. _____ is the term in economics for the amount of fixed or real capital present in relation to other factors of production, especially labor. At the level of either a production process or the aggregate economy, it may be estimated by the capital/labor ratio, such as from the points along a capital/labor isoquant.

Since the use of tools and machinery makes labor more effective, rising _____ pushes up the productivity of labor, so a society that is more capital intensive tends to have a higher standard of living over the long run than one with low _____.

   a. Capital intensity
   b. Capital flight
   c. Capital goods
   d. Firm-specific infrastructure

15. _____ refers to the actions that governments take in the economic field. It covers the systems for setting interest rates and government deficit as well as the labour market, national ownership, and many other areas of government.

Such policies are often influenced by international institutions like the International Monetary Fund or World Bank as well as political beliefs and the consequent policies of parties.

   a. Economic policy
   b. ACEA agreement
   c. AD-IA Model
   d. ACCRA Cost of Living Index

16. The _____ was a period in the late 18th and early 19th centuries when major changes in agriculture, manufacturing, mining, and transportation had a profound effect on the socioeconomic and cultural conditions in Britain. The changes subsequently spread throughout Europe, North America, and eventually the world. The onset of the _____ marked a major turning point in human society; almost every aspect of daily life was eventually influenced in some way.

| a. Industrial Revolution | b. Adolph Fischer |
| c. Adam Smith | d. Adolf Hitler |

17. _____ is a type of private equity investment, most often a minority investment, in relatively mature companies that are looking for capital to expand or restructure operations, enter new markets or finance a significant acquisition without a change of control of the business.

Companies that seek _____, will often do so in order to finance a transformational event in their lifecycle. These companies are likely to be more mature than venture capital funded companies, able to generate revenue and operating profits but unable to generate sufficient cash to fund major expansions, acquisitions or other investments.

| a. Startup company | b. Seed money |
| c. Club deal | d. Growth Capital |

18. In the standard exogenous growth model the type of equilibrium studied is a _____. In the _____ the capital intensity of the economy--its capital stock divided by its total output--is constant. However, other variables like the capital stock, real GDP, and output per worker are growing.

| a. Monetary conditions index | b. Balanced-growth equilibrium |
| c. War economy | d. Marginal propensity to consume |

19. _____ in economics refers to metrics and measures of output from production processes, per unit of input. Labor _____, for example, is typically measured as a ratio of output per labor-hour, an input. _____ may be conceived of as a metrics of the technical or engineering efficiency of production.

| a. Piece work | b. Production-possibility frontier |
| c. Fordism | d. Productivity |

20. _____ is the a method of technical and economic research of the systems for purpose to optimize a parity between system's consumer functions or properties and expenses to achieve those functions or properties.

This methodology for continuous perfection of production, industrial technologies, organizational structures was developed by Juryj Sobolev in 1948 at the 'Perm telephone factory'

- 1948 Juryj Sobolev - the first success in application of a method analysis at the 'Perm telephone factory' .
- 1949 - the first application for the invention as result of use of the new method.

Chapter 4. The Theory of Economic Growth

Today in economically developed countries practically each enterprise or the company use methodology of the kind of functional-cost analysis as a practice of the quality management, most full satisfying to principles of standards of series ISO 9000.

- Interest of consumer not in products itself, but the advantage which it will receive from its usage.
- The consumer aspires to reduce his expenses
- Functions needed by consumer can be executed in the various ways, and, hence, with various efficiency and expenses. Among possible alternatives of realization of functions exist such in which the parity of quality and the price is the optimal for the consumer.

The goal of _____ is achievement of the highest consumer satisfaction of production at simultaneous decrease in all kinds of industrial expenses Classical _____ has three English synonyms - Value Engineering, Value Management, Value Analysis.

a. Monopoly wage
b. Staple financing
c. Willingness to pay
d. Function cost analysis

21. In economics, accounting and Marxian economics, _____ is often equated with investment of profit income, especially in real capital goods. The concentration and centralisation of capital are two of the results of such accumulation

But _____ can refer variously to

- working and consuming less than earned
- relying on the effects of compound interest to increase initial capital
- real investment in tangible means of production.
- financial investment in assets represented on paper.
- investment in non-productive physical assets such as residential real estate that appreciate in value.
- consuming less than produced by productive assets like farm land--saving or accumulating the residual
- 'human _____,' i.e., new education and training increasing the skills of the labour force.

Non-financial and financial _____ is usually needed for economic growth, since additional production usually requires additional funds to enlarge the scale of production. Smarter and more productive organization of production can also increase production without increased capital.

a. Capital accumulation
b. Marxian economics
c. Productive force
d. Cultural Marxism

22. The _____ is 'the basic residential unit in which economic production, consumption, inheritance, child rearing, and shelter are organized and carried out'; [the _____] 'may or may not be synonomous with family'.

The _____ is the basic unit of analysis in many social, microeconomic and government models. The term refers to all individuals who live in the same dwelling.

Chapter 4. The Theory of Economic Growth 57

a. Family economics	b. 130-30 fund
c. 100-year flood	d. Household

23. If the government intervenes by implementing, for example, a tax or a subsidy, then the graph of supply and demand becomes more complicated and will also include an area that represents _____.

Combined, the consumer surplus, the producer surplus, and the _____ make up the social surplus or the total surplus. Total surplus is the primary measure used in welfare economics to evaluate the efficiency of a proposed policy.

a. Customer equity	b. Marginal revenue
c. Long term	d. Government surplus

24. _____ is a term used in accounting, economics and finance to spread the cost of an asset over the span of several years.

In simple words we can say that _____ is the reduction in the value of an asset due to usage, passage of time, wear and tear, technological outdating or obsolescence, depletion, inadequacy, rot, rust, decay or other such factors.

In accounting, _____ is a term used to describe any method of attributing the historical or purchase cost of an asset across its useful life, roughly corresponding to normal wear and tear.

a. Historical cost	b. Salvage value
c. Net income per employee	d. Depreciation

25. The term _____ refers to government debt, expenditures and revenues, or to finance (particularly financial revenue) in general.

- _____ deficit is the budget deficit of federal or local government
- _____ policy is the discretionary spending of governments. Contrasts with monetary policy.
- _____ year and _____ quarter are reporting periods for firms and other agencies.

a. Fiscal	b. Procter ' Gamble
c. Drawdown	d. Bucket shop

26. In economics, _____ is the use of government spending and revenue collection to influence the economy.

_____ can be contrasted with the other main type of economic policy, monetary policy, which attempts to stabilize the economy by controlling interest rates and the supply of money. The two main instruments of _____ are government spending and taxation.

58 *Chapter 4. The Theory of Economic Growth*

a. 100-year flood
c. Sustainable investment rule
b. Fiscalism
d. Fiscal policy

27. A _____ is:

- Rewrite _____, in generative grammar and computer science
- Standardization, a formal and widely-accepted statement, fact, definition, or qualification
- Operation, a determinate _____ for performing a mathematical operation and obtaining a certain result (Mathematics, Logic)
    - Unary operation
    - Binary operation
- _____ of inference, a function from sets of formulae to formulae (Mathematics, Logic)
- _____ of thumb, principle with broad application that is not intended to be strictly accurate or reliable for every situation. Also often simply referred to as a _____
- Moral, an atomic element of a moral code for guiding choices in human behavior
- Heuristic, a quantized '_____' which shows a tendency or probability for successful function
- A regulation, as in sports
- A Production _____, as in computer science
- Procedural law, a _____ set governing the application of laws to cases
    - A law, which may informally be called a '_____'
    - A court ruling, a decision by a court
- In the U.S. Government, a regulation mandated by Congress, but written or expanded upon by the Executive Branch.
- Norm (sociology), an informal but widely accepted _____, concept, truth, definition, or qualification (social norms, legal norms, coding norms)
- Norm (philosophy), a kind of sentence or a reason to act, feel or believe
- 'Rulership' is the concept of governance by a government:
    - Military _____, governance by a military body
    - Monastic _____, a collection of precepts that guides the life of monks or nuns in a religious order where the superior holds the place of Christ
- Slide _____

- '_____,' a song by Ayumi Hamasaki
- '_____,' a song by rapper Nas
- '_____s,' an album by the band The Whitest Boy Alive
- _____s: Pyaar Ka Superhit Formula, a 2003 Bollywood film
- ruler, an instrument for measuring lengths
- _____, a component of an astrolabe, circumferator or similar instrument
- The _____s, a bestselling self-help book
- _____ Project (Run Up-to-date Linux Everywhere), a project that aims to use up-to-date Linux software on old PCs
- _____ engine, a software system that helps managing business _____s
- Ja _____, a hip hop artist
    - R.U.L.E., a 2005 greatest hits album by rapper Ja _____
- '_____s,' a KMFDM song

Chapter 4. The Theory of Economic Growth

a. Technocracy
b. Rule
c. Demand
d. Procter ' Gamble

28. In Marxian economics, _____ originally referred to the means of production. Individuals, organizations and governments use _____ in the production of other goods or commodities. _____ include factories, machinery, tools, equipment, and various buildings which are used to produce other products for consumption.
   a. Wealth inequality in the United States
   b. Capital intensive
   c. Capital deepening
   d. Capital goods

29. A _____ is an object whose consumption increases the utility of the consumer, for which the quantity demanded exceeds the quantity supplied at zero price. _____s are usually modeled as having diminishing marginal utility. The first individual purchase has high utility; the second has less.
   a. Composite good
   b. Merit good
   c. Pie method
   d. Good

30. _____ in economics and business is the result of an exchange and from that trade we assign a numerical monetary value to a good, service or asset. If Alice trades Bob 4 apples for an orange, the _____ of an orange is 4 apples. Inversely, the _____ of an apple is 1/4 oranges.
   a. Price
   b. Premium pricing
   c. Price book
   d. Price war

31. _____, in economics, occurs when assets and/or money rapidly flow out of a country, due to an economic event that disturbs investors and causes them to lower their valuation of the assets in that country, or otherwise to lose confidence in its economic strength. This leads to a disappearance of wealth and is usually accompanied by a sharp drop in the exchange rate of the affected country (depreciation in a variable exchange rate regime, or a forced devaluation in a fixed exchange rate regime.)

This fall is particularly damaging when the capital belongs to the people of the affected country, because not only are the citizens now burdened by the loss of faith in the economy and devaluation of their currency, but probably also their assets have lost much of their nominal value.

   a. Capital flight
   b. Firm-specific infrastructure
   c. Capital formation
   d. Liquid capital

Chapter 5. The Reality of Economic Growth: History and Prospect

1. The _____ was a period in the late 18th and early 19th centuries when major changes in agriculture, manufacturing, mining, and transportation had a profound effect on the socioeconomic and cultural conditions in Britain. The changes subsequently spread throughout Europe, North America, and eventually the world. The onset of the _____ marked a major turning point in human society; almost every aspect of daily life was eventually influenced in some way.
   a. Adolph Fischer
   b. Adam Smith
   c. Adolf Hitler
   d. Industrial Revolution

2. In economics, the _____ functional form of production functions is widely used to represent the relationship of an output to inputs. It was proposed by Knut Wicksell (1851-1926), and tested against statistical evidence by Charles Cobb and Paul Douglas in 1900-1928.

For production, the function is

$$Y = AL^{\alpha}K^{\beta},$$

where:

- Y = total production (the monetary value of all goods produced in a year)
- L = labor input
- K = capital input
- A = total factor productivity
- α and β are the output elasticities of labor and capital, respectively. These values are constants determined by available technology.

Output elasticity measures the responsiveness of output to a change in levels of either labor or capital used in production, ceteris paribus. For example if α = 0.15, a 1% increase in labor would lead to approximately a 0.15% increase in output.

   a. Demand-pull theory
   b. Social savings
   c. Growth accounting
   d. Cobb-Douglas

3. _____s is the social science that studies the production, distribution, and consumption of goods and services. The term _____s comes from the Ancient Greek οἰκονομία from οἶκος (oikos, 'house') + νόμος (nomos, 'custom' or 'law'), hence 'rules of the house(hold)'. Current _____ models developed out of the broader field of political economy in the late 19th century, owing to a desire to use an empirical approach more akin to the physical sciences.
   a. Energy economics
   b. Opportunity cost
   c. Inflation
   d. Economic

4. _____ is the increase in the amount of the goods and services produced by an economy over time. It is conventionally measured as the percent rate of increase in real gross domestic product, or real GDP. Growth is usually calculated in real terms, i.e. inflation-adjusted terms, in order to net out the effect of inflation on the price of the goods and services produced.
   a. Economic growth
   b. AD-IA Model
   c. ACCRA Cost of Living Index
   d. ACEA agreement

Chapter 5. The Reality of Economic Growth: History and Prospect   61

5. _____ is generally measured by standards such as real (i.e. inflation adjusted) income per person and poverty rate. Other measures such as access and quality of health care, income growth inequality and educational standards are also used. Examples are access to certain goods (such as number of refrigerators per 1000 people), or measures of health such as life expectancy.
- a. 100-year flood
- b. 130-30 fund
- c. Standard of living
- d. Remuneration

6. _____ is that which is owed; usually referencing assets owed, but the term can also cover moral obligations and other interactions not requiring money. In the case of assets, _____ is a means of using future purchasing power in the present before a summation has been earned. Some companies and corporations use _____ as a part of their overall corporate finance strategy.
- a. Debenture
- b. Collateral Management
- c. Hard money loan
- d. Debt

7. In microeconomics, _____ is quite simply the conversion of inputs into outputs. It is an economic process that uses resources to create a good or service that is suitable for exchange. This can include manufacturing, storing, shipping, and packaging.
- a. MET
- b. Red Guards
- c. Solved
- d. Production

8. In economics, a _____ is a function that specifies the output of a firm, an industry, or an entire economy for all combinations of inputs. A meta-_____ compares the practice of the existing entities converting inputs X into output y to determine the most efficient practice _____ of the existing entities, whether the most efficient feasible practice production or the most efficient actual practice production. In either case, the maximum output of a technologically-determined production process is a mathematical function of input factors of production.
- a. Short-run
- b. Post-Fordism
- c. Production function
- d. Constant elasticity of substitution

9. _____ is the term in economics for the amount of fixed or real capital present in relation to other factors of production, especially labor. At the level of either a production process or the aggregate economy, it may be estimated by the capital/labor ratio, such as from the points along a capital/labor isoquant.

Since the use of tools and machinery makes labor more effective, rising _____ pushes up the productivity of labor, so a society that is more capital intensive tends to have a higher standard of living over the long run than one with low _____.

- a. Firm-specific infrastructure
- b. Capital flight
- c. Capital goods
- d. Capital intensity

10. _____s (economically referred to as land or raw materials) occur naturally within environments that exist relatively undisturbed by mankind, in a natural form. A _____'s is often characterized by amounts of biodiversity existent in various ecosystems.

Mining, petroleum extraction, fishing, hunting, and forestry are generally considered natural-resource industries.

a. 100-year flood
b. 1921 recession
c. 130-30 fund
d. Natural resource

11. _____ is a type of private equity investment, most often a minority investment, in relatively mature companies that are looking for capital to expand or restructure operations, enter new markets or finance a significant acquisition without a change of control of the business.

Companies that seek _____, will often do so in order to finance a transformational event in their lifecycle. These companies are likely to be more mature than venture capital funded companies, able to generate revenue and operating profits but unable to generate sufficient cash to fund major expansions, acquisitions or other investments.

a. Growth Capital
b. Club deal
c. Startup company
d. Seed money

12. In economic models, the _____ time frame assumes no fixed factors of production. Firms can enter or leave the marketplace, and the cost (and availability) of land, labor, raw materials, and capital goods can be assumed to vary. In contrast, in the short-run time frame, certain factors are assumed to be fixed, because there is not sufficient time for them to change.

a. Price/performance ratio
b. Productivity world
c. Diseconomies of scale
d. Long-run

13. _____ data refers to selected population characteristics as used in government, marketing or opinion research, or the _____ profiles used in such research. Note the distinction from the term 'demography' Commonly-used _____s include race, age, income, disabilities, mobility (in terms of travel time to work or number of vehicles available), educational attainment, home ownership, employment status, and even location.

a. Demographic warfare
b. NEET
c. Generation Z
d. Demographic

14. The _____ model (Demographic transitionM) is a model used to represent the process of explaining the transformation of countries from high birth rates and high death rates to low birth rates and low death rates as part of the economic development of a country from a pre-industrial to an industrialized economy. It is based on an interpretation begun in 1929 by the American demographer Warren Thompson of prior observed changes, or transitions, in birth and death rates in industrialized societies over the past two hundred years.

Most developed countries are beyond stage three of the model; the majority of developing countries are in stage 2 or stage 3.

a. Population mobility
b. Healthy Life Years
c. Demographic economics
d. Demographic transition

15. _____ is the change in population over time, and can be quantified as the change in the number of individuals in a population using 'per unit time' for measurement. The term _____ can technically refer to any species, but almost always refers to humans, and it is often used informally for the more specific demographic term _____ rate , and is often used to refer specifically to the growth of the population of the world.

Chapter 5. The Reality of Economic Growth: History and Prospect 63

Simple models of _____ include the Malthusian Growth Model and the logistic model.

a. 100-year flood
b. 130-30 fund
c. Population dynamics
d. Population growth

16. _____ has several particular meanings:

- in mathematics
    - _____ function
    - Euler _____
    - _____
    - _____ subgroup
    - method of _____s (partial differential equations)
- in physics and engineering
    - any _____ curve that shows the relationship between certain input- and output parameters, e.g.
    - an I-V or current-voltage _____ is the current in a circuit as a function of the applied voltage
    - Receiver-Operator _____
- in fiction
    - in Dungeons ' Dragons, _____ is another name for ability score

a. Russian financial crisis
b. Demand
c. Technocracy
d. Characteristic

17.

_____ was a German philosopher, political economist, historian, political theorist, sociologist, communist and revolutionary credited as the founder of communism.

Marx summarized his approach to history and politics in the opening line of the first chapter of The Communist Manifesto : e;The history of all hitherto existing society is the history of class struggles.e; Marx argued that capitalism, like previous socioeconomic systems, will produce internal tensions which will lead to its destruction. Just as capitalism replaced feudalism, socialism will in its turn replace capitalism and lead to a stateless, classless society which will emerge after a transitional period, the 'dictatorship of the proletariat'.

a. Karl Heinrich Marx
b. Neo-Gramscianism
c. Adam Smith
d. Marxism

18. The _____ is a monetary system in which a region's common medium of exchange are paper notes that are normally freely convertible into pre-set, fixed quantities of gold. The _____ is not currently used by any government, having been replaced completely by fiat currency. Gold certificates were used as paper currency in the United States from 1882 to 1933, these certificates were freely convertable into gold coins.

In the 1790s Britain suffered a massive shortage of silver coinage and ceased to mint larger silver coins.

a. 1921 recession
b. Gold standard
c. 100-year flood
d. 130-30 fund

19. _____ in economics refers to metrics and measures of output from production processes, per unit of input. Labor _____, for example, is typically measured as a ratio of output per labor-hour, an input. _____ may be conceived of as a metrics of the technical or engineering efficiency of production.
    a. Piece work
    b. Fordism
    c. Production-possibility frontier
    d. Productivity

20. The _____ was a worldwide economic downturn starting in most places in 1929 and ending at different times in the 1930s or early 1940s for different countries. It was the largest and most important economic depression in the 20th century, and is used in the 21st century as an example of how far the world's economy can fall. The _____ originated in the United States; historians most often use as a starting date the stock market crash on October 29, 1929, known as Black Tuesday.
    a. Jarrow March
    b. British Empire Economic Conference
    c. Great Depression
    d. Wall Street Crash of 1929

21. In economics, _____ (TFP) is a variable which accounts for effects in total output not caused by inputs. For example, a year with unusually good weather will tend to have higher output, because bad weather hinders agricultural output. A variable like weather does not directly relate to unit inputs, so weather is considered a _____ variable.
    a. 35-hour working week
    b. Flow to Equity-Approach
    c. Human rights
    d. Total-factor productivity

22. A _____ is an expression that compares quantities relative to each other. The most common examples involve two quantities, but any number of quantities can be compared. _____s are represented mathematically by separating each quantity with a colon, for example the _____ 2:3, which is read as the _____ 'two to three'.
    a. Y-intercept
    b. 130-30 fund
    c. Ratio
    d. 100-year flood

23. _____ is a common concept in economics, and gives rise to derived concepts such as consumer debt. Generally _____ is defined by opposition to production. But the precise definition can vary because different schools of economists define production quite differently.
    a. Consumption
    b. Cash or share options
    c. Foreclosure data providers
    d. Federal Reserve Bank Notes

24. The _____ is the market for securities, where companies and governments can raise longterm funds. It is a market in which money is lent for periods longer than a year. The _____ includes the stock market and the bond market.
    a. Performance attribution
    b. Financial instrument
    c. Multi-family office
    d. Capital market

25. In American history, the _____ refers to substantial growth in population in the United States and extravagant displays of wealth and excess of America's upper-class during the post-Civil War and post-Reconstruction era, in the late 19th century (1865-1901.) The wealth polarization derived primarily from industrial and population expansion. The businessmen of the Second Industrial Revolution created industrial towns and cities in the Northeast with new factories, and contributed to the creation of an ethnically diverse industrial working class which produced the wealth owned by rising super-rich industrialists and financiers such as Cornelius Vanderbilt, John D. Rockefeller, Andrew Carnegie, Henry Flagler, and J.P. Morgan.
   a. Adam Smith
   b. Gilded Age
   c. Adolph Fischer
   d. Adolf Hitler

26. _____ is the cost of maintaining a certain standard of living. Changes in the _____ over time are often operationalized in a _____ index. _____ calculations are also used to compare the cost of maintaining a certain standard of living in different geographic areas.
   a. Cost of living
   b. Bear raid
   c. Decision process tool
   d. Restructuring

27. The _____ or gross domestic income (GDI), a basic measure of an economy's economic performance, is the market value of all final goods and services produced within the borders of a nation in a year. _____ can be defined in three ways, all of which are conceptually identical. First, it is equal to the total expenditures for all final goods and services produced within the country in a stipulated period of time (usually a 365-day year.)
   a. Market structure
   b. Monopolistic competition
   c. Countercyclical
   d. Gross domestic product

28. An _____, in economics, is the amount by which the real Gross domestic product exceeds potential GDP. The real GDP is also known as GDP 'adjusted for inflation', 'constant prices' GDP or 'constant dollar' GDP, because it measures the aggregate output in a country's income accounts in a given year, expressed in base-year prices. On the other hand, the potential GDP is the quantity of real GDP when a country's economy is at full-employment.
   a. ACCRA Cost of Living Index
   b. AD-IA Model
   c. Inflationary gap
   d. ACEA agreement

29. A _____ is something for which there is demand, but which is supplied without qualitative differentiation across a market. It is a product that is the same no matter who produces it, such as petroleum, notebook paper, or milk. In other words, copper is copper.
   a. Soft commodity
   b. 100-year flood
   c. Hard commodity
   d. Commodity

30. _____ of an economy refers to a long-term widespread change of the fundamental structure, rather than microscale or short-term output and employment. For example, a subsistence economy is transformed into a manufacturing economy, or a regulated mixed economy is liberalized. A current _____ in the world economy is globalization.
   a. Fiscal adjustment
   b. Robertson lag
   c. Structural change
   d. Dishoarding

31. _____ in economics and business is the result of an exchange and from that trade we assign a numerical monetary value to a good, service or asset. If Alice trades Bob 4 apples for an orange, the _____ of an orange is 4 apples. Inversely, the _____ of an apple is 1/4 oranges.

a. Price
b. Price book
c. Premium pricing
d. Price war

32. An _____ is a manufacturing process in which parts (usually interchangeable parts) are added to a product in a sequential manner using optimally planned logistics to create a finished product much faster than with handcrafting-type methods. The _____ developed by Ford Motor Company between 1908 and 1915 made _____s famous in the following decade through the social ramifications of mass production, such as the affordability of the Ford Model T and the introduction of high wages for Ford workers. However, the various preconditions for the development at Ford stretched far back into the 19th century, from the gradual realization of the dream of interchangeability, to the concept of reinventing workflow and job descriptions using analytical methods.

a. Assembly line
b. ACEA agreement
c. AD-IA Model
d. ACCRA Cost of Living Index

33. _____ was the American founder of the Ford Motor Company and father of modern assembly lines used in mass production. His introduction of the Model T automobile revolutionized transportation and American industry. He was a prolific inventor and was awarded 161 U.S. patents.

a. Henry Ford
b. George Cabot Lodge II
c. Werner Sombart
d. Maximilian Carl Emil Weber

34. _____ is the production of large amounts of standardized products, including and especially on assembly lines. The concepts of _____ are applied to various kinds of products, from fluids and particulates handled in bulk to discrete solid parts to assemblies of such parts

_____ of assemblies typically uses electric-motor-powered moving tracks or conveyor belts to move partially complete products to workers, who perform simple repetitive tasks.

a. 130-30 fund
b. 100-year flood
c. 1921 recession
d. Mass production

35. _____ is a practice of protecting the environment, on individual, organisational or governmental level, for the benefit of the natural environment and (or) humans.

Due to the pressures of population and technology the biophysical environment is being degraded, sometimes permanently. This has been recognised and governments began placing restraints on activities that caused environmental degradation.

a. ACCRA Cost of Living Index
b. ACEA agreement
c. AD-IA Model
d. Environmental protection

36. A variety of measures of _____ and output are used in economics to estimate total economic activity in a country or region, including gross domestic product (GDP), gross national product (GNP), and net _____

There are three main ways of calculating these numbers; the output approach, the income approach and the expenditure approach. In theory, the three must yield the same, because total expenditures on goods and services must equal the total income paid to the producers (Gnational income), and that must also equal the total value of the output of goods and services (GNP.)

Chapter 5. The Reality of Economic Growth: History and Prospect

a. National income
b. Gross world product
c. GNI per capita
d. Volume index

37. _____ use double-entry accounting to report the monetary value and sources of output produced in a country and the distribution of incomes that production generates. Data are available at the national and industry levels.

The NIPA summarizes national income on the left (debit, revenue) side and national product on the right (credit, expense) side of a two-column accounting report.

a. Current account
b. Net national product
c. Gross private domestic investment
d. National income and product accounts

38. In economics, the _____ is a historical inverse relation between the rate of unemployment and the rate of inflation in an economy. Stated simply, the lower the unemployment in an economy, the higher the rate of increase in nominal wages in the economy. Rate of Change of Wages against Unemployment, United Kingdom 1913-1948 from Phillips (1958)

William Phillips, a New Zealand born economist, wrote a paper in 1958 titled The Relationship between Unemployment and the Rate of Change of Money Wages in the United Kingdom 1861-1957, which was published in the quarterly journal Economica.

a. Cost curve
b. Phillips curve
c. Demand curve
d. Lorenz curve

39. A _____ is any period of greatly increased birth rate during a certain period, and usually within certain geographical bounds and when the birth rate exceeds 2% of the population. People born during such a period are sometimes called _____ers, but note the difference between a demographic boom in births and the cultural generations born during such a birth boom. Some contest the general conventional wisdom that _____s signify good times and periods of general economic growth, and stability.

a. Baby boom
b. Demographic warfare
c. Demographic analysis
d. Rate of natural increase

40. In economics, the people in the _____ are the suppliers of labor. The _____ is all the nonmilitary people who are employed or unemployed. In 2005, the worldwide _____ was over 3 billion people.

a. Departmentalization
b. Distributed workforce
c. Grenelle agreements
d. Labor force

41. The _____ is 'the basic residential unit in which economic production, consumption, inheritance, child rearing, and shelter are organized and carried out'; [the _____] 'may or may not be synonymous with family'.

The _____ is the basic unit of analysis in many social, microeconomic and government models. The term refers to all individuals who live in the same dwelling.

a. 130-30 fund
b. Family economics
c. 100-year flood
d. Household

42. The _____ was an evolution of developed countries from an industrial/manufacturing-based wealth producing economy into a service sector asset based economy, brought about by globalization and currency manipulation by governments and their central banks. Some analysts claimed that this change in the economic structure of the United States had created a state of permanent steady growth, low unemployment, and immunity to boom and bust macroeconomic cycles. They believed that the change rendered obsolete many business practices.
   a. 1921 recession
   b. 100-year flood
   c. New economy
   d. 130-30 fund

43. In economics, the term _____ of income or _____ refers to a simple economic model which describes the reciprocal circulation of income between producers and consumers. In the _____ model, the inter-dependent entities of producer and consumer are referred to as 'firms' and 'households' respectively and provide each other with factors in order to facilitate the flow of income. Firms provide consumers with goods and services in exchange for consumer expenditure and 'factors of production' from households.
   a. 1921 recession
   b. 130-30 fund
   c. Circular flow
   d. 100-year flood

44. The _____ is the apparent contradiction that although water is on the whole more useful, in terms of survival, than diamonds, diamonds command a higher price in the market. The economist Adam Smith is often considered to be the classic presenter of this paradox. Nicolaus Copernicus, John Locke, John Law and others had previously tried to explain the disparity.
   a. 130-30 fund
   b. St. Petersburg paradox
   c. 100-year flood
   d. Paradox of value

45. In economics, a _____ is a general slowdown in economic activity over a sustained period of time, or a business cycle contraction. During _____s, many macroeconomic indicators vary in a similar way. Production as measured by Gross Domestic Product (GDP), employment, investment spending, capacity utilization, household incomes and business profits all fall during _____s.
   a. Recession
   b. Leading indicators
   c. Treasury View
   d. Monetary economics

46. In statistics, a _____ is a value that allows data to be measured over time in terms of some base period ussually through a price index in order to distinguish between changes in the money value of GNP which result from a change in prices and those which result from a change in physical output. It is the measure of the price level for some quantity. A _____ serves as a price index in which the effects of inflation are nulled.
   a. Market microstructure
   b. Blanket order
   c. Deflator
   d. Contingent employment

47. In Marxian economics, _____ originally referred to the means of production. Individuals, organizations and governments use _____ in the production of other goods or commodities. _____ include factories, machinery, tools, equipment, and various buildings which are used to produce other products for consumption.
   a. Capital deepening
   b. Capital intensive
   c. Wealth inequality in the United States
   d. Capital goods

48. A _____ is an object whose consumption increases the utility of the consumer, for which the quantity demanded exceeds the quantity supplied at zero price. _____s are usually modeled as having diminishing marginal utility. The first individual purchase has high utility; the second has less.

a. Pie method
b. Merit good
c. Composite good
d. Good

49. The Organisation for Economic Co-operation and Development (_____) is an international organisation of 30 countries that accept the principles of representative democracy and free-market economy. Most _____ members are high-income economies with a high HDI and are regarded as developed countries.

It originated in 1948 as the Organisation for European Economic Co-operation , led by Robert Marjolin of France, to help administer the Marshall Plan for the reconstruction of Europe after World War II.

a. ACCRA Cost of Living Index
b. OECD
c. AD-IA Model
d. ACEA agreement

50. In economics, _____ is how a natione;s total economy is distributed among its population. ._____ has always been a central concern of economic theory and economic policy. Classical economists such as Adam Smith, Thomas Malthus and David Ricardo were mainly concerned with factor _____, that is, the distribution of income between the main factors of production, land, labour and capital.

a. Eco commerce
b. Income distribution
c. Authorised capital
d. Equipment trust certificate

51. In economics and finance, _____ is the practice of taking advantage of a price differential between two or more markets: striking a combination of matching deals that capitalize upon the imbalance, the profit being the difference between the market prices. When used by academics, an _____ is a transaction that involves no negative cash flow at any probabilistic or temporal state and a positive cash flow in at least one state; in simple terms, a risk-free profit. A person who engages in _____ is called an arbitrageur--such as a bank or brokerage firm.

a. Electronic trading
b. Arbitrage
c. Alternext
d. Options Price Reporting Authority

52. The _____ of monetary management established the rules for commercial and financial relations among the world's major industrial states in the mid 20th Century. The _____ was the first example of a fully negotiated monetary order intended to govern monetary relations among independent nation-states.

Preparing to rebuild the international economic system as World War II was still raging, 730 delegates from all 44 Allied nations gathered at the Mount Washington Hotel in Bretton Woods, New Hampshire, United States, for the United Nations Monetary and Financial Conference.

a. 1921 recession
b. Bretton Woods system
c. 130-30 fund
d. 100-year flood

53. A _____, sometimes called a pegged exchange rate, is a type of exchange rate regime wherein a currency's value is matched to the value of another single currency or to a basket of other currencies such as gold.

A _____ is usually used to stabilize the value of a currency, vis-a-vis the currency it is pegged to. This facilitates trade and investments between the two countries, and is especially useful for small economies where external trade forms a large part of their GDP.

a. Leading indicators
b. Law of supply
c. Monetary economics
d. Fixed exchange rate

54. A _____ or a flexible exchange rate is a type of exchange rate regime wherein a currency's value is allowed to fluctuate according to the foreign exchange market. A currency that uses a _____ is known as a floating currency. The opposite of a _____ is a fixed exchange rate.
   a. Foreign exchange market
   b. Trade Weighted US dollar Index
   c. Floating currency
   d. Floating exchange rate

55. A _____ is an economic system that incorporates a mixture of private and government ownership or control, or a mixture of capitalism and socialism.

There is not one single definition for a _____, but relevant aspects include: a degree of private economic freedom (including privately owned industry) intermingled with centralized economic planning and government regulation (which may include regulation of the market for environmental concerns and social welfare, or state ownership and management of some of the means of production for national or social objectives.)

For some states, there is not a consensus on whether they are capitalist, socialist, or mixed economies.

   a. Mixed economy
   b. Dual economy
   c. Hunter-gatherer
   d. Planned liberalism

56. _____ refers to a business or organization attempting to acquire goods or services to accomplish the goals of the enterprise. Though there are several organizations that attempt to set standards in the _____ process, processes can vary greatly between organizations. Typically the word '_____' is not used interchangeably with the word 'procurement', since procurement typically includes Expediting, Supplier Quality, and Traffic and Logistics (T'L) in addition to _____.
   a. 100-year flood
   b. 130-30 fund
   c. Free port
   d. Purchasing

57. _____ is the number of goods/services that can be purchased with a unit of currency. For example, if you had taken one dollar to a store in the 1950s, you would have been able to buy a greater number of items than you would today, indicating that you would have had a greater _____ in the 1950s. Currency can be either a commodity money, like gold or silver, or fiat currency like US dollars.
   a. Genuine progress indicator
   b. Human Poverty Index
   c. Compliance cost
   d. Purchasing power

58. The _____ theory uses the long-term equilibrium exchange rate of two currencies to equalize their purchasing power. Developed by Gustav Cassel in 1920, it is based on the law of one price: the theory states that, in ideally efficient markets, identical goods should have only one price.

This purchasing power SEM rate equalizes the purchasing power of different currencies in their home countries for a given basket of goods.

   a. Gross national product
   b. Purchasing power parity
   c. Measures of national income and output
   d. Bureau of Labor Statistics

Chapter 5. The Reality of Economic Growth: History and Prospect

59. _____ is money accepted for exchange of goods in an economy. The prevalence of one money over another arises, usually, when a government designates through decrees that the government shall accept only particular notes and coins in payment for taxes. Typically, money of _____ consists of stamped coins and minted paper bills.
- a. Local currency
- b. Totnes pound
- c. Currency
- d. Security thread

60. In finance, the _____s between two currencies specifies how much one currency is worth in terms of the other. It is the value of a foreign natione;s currency in terms of the home natione;s currency. For example an _____ of 102 Japanese yen to the United States dollar means that JPY 102 is worth the same as USD 1.
- a. ACCRA Cost of Living Index
- b. Exchange rate
- c. ACEA agreement
- d. Interbank market

61. _____ was the General Secretary of the Communist Party of the Soviet Union's Central Committee from 1922 until his death in 1953. In the years following Lenin's death in 1924, he rose to become the leader of the Soviet Union.

Stalin launched a command economy, replacing the New Economic Policy of the 1920s with Five-Year Plans and launching a period of rapid industrialization and economic collectivization.

- a. Adam Smith
- b. Josef Stalin
- c. Adolph Fischer
- d. Adolf Hitler

62. _____ is a misspelled phrase from Latin 'pro capite' phrase meaning per head with pro meaning 'per' or 'for each' and capite meaning 'head.' Both words together equate to the phrase 'for each head.'

It is usually used in the field of statistics to indicate the average per person for any given concern, such as income, crime rate, etc.

It is also used in wills to indicate that each of the named beneficiaries should receive, by devise or bequest, equal shares of the estate. This is in contrast to a per stirpes division, in which each branch of the inheriting family inherits an equal share of the estate.

- a. Population statistics
- b. False positive rate
- c. Sargan test
- d. Per capita

63. _____ is the process of sharing of skills, knowledge, technologies, methods of manufacturing, samples of manufacturing and facilities among governments and other institutions to ensure that scientific and technological developments are accessible to a wider range of users who can then further develop and exploit the technology into new products, processes, applications, materials or services. It is closely related to (and may arguably be considered a subset of) Knowledge transfer. Related terms, used almost synonymously, include 'technology valorisation' and 'technology commercialisation'.
- a. Technology transfer
- b. Judgment summons
- c. Law of increasing relative cost
- d. Patent

64. Necessary _____s:

If x is a necessary _____ of y, then the presence of y necessarily implies the presence of x. The presence of x, however, does not imply that y will occur.

Sufficient _____s:

If x is a sufficient _____ of y, then the presence of x necessarily implies the presence of y.

   a. Materialism
   c. Political philosophy
   b. Philosophy of economics
   d. Cause

65. _____ refers to the actions that governments take in the economic field. It covers the systems for setting interest rates and government deficit as well as the labour market, national ownership, and many other areas of government.

Such policies are often influenced by international institutions like the International Monetary Fund or World Bank as well as political beliefs and the consequent policies of parties.

   a. ACCRA Cost of Living Index
   c. ACEA agreement
   b. Economic policy
   d. AD-IA Model

66. In finance, _____ is investment originating from other countries. See Foreign direct investment.
   a. Demand side economics
   c. Preclusive purchasing
   b. Horizontal merger
   d. Foreign investment

67. A _____ is an aspect of the tax code designed to incentivize a certain type of behavior. This may be accomplished through means including tax holidays or tax deductions.
   a. Current use
   c. Nil-rate band
   b. General nondiscrimination
   d. Tax incentive

68. In economics, a _____ is a good that is non-rivaled and non-excludable. This means, respectively, that consumption of the good by one individual does not reduce availability of the good for consumption by others; and that no one can be effectively excluded from using the good. In the real world, there may be no such thing as an absolutely non-rivaled and non-excludable good; but economists think that some goods approximate the concept closely enough for the analysis to be economically useful.
   a. Happiness economics
   c. Neoclassical synthesis
   b. Demand-pull theory
   d. Public good

69. The phrase _____, according to the Organization for Economic Co-operation and Development, refers to 'creative work undertaken on a systematic basis in order to increase the stock of knowledge, including knowledge of man, culture and society, and the use of this stock of knowledge to devise new applications [sic]'

New product design and development is more than often a crucial factor in the survival of a company. In an industry that is fast changing, firms must continually revise their design and range of products. This is necessary due to continuous technology change and development as well as other competitors and the changing preference of customers.

Chapter 5. The Reality of Economic Growth: History and Prospect   73

  a. 1921 recession
  c. 100-year flood
  b. Research and development
  d. 130-30 fund

70. _____ is the public sector analogy to market failure and occurs when a government intervention causes a more inefficient allocation of goods and resources than would occur without that intervention. Likewise, the government's failure to intervene in a market failure that would result in a socially preferable mix of output is referred to as passive _____ (Weimer and Vining, 2004.) Just as with market failures, there are many different kinds of _____s that describe corresponding distortions.

  a. Natural monopoly
  c. Government-granted monopoly
  b. Privatizing profits and socializing losses
  d. Government failure

71. A _____ is a set of exclusive rights granted by a state to an inventor or his assignee for a limited period of time in exchange for a disclosure of an invention.

The procedure for granting _____s, the requirements placed on the _____ee and the extent of the exclusive rights vary widely between countries according to national laws and international agreements. Typically, however, a _____ application must include one or more claims defining the invention which must be new, inventive, and useful or industrially applicable.

  a. Bona fide occupational qualification
  c. Long service leave
  b. Patent
  d. Bank regulation

72. _____: Sometimes cleptocracy, occasionally kleptarchy, is a term applied to a government that extends the personal wealth and political power of government officials and the ruling class (collectively, kleptocrats) at the expense of the population, sometimes without even the pretense of honest service. The term derives from the Greek root klepto .

Kleptocracies are often dictatorships or some other form of autocratic and nepotist government, or lapsed democracies that have transformed into oligarchies.

  a. Glass ceiling
  c. Waithood
  b. Criticism of globalization
  d. Kleptocracy

73. The term _____ refers to economy-wide fluctuations in production or economic activity over several months or years. These fluctuations occur around a long-term growth trend, and typically involve shifts over time between periods of relatively rapid economic growth (expansion or boom), and periods of relative stagnation or decline (contraction or recession.)

These fluctuations are often measured using the growth rate of real gross domestic product.

  a. Tobit model
  c. Business cycle
  b. Nominal value
  d. Consumer theory

1. In economics, the _____ functional form of production functions is widely used to represent the relationship of an output to inputs. It was proposed by Knut Wicksell (1851-1926), and tested against statistical evidence by Charles Cobb and Paul Douglas in 1900-1928.

For production, the function is

$$Y = AL^{\alpha}K^{\beta},$$

where:

- Y = total production (the monetary value of all goods produced in a year)
- L = labor input
- K = capital input
- A = total factor productivity
- α and β are the output elasticities of labor and capital, respectively. These values are constants determined by available technology.

Output elasticity measures the responsiveness of output to a change in levels of either labor or capital used in production, ceteris paribus. For example if α = 0.15, a 1% increase in labor would lead to approximately a 0.15% increase in output.

a. Social savings
b. Growth accounting
c. Demand-pull theory
d. Cobb-Douglas

2. Economists distinguish between various types of unemployment, including cyclical unemployment, _____, structural unemployment and classical unemployment. Some additional types of unemployment that are occasionally mentioned are seasonal unemployment, hardcore unemployment, and hidden unemployment. Real-world unemployment may combine different types.

a. Types of unemployment
b. Frictional unemployment
c. Seasonal unemployment
d. Structural unemployment

3. _____ and Keynesian Theory) is a macroeconomic theory based on the ideas of 20th-century British economist John Maynard Keynes. _____ argues that private sector decisions sometimes lead to inefficient macroeconomic outcomes and therefore advocates active policy responses by the public sector, including monetary policy actions by the central bank and fiscal policy actions by the government to stabilize output over the business cycle.

The theories forming the basis of _____ were first presented in The General Theory of Employment, Interest and Money, published in 1936.

a. Rational choice theory
b. Market failure
c. Deflation
d. Keynesian economics

4. The _____ is a concept of economic activity developed in particular by Milton Friedman and Edmund Phelps in the 1960s, both recipients of the Nobel prize in economics. In both cases, the development of the concept is cited as a main motivation behind the prize. It represents the hypothetical unemployment rate consistent with aggregate production being at the 'long-run' level.

a. Romer Model
b. Natural rate of unemployment
c. Robertson lag
d. Real Business Cycle Theory

5. In economics, the _____ is a historical inverse relation between the rate of unemployment and the rate of inflation in an economy. Stated simply, the lower the unemployment in an economy, the higher the rate of increase in nominal wages in the economy. Rate of Change of Wages against Unemployment, United Kingdom 1913-1948 from Phillips (1958)

William Phillips, a New Zealand born economist, wrote a paper in 1958 titled The Relationship between Unemployment and the Rate of Change of Money Wages in the United Kingdom 1861-1957, which was published in the quarterly journal Economica.

a. Demand curve
b. Cost curve
c. Lorenz curve
d. Phillips curve

6. In economics, _____ refers to the highest level of real Gross Domestic Product output that can be sustained over the long term. The existence of a limit is due to natural and institutional constraints. If actual GDP rises and stays above _____, then (in the absence of wage and price controls) inflation tends to increase as demand exceeds supply.

a. Monetary policy reaction function
b. Monetary conditions index
c. Potential output
d. Fundamental psychological law

7. The term _____s refers to wages that have been adjusted for inflation. This term is used in contrast to nominal wages or unadjusted wages.

The use of adjusted figures is in undertaking some form of economic analysis.

a. Federal Wage System
b. Profit sharing
c. Living wage
d. Real wage

8. In economics, _____ is the total demand for final goods and services in the economy (Y) at a given time and price level. It is the amount of goods and services in the economy that will be purchased at all possible price levels. This is the demand for the gross domestic product of a country when inventory levels are static.

a. Aggregate expenditure
b. Aggregate supply
c. Aggregation problem
d. Aggregate demand

9. In economics, _____ is the total supply of goods and services produced by a national economy during a specific time period. It is the total amount of goods and services in the economy available at all possible price levels.

a. Aggregate supply
b. Aggregate expenditure
c. Aggregation problem
d. Aggregate demand

10. The term _____ refers to economy-wide fluctuations in production or economic activity over several months or years. These fluctuations occur around a long-term growth trend, and typically involve shifts over time between periods of relatively rapid economic growth (expansion or boom), and periods of relative stagnation or decline (contraction or recession.)

These fluctuations are often measured using the growth rate of real gross domestic product.

Chapter 6. Building Blocks of the Flexible-Price Model

a. Nominal value
c. Consumer theory
b. Business cycle
d. Tobit model

11. Economics:

- _____, the desire to own something and the ability to pay for it
- _____ curve, a graphic representation of a _____ schedule
- _____ deposit, the money in checking accounts
- _____ pull theory, the theory that inflation occurs when _____ for goods and services exceeds existing supplies
- _____ schedule, a table that lists the quantity of a good a person will buy it each different price
- _____ side economics, the school of economics at believes government spending and tax cuts open economy by raising _____

a. Demand
c. Production
b. Variability
d. McKesson ' Robbins scandal

12. In microeconomics, _____ is quite simply the conversion of inputs into outputs. It is an economic process that uses resources to create a good or service that is suitable for exchange. This can include manufacturing, storing, shipping, and packaging.

a. Production
c. MET
b. Solved
d. Red Guards

13. In economics, a _____ is a function that specifies the output of a firm, an industry, or an entire economy for all combinations of inputs. A meta-_____ compares the practice of the existing entities converting inputs X into output y to determine the most efficient practice _____ of the existing entities, whether the most efficient feasible practice production or the most efficient actual practice production. In either case, the maximum output of a technologically-determined production process is a mathematical function of input factors of production.

a. Post-Fordism
c. Short-run
b. Constant elasticity of substitution
d. Production function

14. A _____ is an expression that compares quantities relative to each other. The most common examples involve two quantities, but any number of quantities can be compared. _____s are represented mathematically by separating each quantity with a colon, for example the _____ 2:3, which is read as the _____ 'two to three'.

a. 130-30 fund
c. Ratio
b. 100-year flood
d. Y-intercept

15. In economics, the _____ or marginal physical product is the extra output produced by one more unit of an input (for instance, the difference in output when a firm's labour is increased from five to six units.) Assuming that no other inputs to production change, the _____ of a given input (X) can be expressed as:

Chapter 6. Building Blocks of the Flexible-Price Model   77

_____ = ΔY/ΔX = (the change of Y)/(the change of X.)

-
  - ○
    - Pending approval by Thomas Sowell***

In neoclassical economics, this is the mathematical derivative of the production function.... Note that the 'product' (Y) is typically defined ignoring external costs and benefits.

a. Marginal product
c. Factor prices
b. Productive capacity
d. Labor problem

16. _____ is the additional output resulting from the use of an additional unit of capital (ceteris paribus assuming all other factors are fixed.) It equals to 1 divided by the Incremental Capital-Output Ratio.

a. CAN SLIM
c. Buy-write
b. Loan officer
d. Marginal product of capital

17. In economics, the _____ also known as MPL or MPN is the change in output from hiring one additional unit of labor. It is the increase in output added by the last unit of labor. Assuming that no other inputs to production change, the marginal product of a given input (X) can be expressed as:

MP = ΔY/ΔX = (the change of Y)/(the change of X.)

a. Marginal product
c. Marginal product of labor
b. Production function
d. Product Pipeline

18. _____ is the a method of technical and economic research of the systems for purpose to optimize a parity between system's consumer functions or properties and expenses to achieve those functions or properties.

This methodology for continuous perfection of production, industrial technologies, organizational structures was developed by Juryj Sobolev in 1948 at the 'Perm telephone factory'

- 1948 Juryj Sobolev - the first success in application of a method analysis at the 'Perm telephone factory' .
- 1949 - the first application for the invention as result of use of the new method.

78 *Chapter 6. Building Blocks of the Flexible-Price Model*

Today in economically developed countries practically each enterprise or the company use methodology of the kind of functional-cost analysis as a practice of the quality management, most full satisfying to principles of standards of series ISO 9000.

- Interest of consumer not in products itself, but the advantage which it will receive from its usage.
- The consumer aspires to reduce his expenses
- Functions needed by consumer can be executed in the various ways, and, hence, with various efficiency and expenses. Among possible alternatives of realization of functions exist such in which the parity of quality and the price is the optimal for the consumer.

The goal of _____ is achievement of the highest consumer satisfaction of production at simultaneous decrease in all kinds of industrial expenses Classical _____ has three English synonyms - Value Engineering, Value Management, Value Analysis.

a. Function cost analysis
b. Willingness to pay
c. Monopoly wage
d. Staple financing

19. The supply of labor is the number of total hours that workers wish to work at a given real wage rate.

_____ curves are derived from the 'labor-leisure' trade-off. More hours worked earn higher incomes but necessitate a cut in the amount of leisure that workers enjoy.

a. Late capitalism
b. Human trafficking
c. Creative capitalism
d. Labor supply

20. In economics, economic equilibrium is simply a state of the world where economic forces are balanced and in the absence of external influences the (equilibrium) values of economic variables will not change. It is the point at which quantity demanded and quantity supplied are equal. _____, for example, refers to a condition where a market price is established through competition such that the amount of goods or services sought by buyers is equal to the amount of goods or services produced by sellers.

a. Market Equilibrium
b. Marketization
c. Product-Market Growth Matrix
d. Regulated market

21. In macroeconomics, _____ is a condition of the national economy, where all or nearly all persons willing and able to work at the prevailing wages and working conditions are able to do so. It is defined either as 0% unemployment, literally, no unemployment (the rate of unemployment is the fraction of the work force unable to find work), as by James Tobin, or as the level of employment rates when there is no cyclical unemployment. It is defined by the majority of mainstream economists as being an acceptable level of natural unemployment above 0%, the discrepancy from 0% being due to non-cyclical types of unemployment.

a. Harrod-Johnson diagram
b. Full employment
c. Marginal propensity to consume
d. Demand shock

Chapter 6. Building Blocks of the Flexible-Price Model

22. The _____ or gross domestic income (GDI), a basic measure of an economy's economic performance, is the market value of all final goods and services produced within the borders of a nation in a year. _____ can be defined in three ways, all of which are conceptually identical. First, it is equal to the total expenditures for all final goods and services produced within the country in a stipulated period of time (usually a 365-day year.)
   a. Countercyclical
   b. Monopolistic competition
   c. Market structure
   d. Gross domestic product

23. An _____, in economics, is the amount by which the real Gross domestic product exceeds potential GDP. The real GDP is also known as GDP 'adjusted for inflation', 'constant prices' GDP or 'constant dollar' GDP, because it measures the aggregate output in a country's income accounts in a given year, expressed in base-year prices. On the other hand, the potential GDP is the quantity of real GDP when a country's economy is at full-employment.
   a. ACCRA Cost of Living Index
   b. ACEA agreement
   c. AD-IA Model
   d. Inflationary gap

24. _____ is a common concept in economics, and gives rise to derived concepts such as consumer debt. Generally _____ is defined by opposition to production. But the precise definition can vary because different schools of economists define production quite differently.
   a. Cash or share options
   b. Federal Reserve Bank Notes
   c. Foreclosure data providers
   d. Consumption

25. A _____ product is a product designed for cheapness and short-term convenience rather than medium to long-term durability, with most products only intended for single use. The term is also sometimes used for products that may last several months (ex. _____ air filters) to distinguish from similar products that last indefinitely (ex.
   a. 130-30 fund
   b. 100-year flood
   c. 1921 recession
   d. Disposable

26. _____ is gross income minus income tax on that income.

Discretionary income is income after subtracting taxes and normal expenses (such as rent or mortgage, utilities, insurance, medical, transportation, property maintenance, child support, inflation, food and sundries, 'c.') to maintain a certain standard of living.

   a. Disposable personal income
   b. Disposable income
   c. Taxation as theft
   d. Stamp Act

27. The _____ is 'the basic residential unit in which economic production, consumption, inheritance, child rearing, and shelter are organized and carried out'; [the _____] 'may or may not be synonomous with family'.

The _____ is the basic unit of analysis in many social, microeconomic and government models. The term refers to all individuals who live in the same dwelling.

   a. Family economics
   b. 130-30 fund
   c. 100-year flood
   d. Household

28. A variety of measures of _____ and output are used in economics to estimate total economic activity in a country or region, including gross domestic product (GDP), gross national product (GNP), and net _____

80 *Chapter 6. Building Blocks of the Flexible-Price Model*

There are three main ways of calculating these numbers; the output approach, the income approach and the expenditure approach. In theory, the three must yield the same, because total expenditures on goods and services must equal the total income paid to the producers (Gnational income), and that must also equal the total value of the output of goods and services (GNP.)

a. Volume index
c. GNI per capita
b. National income
d. Gross world product

29. _____ use double-entry accounting to report the monetary value and sources of output produced in a country and the distribution of incomes that production generates. Data are available at the national and industry levels.

The NIPA summarizes national income on the left (debit, revenue) side and national product on the right (credit, expense) side of a two-column accounting report.

a. Net national product
c. Gross private domestic investment
b. National income and product accounts
d. Current account

30. A _____ is a tax by which the tax rate increases as the taxable amount increases. 'Progressive' describes a distribution effect on income or expenditure, referring to the way the rate progresses from low to high, where the average tax rate is less than the marginal tax rate. It can be applied to individual taxes or to a tax system as a whole; a year, multi-year, or lifetime.

a. Proportional tax
c. 130-30 fund
b. 100-year flood
d. Progressive tax

31. In economics, the term _____ of income or _____ refers to a simple economic model which describes the reciprocal circulation of income between producers and consumers. In the _____ model, the inter-dependent entities of producer and consumer are referred to as 'firms' and 'households' respectively and provide each other with factors in order to facilitate the flow of income. Firms provide consumers with goods and services in exchange for consumer expenditure and 'factors of production' from households.

a. 100-year flood
c. 1921 recession
b. Circular flow
d. 130-30 fund

32. _____ is a specific term used in companies' financial reporting from the company-whole point of view. Because that use excludes the effects of changing ownership interest, an economic measure of _____ is necessary for financial analysis from the shareholders' point of view

_____ is defined by the Financial Accounting Standards Board, or FASB, as e;the change in equity [net assets] of a business enterprise during a period from transactions and other events and circumstances from nonowner sources. It includes all changes in equity during a period except those resulting from investments by owners and distributions to owners.e;

_____ is the sum of net income and other items that must bypass the income statement because they have not been realized, including items like an unrealized holding gain or loss from available for sale securities and foreign currency translation gains or losses.

Chapter 6. Building Blocks of the Flexible-Price Model

a. Windfall gain	b. Real income
c. Net national income	d. Comprehensive income

33. To _____ is to impose a financial charge or other levy upon a taxpayer by a state or the functional equivalent of a state.

_____es are also imposed by many subnational entities. _____es consist of direct _____ or indirect _____, and may be paid in money or as its labour equivalent (often but not always unpaid.)

a. 130-30 fund	b. 100-year flood
c. 1921 recession	d. Tax

34. To tax is to impose a financial charge or other levy upon a taxpayer by a state or the functional equivalent of a state.

_____ are also imposed by many subnational entities. _____ consist of direct tax or indirect tax, and may be paid in money or as its labour equivalent (often but not always unpaid.)

a. 130-30 fund	b. 1921 recession
c. Taxes	d. 100-year flood

35. In economics, the _____ is a single mathematical function used to express consumer spending. It was developed by John Maynard Keynes and detailed most famously in his book The General Theory of Employment, Interest, and Money. The function is used to calculate the amount of total consumption in an economy.
   - a. Procyclical
   - b. DAD-SAS model
   - c. Liquidity preference
   - d. Consumption function

36. In economics, the _____ is an empirical metric that quantifies induced consumption, the concept that the increase in personal consumer spending (consumption) that occurs with an increase in disposable income (income after taxes and transfers.) For example, if a household earns one extra dollar of disposable income, and the _____ is 0.65, then of that dollar, the household will spend 65 cents and save 35 cents.

Mathematically, the _____ (MPC) function is expressed as the derivative of the consumption (C) function with respect to disposable income (Y.)

   - a. Technology shock
   - b. Marginal propensity to consume
   - c. Supply shock
   - d. Marginal propensity to import

37. The '_____' is approximately the nominal interest rate minus the inflation rate Since the inflation rate over the course of a loan is not known initially, volatility in inflation represents a risk to both the lender and the borrower.

In economics and finance, an individual who lends money for repayment at a later point in time expects to be compensated for the time value of money, or not having the use of that money while it is lent.

   - a. Core inflation
   - b. Reflation
   - c. Cost-push inflation
   - d. Real interest rate

82 *Chapter 6. Building Blocks of the Flexible-Price Model*

38. In algebra, a _____ is a function depending on n that associates a scalar, det(A), to an n×n square matrix A. The fundamental geometric meaning of a _____ is a scale factor for measure when A is regarded as a linear transformation. _____s are important both in calculus, where they enter the substitution rule for several variables, and in multilinear algebra.

For a fixed nonnegative integer n, there is a unique _____ function for the n×n matrices over any commutative ring R. In particular, this function exists when R is the field of real or complex numbers.

    a. 1921 recession
    c. Determinant
    b. 100-year flood
    d. 130-30 fund

39. _____ is a fee paid on borrowed assets. It is the price paid for the use of borrowed money , or, money earned by deposited funds . Assets that are sometimes lent with _____ include money, shares, consumer goods through hire purchase, major assets such as aircraft, and even entire factories in finance lease arrangements.
    a. Insolvency
    c. Asset protection
    b. Interest
    d. Internal debt

40. An _____ is the price a borrower pays for the use of money they do not own, for instance a small company might borrow from a bank to kick start their business, and the return a lender receives for deferring the use of funds, by lending it to the borrower. _____s are normally expressed as a percentage rate over the period of one year.

_____s targets are also a vital tool of monetary policy and are used to control variables like investment, inflation, and unemployment.

    a. Enterprise value
    c. Interest rate
    b. ACCRA Cost of Living Index
    d. Arrow-Debreu model

41. A _____ is something for which there is demand, but which is supplied without qualitative differentiation across a market. It is a product that is the same no matter who produces it, such as petroleum, notebook paper, or milk. In other words, copper is copper.
    a. Soft commodity
    c. 100-year flood
    b. Commodity
    d. Hard commodity

42. In statistics, a _____ is a value that allows data to be measured over time in terms of some base period usually through a price index in order to distinguish between changes in the money value of GNP which result from a change in prices and those which result from a change in physical output. It is the measure of the price level for some quantity. A _____ serves as a price index in which the effects of inflation are nulled.
    a. Blanket order
    c. Deflator
    b. Contingent employment
    d. Market microstructure

43. _____ is a term used in accounting, economics and finance to spread the cost of an asset over the span of several years.

In simple words we can say that _____ is the reduction in the value of an asset due to usage, passage of time, wear and tear, technological outdating or obsolescence, depletion, inadequacy, rot, rust, decay or other such factors.

Chapter 6. Building Blocks of the Flexible-Price Model

In accounting, _____ is a term used to describe any method of attributing the historical or purchase cost of an asset across its useful life, roughly corresponding to normal wear and tear.

a. Depreciation
c. Net income per employee
b. Salvage value
d. Historical cost

44. _____ relates to the composition of GDP. What is produced in a certain country is naturally also sold, but some of the goods produced in a given year may not be sold the same year, but in later years. Conversely, some of the goods sold in a given year might have been produced in an earlier year.

a. Inventory investment
c. Obelisk International
b. Investment decisions
d. Investment theory

45. _____, 1st Baron Keynes was a renowned economist from Britain whose many ideas on economic and political theories as well as on many governments' monetary policies influenced America. He advocated a government that played an active role in the lives of people regarding business, economy, etc. In this role, the government would use fiscal measures to reduce the consequences of recessions, economic depressions and booms.

a. Adam Smith
c. Adolph Fischer
b. Adolf Hitler
d. John Maynard Keynes

46. In economics, _____ refers to an activity of spending which increases the availability of fixed capital goods or means of production. It is the total spending on new fixed investment minus replacement investment, which simply replaces depreciated capital goods.

a. Tangible investments
c. Net investment
b. Greenfield investment
d. Lehman Formula

47. _____ is a financial mechanism in which a debtor obtains the right to delay payments to a creditor, for a defined period of time, in exchange for a charge or fee. Essentially, the party that owes money in the present purchases the right to delay the payment until some future date. The discount, or charge, is simply the difference between the original amount owed in the present and the amount that has to be paid in the future to settle the debt.

a. Generalized linear model
c. Maximum life span
b. Certified Risk Manager
d. Discounting

48. _____ is the value on a given date of a future payment or series of future payments, discounted to reflect the time value of money and other factors such as investment risk. _____ calculations are widely used in business and economics to provide a means to compare cash flows at different times on a meaningful 'like to like' basis.

Money value fluctuates over time: $100 today are not worth $100 in five years.

a. Future value
c. Present value of costs
b. Tax shield
d. Present value

49. _____ refers to a business or organization attempting to acquire goods or services to accomplish the goals of the enterprise. Though there are several organizations that attempt to set standards in the _____ process, processes can vary greatly between organizations. Typically the word '_____' is not used interchangeably with the word 'procurement', since procurement typically includes Expediting, Supplier Quality, and Traffic and Logistics (T'L) in addition to _____.

a. 100-year flood
b. 130-30 fund
c. Purchasing
d. Free port

50. _____ is the number of goods/services that can be purchased with a unit of currency. For example, if you had taken one dollar to a store in the 1950s, you would have been able to buy a greater number of items than you would today, indicating that you would have had a greater _____ in the 1950s. Currency can be either a commodity money, like gold or silver, or fiat currency like US dollars.

a. Compliance cost
b. Human Poverty Index
c. Genuine progress indicator
d. Purchasing power

51. In finance, a _____ is a debt security, in which the authorized issuer owes the holders a debt and, depending on the terms of the _____, is obliged to pay interest (the coupon) and/or to repay the principal at a later date, termed maturity. A _____ is a formal contract to repay borrowed money with interest at fixed intervals.

Thus a _____ is like a loan: the issuer is the borrower (debtor), the holder is the lender (creditor), and the coupon is the interest.

a. Prize Bond
b. Bond
c. Callable
d. Zero-coupon

52. A _____ is a public market for the trading of company stock and derivatives at an agreed price; these are securities listed on a stock exchange as well as those only traded privately.

The size of the world _____ was estimated at about $36.6 trillion US at the beginning of October 2008 . The total world derivatives market has been estimated at about $791 trillion face or nominal value, 11 times the size of the entire world economy.

a. Stock market
b. Adolf Hitler
c. Adam Smith
d. Adolph Fischer

53. A _____ is a type of economic bubble taking place in stock markets when price of stocks rise and become overvalued by any measure of stock valuation.

The existence of _____ s is at odds with the assumptions of efficient market theory which assumes rational investor behaviour. Behavioral finance theory attribute _____ s to cognitive biases that lead to groupthink and herd behavior.

a. Growth investing
b. Stock market bubble
c. Fill or kill
d. Scrip issue

54. _____ in economics and business is the result of an exchange and from that trade we assign a numerical monetary value to a good, service or asset. If Alice trades Bob 4 apples for an orange, the _____ of an orange is 4 apples. Inversely, the _____ of an apple is 1/4 oranges.

a. Price book
b. Price war
c. Premium pricing
d. Price

Chapter 6. Building Blocks of the Flexible-Price Model

55. _____s is the social science that studies the production, distribution, and consumption of goods and services. The term _____s comes from the Ancient Greek oá¼°κονομῖα from oá¼¶κος (oikos, 'house') + vÏŒμος (nomos, 'custom' or 'law'), hence 'rules of the house(hold)'. Current _____ models developed out of the broader field of political economy in the late 19th century, owing to a desire to use an empirical approach more akin to the physical sciences.
   a. Opportunity cost
   b. Energy economics
   c. Inflation
   d. Economic

56. _____ refers to the actions that governments take in the economic field. It covers the systems for setting interest rates and government deficit as well as the labour market, national ownership, and many other areas of government.

Such policies are often influenced by international institutions like the International Monetary Fund or World Bank as well as political beliefs and the consequent policies of parties.

   a. ACCRA Cost of Living Index
   b. ACEA agreement
   c. AD-IA Model
   d. Economic policy

57. The term _____ refers to government debt, expenditures and revenues, or to finance (particularly financial revenue) in general.

   - _____ deficit is the budget deficit of federal or local government
   - _____ policy is the discretionary spending of governments. Contrasts with monetary policy.
   - _____ year and _____ quarter are reporting periods for firms and other agencies.

   a. Fiscal
   b. Procter ' Gamble
   c. Drawdown
   d. Bucket shop

58. In economics, _____ is the use of government spending and revenue collection to influence the economy.

_____ can be contrasted with the other main type of economic policy, monetary policy, which attempts to stabilize the economy by controlling interest rates and the supply of money. The two main instruments of _____ are government spending and taxation.

   a. Sustainable investment rule
   b. Fiscal policy
   c. Fiscalism
   d. 100-year flood

59. _____ was the 31st President of the United States (1929-1933.) Besides his political career, Hoover was a professional mining engineer and author. As the United States Secretary of Commerce in the 1920s under Presidents Warren Harding and Calvin Coolidge, he promoted government intervention under the rubric 'economic modernization'.
   a. Herbert Hoover
   b. Adam Smith
   c. Adolph Fischer
   d. Adolf Hitler

60. _____ is the process by which the government, central bank (ii) availability of money, and (iii) cost of money or rate of interest, in order to attain a set of objectives oriented towards the growth and stability of the economy. Monetary theory provides insight into how to craft optimal _____.

Chapter 6. Building Blocks of the Flexible-Price Model

_____ is referred to as either being an expansionary policy where an expansionary policy increases the total supply of money in the economy, and a contractionary policy decreases the total money supply.

a. 1921 recession
b. 100-year flood
c. 130-30 fund
d. Monetary policy

61. A _____ is a package or set of measures introduced to stabilise a financial system or economy. The term can refer to policies in two distinct sets of circumstances: business cycle stabilization and crisis stabilization.

Stabilization can refer to correcting the normal behavior of the business cycle.

a. Capacity Development
b. Volunteers for Economic Growth Alliance
c. New International Economic Order
d. Stabilization policy

62. A _____ is a set of exclusive rights granted by a state to an inventor or his assignee for a limited period of time in exchange for a disclosure of an invention.

The procedure for granting _____s, the requirements placed on the _____ee and the extent of the exclusive rights vary widely between countries according to national laws and international agreements. Typically, however, a _____ application must include one or more claims defining the invention which must be new, inventive, and useful or industrially applicable.

a. Bona fide occupational qualification
b. Patent
c. Long service leave
d. Bank regulation

63. A _____ is the transfer of wealth from one party (such as a person or company) to another. A _____ is usually made in exchange for the provision of goods, services or both, or to fulfill a legal obligation.

The simplest and oldest form of _____ is barter, the exchange of one good or service for another.

a. Going concern
b. Social gravity
c. Soft count
d. Payment

64. In economics, a _____ is a redistribution of income in the market system. These payments are considered to be nonexhaustive because they do not directly absorb resources or create output. Examples of certain _____s include welfare (financial aid), social security, and government subsidies for certain businesses (firms.)

a. 1921 recession
b. 130-30 fund
c. 100-year flood
d. Transfer payment

65. In economics, an _____ is any good or commodity, transported from one country to another country in a legitimate fashion, typically for use in trade. _____ goods or services are provided to foreign consumers by domestic producers. _____ is an important part of international trade.

a. ACCRA Cost of Living Index
b. AD-IA Model
c. Export
d. ACEA agreement

Chapter 6. Building Blocks of the Flexible-Price Model

66. In economics, an _____ is any good (e.g. a commodity) or service brought into one country from another country in a legitimate fashion, typically for use in trade.It is a good that is brought in from another country for sale. _____ goods or services are provided to domestic consumers by foreign producers. An _____ in the receiving country is an export to the sending country.
   a. Import
   b. Economic integration
   c. Incoterms
   d. Import quota

67. _____ is exchange of capital, goods, and services across international borders or territories. In most countries, it represents a significant share of gross domestic product (GDP.) While _____ has been present throughout much of history , its economic, social, and political importance has been on the rise in recent centuries.
   a. Intra-industry trade
   b. International trade
   c. Import license
   d. Incoterms

68. _____ is a concept found in moral, political, and bioethical philosophy. Within these contexts, it refers to the capacity of a rational individual to make an informed, un-coerced decision. In moral and political philosophy, _____ is often used as the basis for determining moral responsibility for one's actions.
   a. ACEA agreement
   b. AD-IA Model
   c. ACCRA Cost of Living Index
   d. Autonomy

69. The _____ of monetary management established the rules for commercial and financial relations among the world's major industrial states in the mid 20th Century. The _____ was the first example of a fully negotiated monetary order intended to govern monetary relations among independent nation-states.

Preparing to rebuild the international economic system as World War II was still raging, 730 delegates from all 44 Allied nations gathered at the Mount Washington Hotel in Bretton Woods, New Hampshire, United States, for the United Nations Monetary and Financial Conference.

   a. 130-30 fund
   b. 100-year flood
   c. 1921 recession
   d. Bretton Woods system

70. A _____, sometimes called a pegged exchange rate, is a type of exchange rate regime wherein a currency's value is matched to the value of another single currency or to a basket of other currencies such as gold.

A _____ is usually used to stabilize the value of a currency, vis-a-vis the currency it is pegged to. This facilitates trade and investments between the two countries, and is especially useful for small economies where external trade forms a large part of their GDP.

   a. Leading indicators
   b. Monetary economics
   c. Law of supply
   d. Fixed exchange rate

71. A _____ or a flexible exchange rate is a type of exchange rate regime wherein a currency's value is allowed to fluctuate according to the foreign exchange market. A currency that uses a _____ is known as a floating currency. The opposite of a _____ is a fixed exchange rate.
   a. Trade Weighted US dollar Index
   b. Foreign exchange market
   c. Floating exchange rate
   d. Floating currency

Chapter 6. Building Blocks of the Flexible-Price Model

72. In finance, the _____s between two currencies specifies how much one currency is worth in terms of the other. It is the value of a foreign natione;s currency in terms of the home natione;s currency. For example an _____ of 102 Japanese yen to the United States dollar means that JPY 102 is worth the same as USD 1.
   a. ACCRA Cost of Living Index
   b. Interbank market
   c. ACEA agreement
   d. Exchange rate

73. The _____ is where currency trading takes place. It is where banks and other official institutions facilitate the buying and selling of foreign currencies. FX transactions typically involve one party purchasing a quantity of one currency in exchange for paying a quantity of another.
   a. Covered interest arbitrage
   b. Floating currency
   c. Currency swap
   d. Foreign exchange market

74. _____ are supposed, together with herd instinct, to be the three main emotional motivators of stock markets and business behavior, and one of the cause of bull markets, bear markets and business cycles.

The phrase, traditionally used by traders and market commentators, has become a topic of economic research about investor irrationalities (cognitive and emotional biases.) Its effects on market prices and returns contradict, or at least moderate, the efficient market hypothesis.

   a. Corporate haven
   b. Business failure
   c. Greed and fear
   d. Debtor-in-possession financing

75. A _____ represents the combinations of goods and services that a consumer can purchase given current prices and his income. Consumer theory uses the concepts of a _____ and a preference map to analyze consumer choices. Both concepts have a ready graphical representation in the two-good case.
   a. Revealed preference
   b. Quality bias
   c. Budget constraint
   d. Joint demand

76. In economics, the _____ of a good or of a service is the utility of the specific use to which an agent would put a given increase in that good or service, or of the specific use that would be abandoned in response to a given decrease. In other words, _____ is the utility of the marginal use -- which, on the assumption of economic rationality, would be the least urgent use of the good or service, from the best feasible combination of actions in which its use is included. Under the mainstream assumptions, the _____ of a good or service is the posited quantified change in utility obtained by increasing or by decreasing use of that good or service.
   a. 1921 recession
   b. Marginal utility
   c. 130-30 fund
   d. 100-year flood

77. In economics, _____ is a measure of the relative satisfaction from consumption of various goods and services. Given this measure, one may speak meaningfully of increasing or decreasing _____, and thereby explain economic behavior in terms of attempts to increase one's _____. For illustrative purposes, changes in _____ are sometimes expressed in units called utils.
   a. Utility function
   b. Utility
   c. Expected utility hypothesis
   d. Ordinal utility

Chapter 6. Building Blocks of the Flexible-Price Model

78. _____ is an economic concept which refers to balancing out spending and saving to attain and maintain the highest possible living standard over the course of one's life. This idea is notable because of its difference in approach to common knowledge about preparing for retirement, in which individuals are encouraged to save a particular % of their income throughout their life. Some believe that this approach is flawed and typically leads to one of two outcomes: over-saving or over-spending.
  a. Conspicuous consumption
  b. Multidimensional scaling
  c. Rule Developing Experimentation
  d. Consumption smoothing

79. In statistics and image processing, to smooth a data set is to create an approximating function that attempts to capture important patterns in the data, while leaving out noise or other fine-scale structures/rapid phenomena. Many different algorithms are used in _____. One of the most common algorithms is the 'moving average', often used to try to capture important trends in repeated statistical surveys.
  a. Partial regression plot
  b. X-bar chart
  c. Smoothing
  d. Partial residual plot

80. _____ is a broad label that refers to any individuals or households that use goods and services generated within the economy. The concept of a _____ is used in different contexts, so that the usage and significance of the term may vary.

Typically when business people and economists talk of _____s they are talking about person as _____, an aggregated commodity item with little individuality other than that expressed in the buy/not-buy decision.

  a. 130-30 fund
  b. 1921 recession
  c. 100-year flood
  d. Consumer

81. In economics, the _____ is the change in consumption resulting from a change in real income.

Another important item that can change is the money income of the consumer. The _____ is the phenomenon observed through changes in purchasing power.

  a. Income effect
  b. Equilibrium wage
  c. Inflation hedge
  d. Export subsidy

82. The _____ problem (often 'double _____') is an important category of transaction costs that impose severe limitations on economies lacking money and thus dominated by barter or other in-kind transactions. The problem is caused by the improbability of the wants, needs or events that cause or motivate a transaction occurring at the same time and the same place.

In-kind transactions have several problems, most notably timing constraints.

  a. RFM
  b. Coincidence of wants
  c. Going concern
  d. Buy-sell agreement

Chapter 7. Equilibrium in the Flexible-Price Model

1. In economics, a _____ is a mechanism that allows people to easily buy and sell (trade) financial securities (such as stocks and bonds), commodities (such as precious metals or agricultural goods), and other fungible items of value at low transaction costs and at prices that reflect the efficient-market hypothesis.

   _____s have evolved significantly over several hundred years and are undergoing constant innovation to improve liquidity.

   Both general markets (where many commodities are traded) and specialized markets (where only one commodity is traded) exist.

   a. Noise trader
   b. Financial market
   c. Market anomaly
   d. Convertible arbitrage

2. In economics, the term _____ of income or _____ refers to a simple economic model which describes the reciprocal circulation of income between producers and consumers. In the _____ model, the inter-dependent entities of producer and consumer are referred to as 'firms' and 'households' respectively and provide each other with factors in order to facilitate the flow of income. Firms provide consumers with goods and services in exchange for consumer expenditure and 'factors of production' from households.
   a. Circular flow
   b. 130-30 fund
   c. 1921 recession
   d. 100-year flood

3. In economics, _____ is the total demand for final goods and services in the economy (Y) at a given time and price level. It is the amount of goods and services in the economy that will be purchased at all possible price levels. This is the demand for the gross domestic product of a country when inventory levels are static.
   a. Aggregate supply
   b. Aggregation problem
   c. Aggregate demand
   d. Aggregate expenditure

4. In economics, the _____ market is a hypothetical market that brings savers and borrowers together, also bringing together the money available in commercial banks and lending institutions available for firms and households to finance expenditures, either investments or consumption. Savers supply the _____; for instance, buying bonds will transfer their money to the institution issuing the bond, which can be a firm or government. In return, borrowers demand _____; when an institution sells a bond, it is demanding _____.
   a. Spatial inequality
   b. Reservation wage
   c. Buffer stock scheme
   d. Loanable funds

5. The term _____ refers to economy-wide fluctuations in production or economic activity over several months or years. These fluctuations occur around a long-term growth trend, and typically involve shifts over time between periods of relatively rapid economic growth (expansion or boom), and periods of relative stagnation or decline (contraction or recession.)

   These fluctuations are often measured using the growth rate of real gross domestic product.

   a. Nominal value
   b. Consumer theory
   c. Tobit model
   d. Business cycle

Chapter 7. Equilibrium in the Flexible-Price Model

6. In macroeconomics, the _____ refers to an idea attributed to classical and pre-Keynesian economics that real and nominal variables can be analyzed separately. To be precise, an economy exhibits the _____ if real variables such as output and real interest rates can be completely analyzed without considering what is happening to their nominal counterparts, the money value of output and the interest rate. In particular, this means that real GDP and other real variables can be determined without knowing the level of the nominal money supply or the rate of inflation.
   a. Break-even
   b. Classical dichotomy
   c. Market cannibalism
   d. Deflator

7. Economics:

   • _____, the desire to own something and the ability to pay for it
   • _____ curve, a graphic representation of a _____ schedule
   • _____ deposit, the money in checking accounts
   • _____ pull theory, the theory that inflation occurs when _____ for goods and services exceeds existing supplies
   • _____ schedule, a table that lists the quantity of a good a person will buy it each different price
   • _____ side economics, the school of economics at believes government spending and tax cuts open economy by raising _____

   a. Demand
   b. Variability
   c. Production
   d. McKesson ' Robbins scandal

8. _____ in economics and business is the result of an exchange and from that trade we assign a numerical monetary value to a good, service or asset. If Alice trades Bob 4 apples for an orange, the _____ of an orange is 4 apples. Inversely, the _____ of an apple is 1/4 oranges.
   a. Price book
   b. Price
   c. Premium pricing
   d. Price war

9. If the government intervenes by implementing, for example, a tax or a subsidy, then the graph of supply and demand becomes more complicated and will also include an area that represents _____.

Combined, the consumer surplus, the producer surplus, and the _____ make up the social surplus or the total surplus. Total surplus is the primary measure used in welfare economics to evaluate the efficiency of a proposed policy.

   a. Government surplus
   b. Long term
   c. Customer equity
   d. Marginal revenue

10. The _____ is 'the basic residential unit in which economic production, consumption, inheritance, child rearing, and shelter are organized and carried out'; [the _____] 'may or may not be synonymous with family'.

The _____ is the basic unit of analysis in many social, microeconomic and government models. The term refers to all individuals who live in the same dwelling.

a. 100-year flood
c. 130-30 fund
b. Family economics
d. Household

11. _____ is a common concept in economics, and gives rise to derived concepts such as consumer debt. Generally _____ is defined by opposition to production. But the precise definition can vary because different schools of economists define production quite differently.
   a. Foreclosure data providers
   c. Consumption
   b. Cash or share options
   d. Federal Reserve Bank Notes

12. A _____ is an event or condition under the contract between a buyer and a seller to exchange an asset for payment. In accounting, it is recognized by an entry in the books of account. It involves a change in the status of the finances of two or more businesses or individuals.
   a. Biflation
   c. Negative gearing
   b. Present value of costs
   d. Financial transaction

13. _____ is an economic model based on price, utility and quantity in a market. It predicts that in a competitive market, price will function to equalize the quantity demanded by consumers, and the quantity supplied by producers, resulting in an economic equilibrium of price and quantity. The model incorporates other factors changing equilibrium as a shift of demand and/or supply.
   a. Rational addiction
   c. Joint demand
   b. Deferred gratification
   d. Supply and demand

14. The '_____' is approximately the nominal interest rate minus the inflation rate Since the inflation rate over the course of a loan is not known initially, volatility in inflation represents a risk to both the lender and the borrower.

In economics and finance, an individual who lends money for repayment at a later point in time expects to be compensated for the time value of money, or not having the use of that money while it is lent.

   a. Core inflation
   c. Cost-push inflation
   b. Reflation
   d. Real interest rate

15. _____ is a fee paid on borrowed assets. It is the price paid for the use of borrowed money , or, money earned by deposited funds . Assets that are sometimes lent with _____ include money, shares, consumer goods through hire purchase, major assets such as aircraft, and even entire factories in finance lease arrangements.
   a. Interest
   c. Asset protection
   b. Internal debt
   d. Insolvency

16. An _____ is the price a borrower pays for the use of money they do not own, for instance a small company might borrow from a bank to kick start their business, and the return a lender receives for deferring the use of funds, by lending it to the borrower. _____s are normally expressed as a percentage rate over the period of one year.

_____s targets are also a vital tool of monetary policy and are used to control variables like investment, inflation, and unemployment.

Chapter 7. Equilibrium in the Flexible-Price Model

a. Arrow-Debreu model
b. ACCRA Cost of Living Index
c. Enterprise value
d. Interest rate

17. The balance of trade (or net exports, sometimes symbolized as NX) is the difference between the monetary value of exports and imports in an economy over a certain period of time. It is the relationship between a nation's imports and exports. A favorable balance of trade is known as a trade surplus and consists of exporting more than is imported; an unfavorable balance of trade is known as a _____ or, informally, a trade gap.
   a. Demographics of India
   b. Trade deficit
   c. Complementary asset
   d. Computational economic

18. The _____ of monetary management established the rules for commercial and financial relations among the world's major industrial states in the mid 20th Century. The _____ was the first example of a fully negotiated monetary order intended to govern monetary relations among independent nation-states.

Preparing to rebuild the international economic system as World War II was still raging, 730 delegates from all 44 Allied nations gathered at the Mount Washington Hotel in Bretton Woods, New Hampshire, United States, for the United Nations Monetary and Financial Conference.

   a. 100-year flood
   b. 130-30 fund
   c. 1921 recession
   d. Bretton Woods system

19. A _____, sometimes called a pegged exchange rate, is a type of exchange rate regime wherein a currency's value is matched to the value of another single currency or to a basket of other currencies such as gold.

A _____ is usually used to stabilize the value of a currency, vis-a-vis the currency it is pegged to. This facilitates trade and investments between the two countries, and is especially useful for small economies where external trade forms a large part of their GDP.

   a. Monetary economics
   b. Law of supply
   c. Leading indicators
   d. Fixed exchange rate

20. A _____ or a flexible exchange rate is a type of exchange rate regime wherein a currency's value is allowed to fluctuate according to the foreign exchange market. A currency that uses a _____ is known as a floating currency. The opposite of a _____ is a fixed exchange rate.
   a. Floating currency
   b. Trade Weighted US dollar Index
   c. Floating exchange rate
   d. Foreign exchange market

21. In finance, the _____s between two currencies specifies how much one currency is worth in terms of the other. It is the value of a foreign natione;s currency in terms of the home natione;s currency. For example an _____ of 102 Japanese yen to the United States dollar means that JPY 102 is worth the same as USD 1.
   a. Exchange rate
   b. ACEA agreement
   c. Interbank market
   d. ACCRA Cost of Living Index

22. In economics, the _____ functional form of production functions is widely used to represent the relationship of an output to inputs. It was proposed by Knut Wicksell (1851-1926), and tested against statistical evidence by Charles Cobb and Paul Douglas in 1900-1928.

Chapter 7. Equilibrium in the Flexible-Price Model

For production, the function is

$$Y = AL^{\alpha}K^{\beta},$$

where:

- Y = total production (the monetary value of all goods produced in a year)
- L = labor input
- K = capital input
- A = total factor productivity
- α and β are the output elasticities of labor and capital, respectively. These values are constants determined by available technology.

Output elasticity measures the responsiveness of output to a change in levels of either labor or capital used in production, ceteris paribus. For example if α = 0.15, a 1% increase in labor would lead to approximately a 0.15% increase in output.

a. Growth accounting
c. Social savings
b. Demand-pull theory
d. Cobb-Douglas

23. In microeconomics, _____ is quite simply the conversion of inputs into outputs. It is an economic process that uses resources to create a good or service that is suitable for exchange. This can include manufacturing, storing, shipping, and packaging.

a. MET
c. Solved
b. Production
d. Red Guards

24. In economics, a _____ is a function that specifies the output of a firm, an industry, or an entire economy for all combinations of inputs. A meta-_____ compares the practice of the existing entities converting inputs X into output y to determine the most efficient practice _____ of the existing entities, whether the most efficient feasible practice production or the most efficient actual practice production. In either case, the maximum output of a technologically-determined production process is a mathematical function of input factors of production.

a. Short-run
c. Post-Fordism
b. Production function
d. Constant elasticity of substitution

Chapter 8. Money, Prices, and Inflation

1. In economics, _____ is a sustained decrease in the general price level of goods and services. _____ occurs when the annual inflation rate falls below zero percent, resulting in an increase in the real value of money -- a negative inflation rate. This should not be confused with disinflation, a slow-down in the inflation rate (i.e. when the inflation decreases, but still remains positive.)
   a. Literacy rate
   b. Price revolution
   c. Tobit model
   d. Deflation

2. The _____ is the central banking system of the United States. Created in 1913 by the enactment of the Federal Reserve Act (signed by Woodrow Wilson), it is a quasi-public and quasi-private (government entity with private components) banking system that comprises (1) the presidentially appointed Board of Governors of the _____ in Washington, D.C.; (2) the Federal Open Market Committee; (3) twelve regional Federal Reserve Banks located in major cities throughout the nation acting as fiscal agents for the U.S. Treasury, each with its own nine-member board of directors; (4) numerous other private U.S. member banks, which subscribe to required amounts of non-transferable stock in their regional Federal Reserve Banks; and (5) various advisory councils. Since February 2006, Ben Bernanke has served as the Chairman of the Board of Governors of the _____.
   a. Term auction facility
   b. Monetary Policy Report to the Congress
   c. Federal Reserve System Open Market Account
   d. Federal Reserve System

3. _____, 1st Baron Keynes was a renowned economist from Britain whose many ideas on economic and political theories as well as on many governments' monetary policies influenced America. He advocated a government that played an active role in the lives of people regarding business, economy, etc. In this role, the government would use fiscal measures to reduce the consequences of recessions, economic depressions and booms.
   a. Adolph Fischer
   b. Adolf Hitler
   c. Adam Smith
   d. John Maynard Keynes

4. _____ describes any movement or theory that proposes a different system of supplying money and financing the economy than the current system.

   _____ers may advocate any of the following, among other proposals:

   - A return to the gold standard (or silver standard or bimetallism.)

   - The issuance of interest-free credit from a government-controlled and fully owned central bank. These interest free but repayable loans would be used for public infrastructure and productive private investment. This proposal seeks to overcome the charge that debt-free money would cause inflation.

   a. Quantum economics
   b. Monetary Reform
   c. Fiscal theory of the price level
   d. Silver standard

5. _____ in economics and business is the result of an exchange and from that trade we assign a numerical monetary value to a good, service or asset. If Alice trades Bob 4 apples for an orange, the _____ of an orange is 4 apples. Inversely, the _____ of an apple is 1/4 oranges.
   a. Premium pricing
   b. Price book
   c. Price war
   d. Price

6. A _____ is a hypothetical measure of overall prices for some set of goods and services, in a given region during a given interval, normalized relative to some base set. Typically, a _____ is approximated with a price index.

The classical dichotomy is the assumption that there is a relatively clean distinction between overall increases or decreases in prices and underlying, e;reale; economic variables.

a. Price elasticity of supply
b. Discretionary spending
c. Price level
d. Discouraged worker

7. In economics, _____ is a rise in the general level of prices of goods and services in an economy over a period of time. When the general price level rises, each unit of currency buys fewer goods and services; consequently, _____ is also a decline in the real value of money--a loss of purchasing power in the medium of exchange which is also the monetary unit of account in the economy. A chief measure of general price-level _____ is the general _____ rate, which is the percentage change in a general price index (normally the Consumer Price Index) over time.

a. Energy economics
b. Inflation
c. Opportunity cost
d. Economic

8. In macroeconomics, the _____ refers to an idea attributed to classical and pre-Keynesian economics that real and nominal variables can be analyzed separately. To be precise, an economy exhibits the _____ if real variables such as output and real interest rates can be completely analyzed without considering what is happening to their nominal counterparts, the money value of output and the interest rate. In particular, this means that real GDP and other real variables can be determined without knowing the level of the nominal money supply or the rate of inflation.

a. Classical dichotomy
b. Market cannibalism
c. Deflator
d. Break-even

9. In economics, _____ is inflation that is very high or 'out of control', a condition in which prices increase rapidly as a currency loses its value. Definitions used by the media vary from a cumulative inflation rate over three years approaching 100% to 'inflation exceeding 50% a month.' In informal usage the term is often applied to much lower rates. As a rule of thumb, normal inflation is reported per year, but _____ is often reported for much shorter intervals, often per month.

a. 100-year flood
b. 130-30 fund
c. 1921 recession
d. Hyperinflation

10. Later Keynesians economists took up the notion and redefined it in terms that ignored the microeconomic time structure of production. On this later definition, _____ is the idea that a change in the stock of money affects only nominal variables in the economy such as prices, wages and exchange rates but no effect on real (inflation-adjusted) variables, like employment, real GDP, and real consumption. It is an important idea in classical economics and is related to the classical dichotomy.

a. Chartalism
b. Monetary reform
c. Veil of money
d. Neutrality of money

11. The term _____ refers to economy-wide fluctuations in production or economic activity over several months or years. These fluctuations occur around a long-term growth trend, and typically involve shifts over time between periods of relatively rapid economic growth (expansion or boom), and periods of relative stagnation or decline (contraction or recession.)

These fluctuations are often measured using the growth rate of real gross domestic product.

Chapter 8. Money, Prices, and Inflation

a. Consumer theory
c. Nominal value
b. Tobit model
d. Business cycle

12. _____ is money accepted for exchange of goods in an economy. The prevalence of one money over another arises, usually, when a government designates through decrees that the government shall accept only particular notes and coins in payment for taxes. Typically, money of _____ consists of stamped coins and minted paper bills.
   a. Security thread
   c. Local currency
   b. Totnes pound
   d. Currency

13. Economics:

   - _____,the desire to own something and the ability to pay for it
   - _____ curve,a graphic representation of a _____ schedule
   - _____ deposit, the money in checking accounts
   - _____ pull theory,the theory that inflation occurs when _____ for goods and services exceeds existing supplies
   - _____ schedule,a table that lists the quantity of a good a person will buy it each different price
   - _____ side economics,the school of economics at believes government spending and tax cuts open economy by raising _____

   a. McKesson ' Robbins scandal
   c. Production
   b. Demand
   d. Variability

14. _____ is a type of bank account where the money in the account is legally able to be withdrawn immediately upon demand (or 'at call'.) This type of bank account can also be referred to as a 'cheque' or 'checking' or transactional account.

This type of bank account, allowing immediate conversion of the account balance into cash or withdrawal to another account, can be contrasted with a time deposit (also known as a certificate of deposit or term deposit), where the funds are not legally available for immediate withdrawal by the depositor.

   a. Tangible Common Equity
   c. Demand deposit
   b. Debt rescheduling
   d. Clawbacks in economic development

15. Market _____ is a business, economics or investment term that refers to an asset's ability to be easily converted through an act of buying or selling without causing a significant movement in the price and with minimum loss of value. Money, or cash on hand, is the most liquid asset. An act of exchange of a less liquid asset with a more liquid asset is called liquidation.
   a. 130-30 fund
   c. Liquidity
   b. 100-year flood
   d. 1921 recession

16. Bartering is a medium in which goods or services are directly exchanged for other goods and/or services, without the use of money. It can be bilateral or multilateral, and usually exists parallel to monetary systems in most developed countries, though to a very limited extent. _____ usually replaces money as the method of exchange in times of monetary crisis, when the currency is unstable and devalued by hyperinflation.

Chapter 8. Money, Prices, and Inflation

a. Community-based economics
c. Meitheal
b. New Economics Foundation
d. Barter

17. The _____ of monetary management established the rules for commercial and financial relations among the world's major industrial states in the mid 20th Century. The _____ was the first example of a fully negotiated monetary order intended to govern monetary relations among independent nation-states.

Preparing to rebuild the international economic system as World War II was still raging, 730 delegates from all 44 Allied nations gathered at the Mount Washington Hotel in Bretton Woods, New Hampshire, United States, for the United Nations Monetary and Financial Conference.

a. 1921 recession
c. Bretton Woods system
b. 100-year flood
d. 130-30 fund

18. The _____ problem (often 'double _____') is an important category of transaction costs that impose severe limitations on economies lacking money and thus dominated by barter or other in-kind transactions. The problem is caused by the improbability of the wants, needs or events that cause or motivate a transaction occurring at the same time and the same place.

In-kind transactions have several problems, most notably timing constraints.

a. Going concern
c. Buy-sell agreement
b. RFM
d. Coincidence of wants

19. _____ is a broad label that refers to any individuals or households that use goods and services generated within the economy. The concept of a _____ is used in different contexts, so that the usage and significance of the term may vary.

Typically when business people and economists talk of _____s they are talking about person as _____, an aggregated commodity item with little individuality other than that expressed in the buy/not-buy decision.

a. Consumer
c. 130-30 fund
b. 1921 recession
d. 100-year flood

20. _____ is a common concept in economics, and gives rise to derived concepts such as consumer debt. Generally _____ is defined by opposition to production. But the precise definition can vary because different schools of economists define production quite differently.

a. Federal Reserve Bank Notes
c. Cash or share options
b. Consumption
d. Foreclosure data providers

21. A currency crisis, which is also called a balance-of-payments crisis, occurs when the value of a currency changes quickly, undermining its ability to serve as a medium of exchange or a store of value. It is a type of financial crisis and is often associated with a real economic crisis. _____ can be especially destructive to small open economies or bigger, but not sufficiently stable ones.

a. 100-year flood
b. 1921 recession
c. 130-30 fund
d. Currency crises

22. A _____, sometimes called a pegged exchange rate, is a type of exchange rate regime wherein a currency's value is matched to the value of another single currency or to a basket of other currencies such as gold.

A _____ is usually used to stabilize the value of a currency, vis-a-vis the currency it is pegged to. This facilitates trade and investments between the two countries, and is especially useful for small economies where external trade forms a large part of their GDP.

a. Fixed exchange rate
b. Monetary economics
c. Law of supply
d. Leading indicators

23. A _____ or a flexible exchange rate is a type of exchange rate regime wherein a currency's value is allowed to fluctuate according to the foreign exchange market. A currency that uses a _____ is known as a floating currency. The opposite of a _____ is a fixed exchange rate.

a. Floating currency
b. Foreign exchange market
c. Trade Weighted US dollar Index
d. Floating exchange rate

24. A _____ is an intermediary used in trade to avoid the inconveniences of a pure barter system.

By contrast, as William Stanley Jevons argued, in a barter system there must be a coincidence of wants before two people can trade - one must want exactly what the other has to offer, when and where it is offered, so that the exchange can occur. A _____ permits the value of goods to be assessed and rendered in terms of the intermediary, most often, a form of money widely accepted to buy any other good.

a. Consumer theory
b. Medium of exchange
c. Price revolution
d. Labour economics

25. A _____ is a standard monetary unit of measurement of the market value/cost of goods, services, or assets. It is one of three well-known functions of money. It lends meaning to profits, losses, liability, or assets.

a. ACEA agreement
b. ACCRA Cost of Living Index
c. AD-IA Model
d. Unit of account

26. In finance, the _____s between two currencies specifies how much one currency is worth in terms of the other. It is the value of a foreign natione;s currency in terms of the home natione;s currency. For example an _____ of 102 Japanese yen to the United States dollar means that JPY 102 is worth the same as USD 1.

a. Interbank market
b. ACCRA Cost of Living Index
c. ACEA agreement
d. Exchange rate

27. _____ or economic opportunity loss is the value of the next best alternative foregone as the result of making a decision. _____ analysis is an important part of a company's decision-making processes but is not treated as an actual cost in any financial statement. The next best thing that a person can engage in is referred to as the _____ of doing the best thing and ignoring the next best thing to be done.

Chapter 8. Money, Prices, and Inflation

a. Industrial organization
b. Opportunity cost
c. Economic
d. Economic ideology

28. _____ refers to a business or organization attempting to acquire goods or services to accomplish the goals of the enterprise. Though there are several organizations that attempt to set standards in the _____ process, processes can vary greatly between organizations. Typically the word '_____' is not used interchangeably with the word 'procurement', since procurement typically includes Expediting, Supplier Quality, and Traffic and Logistics (T'L) in addition to _____.

a. Free port
b. Purchasing
c. 130-30 fund
d. 100-year flood

29. _____ is the number of goods/services that can be purchased with a unit of currency. For example, if you had taken one dollar to a store in the 1950s, you would have been able to buy a greater number of items than you would today, indicating that you would have had a greater _____ in the 1950s. Currency can be either a commodity money, like gold or silver, or fiat currency like US dollars.

a. Human Poverty Index
b. Compliance cost
c. Genuine progress indicator
d. Purchasing power

30. In economics, the _____ of money is a theory emphasizing the positive relationship of overall prices or the nominal value of expenditures to the quantity of money.

It is the mainstream economic theory of the price level. Alternative theories include the real bills doctrine and the more recent fiscal theory of the price level.

a. Quantity theory
b. Real business cycle
c. Romer Model
d. Dishoarding

31. In economics, the _____ is a theory emphasizing the positive relationship of overall prices or the nominal value of expenditures to the quantity of money.

It is the mainstream economic theory of the price level. Alternative theories include the real bills doctrine and the more recent fiscal theory of the price level.

a. Consumer spending
b. Microsimulation
c. Fundamental psychological law
d. Quantity theory of money

Chapter 8. Money, Prices, and Inflation

32. _____ has several particular meanings:

- in mathematics
    - _____ function
    - Euler _____
    - _____
    - _____ subgroup
    - method of _____s (partial differential equations)
- in physics and engineering
    - any _____ curve that shows the relationship between certain input- and output parameters, e.g.
    - an I-V or current-voltage _____ is the current in a circuit as a function of the applied voltage
    - Receiver-Operator _____
- in fiction
    - in Dungeons ' Dragons, _____ is another name for ability score

a. Characteristic
b. Technocracy
c. Russian financial crisis
d. Demand

33. The _____ is the average frequency with which a unit of money is spent in a specific period of time. Velocity associates the amount of economic activity associated with a given money supply. When the period is understood, the velocity may be present as a pure number; otherwise it should be given as a pure number over time.
a. Money supply
b. Chartalism
c. Neutrality of money
d. Velocity of money

34. The _____ is 'the basic residential unit in which economic production, consumption, inheritance, child rearing, and shelter are organized and carried out'; [the _____] 'may or may not be synonymous with family'.

The _____ is the basic unit of analysis in many social, microeconomic and government models. The term refers to all individuals who live in the same dwelling.

a. 100-year flood
b. Family economics
c. 130-30 fund
d. Household

35. In economics, the term _____ of income or _____ refers to a simple economic model which describes the reciprocal circulation of income between producers and consumers. In the _____ model, the inter-dependent entities of producer and consumer are referred to as 'firms' and 'households' respectively and provide each other with factors in order to facilitate the flow of income. Firms provide consumers with goods and services in exchange for consumer expenditure and 'factors of production' from households.
a. 100-year flood
b. Circular flow
c. 1921 recession
d. 130-30 fund

Chapter 8. Money, Prices, and Inflation

36. A _____, reserve bank, or monetary authority is the entity responsible for the monetary policy of a country or of a group of member states. It is a bank that can lend money to other banks in times of need. Its primary responsibility is to maintain the stability of the national currency and money supply, but more active duties include controlling subsidized-loan interest rates, and acting as a lender of last resort to the banking sector during times of financial crisis (private banks often being integral to the national financial system.)

    a. 1921 recession
    b. 130-30 fund
    c. 100-year flood
    d. Central bank

37. In economics, the _____ is a term relating to the money supply, the amount of money in the economy. The _____ comprises only coins, paper money, and commercial banks' reserves with the central bank. Broader measures of the money supply include the public's bank deposits .

    a. Chartalism
    b. Monetary economy
    c. Monetary base
    d. Quantum economics

38. In economics, _____ is the total amount of money available in an economy at a particular point in time. There are several ways to define 'money', but standard measures usually include currency in circulation and demand deposits.

_____ data are recorded and published, usually by the government or the central bank of the country.

    a. Money supply
    b. Neutrality of money
    c. Velocity of money
    d. Veil of money

39. In economics, the _____ is the term used to refer to the environment in which bonds are bought and sold between a central bank ' its regulated banks. It is not a free market process.

- To intervene in the 'business cycle', a central bank may choose to go into the _____ and buy or sell government bonds, which is known as _____ operations to increase reserves.

    a. Outside money
    b. Inside money
    c. ACCRA Cost of Living Index
    d. Open market

40. _____ are the means of implementing monetary policy by which a central bank controls its national money supply by buying and selling government securities, or other financial instruments. Monetary targets, such as interest rates or exchange rates, are used to guide this implementation.

Since most money is now in the form of electronic records, rather than paper records such as banknotes, _____ are conducted simply by electronically increasing or decreasing ('crediting' or 'debiting') the amount of money that a bank has, e.g., in its reserve account at the central bank, in exchange for a bank selling or buying a financial instrument.

    a. ACCRA Cost of Living Index
    b. AD-IA Model
    c. Open market operations
    d. ACEA agreement

41. The _____ is a bank regulation that sets the minimum reserves each bank must hold to customer deposits and notes. It would normally be in the form of fiat currency stored in a bank vault (vault cash), or with a central bank.

Chapter 8. Money, Prices, and Inflation

The reserve ratio is sometimes used as a tool in the monetary policy, influencing the country's economy, borrowing, and interest rates.

a. Probability of default
b. Reserve requirement
c. Private money
d. Fractional-reserve banking

42. In banking, _____ are bank reserves in excess of the reserve requirement set by a central bank (in the United States, the Federal Reserve System, called the Fed; in Canada, the Bank of Canada.) They are reserves of cash more than the required amounts. Holding _____ is generally considered costly and uneconomical as no interest is earned on the excess amount.

a. Universal bank
b. Annual percentage rate
c. Origination fee
d. Excess reserves

43. The _____ , a component of the Federal Reserve System, is charged under United States law with overseeing the nation's open market operations. It is the Federal Reserve Committee that makes key decisions about interest rates and the growth jam of the United States money supply. It is the principal organ of United States national monetary policy.

a. Federal Reserve Transparency Act
b. Fed Funds Probability
c. Primary Dealer Credit Facility
d. Federal Open Market Committee

44. The Federal Reserve System (also the Federal Reserve; informally The Fed) is the central banking system of the United States. Created in 1913 by the enactment of the Federal Reserve Act (signed by Woodrow Wilson), it is a quasi-public and quasi-private (government entity with private components) banking system that comprises (1) the presidentially appointed Board of Governors of the Federal Reserve System in Washington, D.C.; (2) the Federal Open Market Committee; (3) twelve regional _____ located in major cities throughout the nation acting as fiscal agents for the U.S. Treasury, each with its own nine-member board of directors; (4) numerous other private U.S. member banks, which subscribe to required amounts of non-transferable stock in their regional _____; and (5) various advisory councils. Since February 2006, Ben Bernanke has served as the Chairman of the Board of Governors of the Federal Reserve System.

a. Federal funds
b. Fed Funds Probability
c. Federal Reserve banks
d. Federal Open Market Committee

45. In calculus, a function f defined on a subset of the real numbers with real values is called _____, if for all x and y such that x >≤ y one has f(x) >≤ f(y), so f preserves the order. In layman's terms, the sign of the slope is always positive (the curve tending upwards) or zero (i.e., non-decreasing, or asymptotic, or depicted as a horizontal, flat line) Likewise, a function is called monotonically decreasing (non-increasing) if, whenever x >≤ y, then f(x) >≥ f(y), so it reverses the order.

a. 100-year flood
b. 130-30 fund
c. Monotonic
d. 1921 recession

46. _____, in law and economics, is a form of risk management primarily used to hedge against the risk of a contingent loss. _____ is defined as the equitable transfer of the risk of a loss, from one entity to another, in exchange for a premium, and can be thought of as a guaranteed small loss to prevent a large, possibly devastating loss. An insurer is a company selling the _____; an insured or policyholder is the person or entity buying the _____.

a. AD-IA Model
b. ACEA agreement
c. ACCRA Cost of Living Index
d. Insurance

47. _____ is the process by which the government, central bank (ii) availability of money, and (iii) cost of money or rate of interest, in order to attain a set of objectives oriented towards the growth and stability of the economy. Monetary theory provides insight into how to craft optimal _____.

_____ is referred to as either being an expansionary policy where an expansionary policy increases the total supply of money in the economy, and a contractionary policy decreases the total money supply.

a. Monetary policy
b. 1921 recession
c. 100-year flood
d. 130-30 fund

48. The _____ is the upward-sloping relationship between the inflation rate and the unemployment rate. When the inflation rate rises, a central bank wishing to fight inflation will raise interest rates to reduce output and thus increase the unemployment rate. The _____ is a function of the Taylor Rule, the Investment-Spending Curve (IS Curve) and Okun's Law

The _____ has the equation:

$$u = u_0 + \Phi(\pi - \pi t)$$

Where Φ is a parameter that tells us how much unemployment rises when the central bank raises the real interest rate r because it thinks that inflation is too high and needs to be reduced.

a. Secular basis
b. Monetary policy reaction function
c. Marginal propensity to import
d. Value added

49. _____ is a macroeconomic term referring to the monetary base -- that is, to highly liquid money and includes currency and vault cash. In the United States, with the beginning of the Federal Reserve System in 1913, _____ also includes deposit liabilities of the Federal Reserve System to banks.

The monetary base is typically controlled by the institution in a country that controls monetary policy.

a. Rational expectations
b. Complex multiplier
c. Hodrick-Prescott filter
d. High-powered money

50. In economics, the _____ is a measure of inflation, the rate of increase of a price index (for example, a consumer price index.)It is the percentage rate of change in price level over time. The rate of decrease in the purchasing power of money is approximately equal.

It's used to calculate the real interest rate, as well as real increases in wages, and official measurements of this rate act as input variables to COLA adjustments and Inflation derivatives prices.

a. Edgeworth paradox
b. Interest rate option
c. Inflation rate
d. Equity value

51. Necessary _____s:

Chapter 8. Money, Prices, and Inflation 105

If x is a necessary _____ of y, then the presence of y necessarily implies the presence of x. The presence of x, however, does not imply that y will occur.

Sufficient _____s:

If x is a sufficient _____ of y, then the presence of x necessarily implies the presence of y.

 a. Philosophy of economics
 b. Materialism
 c. Political philosophy
 d. Cause

52. A _____ is a measure of the average price of consumer goods and services purchased by households. A _____ measures a price change for a constant market basket of goods and services from one period to the next within the same area (city, region, or nation.) It is a price index determined by measuring the price of a standard group of goods meant to represent the typical market basket of a typical urban consumer.
 a. Cost-of-living index
 b. Consumer price index
 c. CPI
 d. Lipstick index

53. A _____ is a normalized average (typically a weighted average) of prices for a given class of goods or services in a given region, during a given interval of time. It is a statistic designed to help to compare how these prices, taken as a whole, differ between time periods or geographical locations.

Price indices have several potential uses.

 a. Two-part tariff
 b. Product sabotage
 c. Price index
 d. Transactional Net Margin Method

54. The _____ or gross domestic income (GDI), a basic measure of an economy's economic performance, is the market value of all final goods and services produced within the borders of a nation in a year. _____ can be defined in three ways, all of which are conceptually identical. First, it is equal to the total expenditures for all final goods and services produced within the country in a stipulated period of time (usually a 365-day year.)
 a. Countercyclical
 b. Market structure
 c. Gross domestic product
 d. Monopolistic competition

55. An _____, in economics, is the amount by which the real Gross domestic product exceeds potential GDP. The real GDP is also known as GDP 'adjusted for inflation', 'constant prices' GDP or 'constant dollar' GDP, because it measures the aggregate output in a country's income accounts in a given year, expressed in base-year prices. On the other hand, the potential GDP is the quantity of real GDP when a country's economy is at full-employment.
 a. ACCRA Cost of Living Index
 b. ACEA agreement
 c. AD-IA Model
 d. Inflationary gap

56. The _____ was a worldwide economic downturn starting in most places in 1929 and ending at different times in the 1930s or early 1940s for different countries. It was the largest and most important economic depression in the 20th century, and is used in the 21st century as an example of how far the world's economy can fall. The _____ originated in the United States; historians most often use as a starting date the stock market crash on October 29, 1929, known as Black Tuesday.

Chapter 8. Money, Prices, and Inflation

a. British Empire Economic Conference
c. Jarrow March
b. Great Depression
d. Wall Street Crash of 1929

57. The term _____s refers to wages that have been adjusted for inflation. This term is used in contrast to nominal wages or unadjusted wages.

The use of adjusted figures is in undertaking some form of economic analysis.

a. Profit sharing
c. Living wage
b. Federal Wage System
d. Real wage

58. _____ is a fee paid on borrowed assets. It is the price paid for the use of borrowed money, or, money earned by deposited funds. Assets that are sometimes lent with _____ include money, shares, consumer goods through hire purchase, major assets such as aircraft, and even entire factories in finance lease arrangements.
a. Asset protection
c. Insolvency
b. Interest
d. Internal debt

59. An _____ is the price a borrower pays for the use of money they do not own, for instance a small company might borrow from a bank to kick start their business, and the return a lender receives for deferring the use of funds, by lending it to the borrower. _____s are normally expressed as a percentage rate over the period of one year.

_____s targets are also a vital tool of monetary policy and are used to control variables like investment, inflation, and unemployment.

a. Enterprise value
c. Interest rate
b. Arrow-Debreu model
d. ACCRA Cost of Living Index

60. In finance and economics _____ or nominal rate of interest refers to the rate of interest before adjustment for inflation (in contrast with the real interest rate); or, for interest rates 'as stated' without adjustment for the full effect of compounding (also referred to as the nominal annual rate.) An interest rate is called nominal if the frequency of compounding (e.g. a month) is not identical to the basic time unit (normally a year.)

The real interest rate includes compensation for the lender's lost value due to inflation, whereas the _____ excludes inflation.

a. Risk-free interest rate
c. Fixed interest
b. Nominal interest rate
d. London Interbank Offered Rate

61. _____ is the net revenue derived from the issuing of currency.

_____ derived from specie - metal coins - arises from the difference between the face value of a coin and the cost of producing, distributing and retiring it from circulation.

_____ derived from notes is more indirect, being the difference between interest earned on securities acquired in exchange for bank notes and the costs of producing and distributing those notes.

Chapter 8. Money, Prices, and Inflation

a. Money Tracker
c. Seigniorage
b. 130-30 fund
d. 100-year flood

62. To _____ is to impose a financial charge or other levy upon a taxpayer by a state or the functional equivalent of a state.

_____es are also imposed by many subnational entities. _____es consist of direct _____ or indirect _____, and may be paid in money or as its labour equivalent (often but not always unpaid.)

a. 130-30 fund
c. 1921 recession
b. 100-year flood
d. Tax

63. In finance, _____ rate of profit or sometimes just return, is the ratio of money gained or lost on an investment relative to the amount of money invested. The amount of money gained or lost may be referred to as interest, profit/loss, gain/loss, or net income/loss. The money invested may be referred to as the asset, capital, principal, or the cost basis of the investment.

a. Cost accrual ratio
c. Rate of return
b. Current ratio
d. Sortino ratio

64. In economics, a _____ is a monetary-policy rule that stipulates how much the central bank would or should change the nominal interest rate in response to divergences of actual inflation rates from target inflation rates and of actual Gross Domestic Product (GDP) from potential GDP. It was first proposed by the by U.S. economist John B. Taylor in 1993. The rule can be written as follows:

$$i_t = \pi_t + r_t^* + a_\pi(\pi_t - \pi_t^*) + a_y(y_t - \bar{y}_t).$$

In this equation, i_t is the target short-term nominal interest rate (e.g. the federal funds rate in the US), π_t is the rate of inflation as measured by the GDP deflator, π_t^* is the desired rate of inflation, r_t^* is the assumed equilibrium real interest rate, y_t is the logarithm of real GDP, and $\bar{y}_t$ is the logarithm of potential output, as determined by a linear trend.

a. Fed Funds Probability
c. Federal Reserve Banks
b. Term Securities Lending Facility
d. Taylor rule

Chapter 8. Money, Prices, and Inflation

65. A _____ is:

- Rewrite _____, in generative grammar and computer science
- Standardization, a formal and widely-accepted statement, fact, definition, or qualification
- Operation, a determinate _____ for performing a mathematical operation and obtaining a certain result (Mathematics, Logic)
    - Unary operation
    - Binary operation
- _____ of inference, a function from sets of formulae to formulae (Mathematics, Logic)
- _____ of thumb, principle with broad application that is not intended to be strictly accurate or reliable for every situation. Also often simply referred to as a _____
- Moral, an atomic element of a moral code for guiding choices in human behavior
- Heuristic, a quantized '_____' which shows a tendency or probability for successful function
- A regulation, as in sports
- A Production _____, as in computer science
- Procedural law, a _____ set governing the application of laws to cases
    - A law, which may informally be called a '_____'
    - A court ruling, a decision by a court
- In the U.S. Government, a regulation mandated by Congress, but written or expanded upon by the Executive Branch.
- Norm (sociology), an informal but widely accepted _____, concept, truth, definition, or qualification (social norms, legal norms, coding norms)
- Norm (philosophy), a kind of sentence or a reason to act, feel or believe
- 'Rulership' is the concept of governance by a government:
    - Military _____, governance by a military body
    - Monastic _____, a collection of precepts that guides the life of monks or nuns in a religious order where the superior holds the place of Christ
- Slide _____

- '_____,' a song by Ayumi Hamasaki
- '_____,' a song by rapper Nas
- '_____s,' an album by the band The Whitest Boy Alive
- _____s: Pyaar Ka Superhit Formula, a 2003 Bollywood film
- ruler, an instrument for measuring lengths
- _____, a component of an astrolabe, circumferator or similar instrument
- The _____s, a bestselling self-help book
- _____ Project (Run Up-to-date Linux Everywhere), a project that aims to use up-to-date Linux software on old PCs
- _____ engine, a software system that helps managing business _____s
- Ja _____, a hip hop artist
    - R.U.L.E., a 2005 greatest hits album by rapper Ja _____
- '_____s,' a KMFDM song

a. Technocracy
c. Procter ' Gamble
b. Rule
d. Demand

Chapter 9. The Sticky-Price Income-Expenditure Framework: Consumption and the Multiplier 109

1. The _____ or gross domestic income (GDI), a basic measure of an economy's economic performance, is the market value of all final goods and services produced within the borders of a nation in a year. _____ can be defined in three ways, all of which are conceptually identical. First, it is equal to the total expenditures for all final goods and services produced within the country in a stipulated period of time (usually a 365-day year.)
   a. Market structure
   b. Gross domestic product
   c. Countercyclical
   d. Monopolistic competition

2. The _____ is a concept of economic activity developed in particular by Milton Friedman and Edmund Phelps in the 1960s, both recipients of the Nobel prize in economics. In both cases, the development of the concept is cited as a main motivation behind the prize. It represents the hypothetical unemployment rate consistent with aggregate production being at the 'long-run' level.
   a. Romer Model
   b. Natural rate of unemployment
   c. Robertson lag
   d. Real Business Cycle Theory

3. An _____, in economics, is the amount by which the real Gross domestic product exceeds potential GDP. The real GDP is also known as GDP 'adjusted for inflation', 'constant prices' GDP or 'constant dollar' GDP, because it measures the aggregate output in a country's income accounts in a given year, expressed in base-year prices. On the other hand, the potential GDP is the quantity of real GDP when a country's economy is at full-employment.
   a. ACCRA Cost of Living Index
   b. ACEA agreement
   c. AD-IA Model
   d. Inflationary gap

4. In economics, a _____ is a general slowdown in economic activity over a sustained period of time, or a business cycle contraction. During _____s, many macroeconomic indicators vary in a similar way. Production as measured by Gross Domestic Product (GDP), employment, investment spending, capacity utilization, household incomes and business profits all fall during _____s.
   a. Leading indicators
   b. Recession
   c. Monetary economics
   d. Treasury View

5. In economics, a _____ is a monetary-policy rule that stipulates how much the central bank would or should change the nominal interest rate in response to divergences of actual inflation rates from target inflation rates and of actual Gross Domestic Product (GDP) from potential GDP. It was first proposed by the by U.S. economist John B. Taylor in 1993. The rule can be written as follows:

$$i_t = \pi_t + r_t^* + a_\pi(\pi_t - \pi_t^*) + a_y(y_t - \bar{y}_t).$$

In this equation, i_t is the target short-term nominal interest rate (e.g. the federal funds rate in the US), π_t is the rate of inflation as measured by the GDP deflator, π_t^* is the desired rate of inflation, r_t^* is the assumed equilibrium real interest rate, y_t is the logarithm of real GDP, and $\bar{y}_t$ is the logarithm of potential output, as determined by a linear trend.

   a. Taylor rule
   b. Term Securities Lending Facility
   c. Federal Reserve Banks
   d. Fed Funds Probability

Chapter 9. The Sticky-Price Income-Expenditure Framework: Consumption and the Multiplier

6. Unemployment occurs when a person is available to work and seeking work but currently without work. The prevalence of unemployment is usually measured using the _____, which is defined as the percentage of those in the labor force who are unemployed. The _____ is also used in economic studies and economic indexes such as the United States' Conference Board's Index of Leading Indicators as a measure of the state of the macroeconomics.
   a. ACEA agreement
   b. AD-IA Model
   c. ACCRA Cost of Living Index
   d. Unemployment rate

7. The term _____ refers to economy-wide fluctuations in production or economic activity over several months or years. These fluctuations occur around a long-term growth trend, and typically involve shifts over time between periods of relatively rapid economic growth (expansion or boom), and periods of relative stagnation or decline (contraction or recession.)

   These fluctuations are often measured using the growth rate of real gross domestic product.

   a. Tobit model
   b. Nominal value
   c. Consumer theory
   d. Business cycle

8. In statistics, a _____ is a value that allows data to be measured over time in terms of some base period ussually through a price index in order to distinguish between changes in the money value of GNP which result from a change in prices and those which result from a change in physical output. It is the measure of the price level for some quantity. A _____ serves as a price index in which the effects of inflation are nulled.
   a. Market microstructure
   b. Blanket order
   c. Contingent employment
   d. Deflator

9. _____ in economics and business is the result of an exchange and from that trade we assign a numerical monetary value to a good, service or asset. If Alice trades Bob 4 apples for an orange, the _____ of an orange is 4 apples. Inversely, the _____ of an apple is 1/4 oranges.
   a. Premium pricing
   b. Price war
   c. Price book
   d. Price

Chapter 9. The Sticky-Price Income-Expenditure Framework: Consumption and the Multiplier

10. A _____ is:

   - Rewrite _____, in generative grammar and computer science
   - Standardization, a formal and widely-accepted statement, fact, definition, or qualification
   - Operation, a determinate _____ for performing a mathematical operation and obtaining a certain result (Mathematics, Logic)
     - Unary operation
     - Binary operation
   - _____ of inference, a function from sets of formulae to formulae (Mathematics, Logic)
   - _____ of thumb, principle with broad application that is not intended to be strictly accurate or reliable for every situation. Also often simply referred to as a _____
   - Moral, an atomic element of a moral code for guiding choices in human behavior
   - Heuristic, a quantized '_____' which shows a tendency or probability for successful function
   - A regulation, as in sports
   - A Production _____, as in computer science
   - Procedural law, a _____ set governing the application of laws to cases
     - A law, which may informally be called a '_____'
     - A court ruling, a decision by a court
   - In the U.S. Government, a regulation mandated by Congress, but written or expanded upon by the Executive Branch.
   - Norm (sociology), an informal but widely accepted _____, concept, truth, definition, or qualification (social norms, legal norms, coding norms)
   - Norm (philosophy), a kind of sentence or a reason to act, feel or believe
   - 'Rulership' is the concept of governance by a government:
     - Military _____, governance by a military body
     - Monastic _____, a collection of precepts that guides the life of monks or nuns in a religious order where the superior holds the place of Christ
   - Slide _____

   - '_____,' a song by Ayumi Hamasaki
   - '_____,' a song by rapper Nas
   - '_____s,' an album by the band The Whitest Boy Alive
   - _____s: Pyaar Ka Superhit Formula, a 2003 Bollywood film
   - ruler, an instrument for measuring lengths
   - _____, a component of an astrolabe, circumferator or similar instrument
   - The _____s, a bestselling self-help book
   - _____ Project (Run Up-to-date Linux Everywhere), a project that aims to use up-to-date Linux software on old PCs
   - _____ engine, a software system that helps managing business _____s
   - Ja _____, a hip hop artist
     - R.U.L.E., a 2005 greatest hits album by rapper Ja _____
   - '_____s,' a KMFDM song

a. Procter ' Gamble
b. Demand
c. Technocracy
d. Rule

Chapter 9. The Sticky-Price Income-Expenditure Framework: Consumption and the Multiplier

11. In economics, _____ refers to the highest level of real Gross Domestic Product output that can be sustained over the long term. The existence of a limit is due to natural and institutional constraints. If actual GDP rises and stays above _____, then (in the absence of wage and price controls) inflation tends to increase as demand exceeds supply.
  - a. Fundamental psychological law
  - b. Potential output
  - c. Monetary conditions index
  - d. Monetary policy reaction function

12. In economics, _____ is the total demand for final goods and services in the economy (Y) at a given time and price level. It is the amount of goods and services in the economy that will be purchased at all possible price levels. This is the demand for the gross domestic product of a country when inventory levels are static.
  - a. Aggregation problem
  - b. Aggregate supply
  - c. Aggregate expenditure
  - d. Aggregate demand

13. Economics:
  - _____, the desire to own something and the ability to pay for it
  - _____ curve, a graphic representation of a _____ schedule
  - _____ deposit, the money in checking accounts
  - _____ pull theory, the theory that inflation occurs when _____ for goods and services exceeds existing supplies
  - _____ schedule, a table that lists the quantity of a good a person will buy it each different price
  - _____ side economics, the school of economics at believes government spending and tax cuts open economy by raising _____

  - a. McKesson ' Robbins scandal
  - b. Production
  - c. Variability
  - d. Demand

14. _____ is a misspelled phrase from Latin 'pro capite' phrase meaning per head with pro meaning 'per' or 'for each' and capite meaning 'head.' Both words together equate to the phrase 'for each head.'

It is usually used in the field of statistics to indicate the average per person for any given concern, such as income, crime rate, etc.

It is also used in wills to indicate that each of the named beneficiaries should receive, by devise or bequest, equal shares of the estate. This is in contrast to a per stirpes division, in which each branch of the inheriting family inherits an equal share of the estate.

  - a. Sargan test
  - b. Per capita
  - c. False positive rate
  - d. Population statistics

15. _____ is a common concept in economics, and gives rise to derived concepts such as consumer debt. Generally _____ is defined by opposition to production. But the precise definition can vary because different schools of economists define production quite differently.
  - a. Foreclosure data providers
  - b. Cash or share options
  - c. Federal Reserve Bank Notes
  - d. Consumption

Chapter 9. The Sticky-Price Income-Expenditure Framework: Consumption and the Multiplier 113

16. In economics, the _____ is a single mathematical function used to express consumer spending. It was developed by John Maynard Keynes and detailed most famously in his book The General Theory of Employment, Interest, and Money. The function is used to calculate the amount of total consumption in an economy.
- a. DAD-SAS model
- b. Liquidity preference
- c. Procyclical
- d. Consumption function

17. _____, or a _____ is the concept of a resulting effect (cf. cause and effect, arising from another action. In general terms, it is used to indicate that all human actions, particularly crime and sin, have profound effects.
- a. Variability
- b. Rule
- c. Consequence
- d. Solved

18. The '_____' is approximately the nominal interest rate minus the inflation rate Since the inflation rate over the course of a loan is not known initially, volatility in inflation represents a risk to both the lender and the borrower.

In economics and finance, an individual who lends money for repayment at a later point in time expects to be compensated for the time value of money, or not having the use of that money while it is lent.

- a. Reflation
- b. Cost-push inflation
- c. Real interest rate
- d. Core inflation

19. In macroeconomics, the _____ refers to an idea attributed to classical and pre-Keynesian economics that real and nominal variables can be analyzed separately. To be precise, an economy exhibits the _____ if real variables such as output and real interest rates can be completely analyzed without considering what is happening to their nominal counterparts, the money value of output and the interest rate. In particular, this means that real GDP and other real variables can be determined without knowing the level of the nominal money supply or the rate of inflation.
- a. Market cannibalism
- b. Break-even
- c. Deflator
- d. Classical dichotomy

20. _____ is a fee paid on borrowed assets. It is the price paid for the use of borrowed money , or, money earned by deposited funds . Assets that are sometimes lent with _____ include money, shares, consumer goods through hire purchase, major assets such as aircraft, and even entire factories in finance lease arrangements.
- a. Insolvency
- b. Interest
- c. Internal debt
- d. Asset protection

21. An _____ is the price a borrower pays for the use of money they do not own, for instance a small company might borrow from a bank to kick start their business, and the return a lender receives for deferring the use of funds, by lending it to the borrower. _____s are normally expressed as a percentage rate over the period of one year.

_____s targets are also a vital tool of monetary policy and are used to control variables like investment, inflation, and unemployment.

- a. ACCRA Cost of Living Index
- b. Arrow-Debreu model
- c. Enterprise value
- d. Interest rate

114 Chapter 9. The Sticky-Price Income-Expenditure Framework: Consumption and the Multiplier

22. In economics, economic equilibrium is simply a state of the world where economic forces are balanced and in the absence of external influences the (equilibrium) values of economic variables will not change. It is the point at which quantity demanded and quantity supplied are equal. _____, for example, refers to a condition where a market price is established through competition such that the amount of goods or services sought by buyers is equal to the amount of goods or services produced by sellers.

a. Market equilibrium
b. Product-Market Growth Matrix
c. Marketization
d. Regulated market

23. The _____ is 'the basic residential unit in which economic production, consumption, inheritance, child rearing, and shelter are organized and carried out'; [the _____] 'may or may not be synonomous with family'.

The _____ is the basic unit of analysis in many social, microeconomic and government models. The term refers to all individuals who live in the same dwelling.

a. 100-year flood
b. 130-30 fund
c. Family economics
d. Household

24. A variety of measures of _____ and output are used in economics to estimate total economic activity in a country or region, including gross domestic product (GDP), gross national product (GNP), and net _____

There are three main ways of calculating these numbers; the output approach, the income approach and the expenditure approach. In theory, the three must yield the same, because total expenditures on goods and services must equal the total income paid to the producers (Gnational income), and that must also equal the total value of the output of goods and services (GNP.)

a. Volume index
b. Gross world product
c. National income
d. GNI per capita

25. _____ is an assumption used in many contemporary macroeconomic models, and also in other areas of contemporary economics and game theory and in other applications of rational choice theory.

Since most macroeconomic models today study decisions over many periods, the expectations of workers, consumers, and firms about future economic conditions are an essential part of the model. How to model these expectations has long been controversial, and it is well known that the macroeconomic predictions of the model may differ depending on the assumptions made about expectations

a. Potential output
b. Rational expectations
c. Balanced-growth equilibrium
d. Minimum wage

26. In macroeconomics, _____ is a condition of the national economy, where all or nearly all persons willing and able to work at the prevailing wages and working conditions are able to do so. It is defined either as 0% unemployment, literally, no unemployment (the rate of unemployment is the fraction of the work force unable to find work), as by James Tobin, or as the level of employment rates when there is no cyclical unemployment. It is defined by the majority of mainstream economists as being an acceptable level of natural unemployment above 0%, the discrepancy from 0% being due to non-cyclical types of unemployment.

Chapter 9. The Sticky-Price Income-Expenditure Framework: Consumption and the Multiplier

a. Full employment
b. Marginal propensity to consume
c. Demand shock
d. Harrod-Johnson diagram

27. _____, 1st Baron Keynes was a renowned economist from Britain whose many ideas on economic and political theories as well as on many governments' monetary policies influenced America. He advocated a government that played an active role in the lives of people regarding business, economy, etc. In this role, the government would use fiscal measures to reduce the consequences of recessions, economic depressions and booms.

a. Adam Smith
b. Adolf Hitler
c. Adolph Fischer
d. John Maynard Keynes

28. _____ and Keynesian Theory) is a macroeconomic theory based on the ideas of 20th-century British economist John Maynard Keynes. _____ argues that private sector decisions sometimes lead to inefficient macroeconomic outcomes and therefore advocates active policy responses by the public sector, including monetary policy actions by the central bank and fiscal policy actions by the government to stabilize output over the business cycle.

The theories forming the basis of _____ were first presented in The General Theory of Employment, Interest and Money, published in 1936.

a. Market failure
b. Rational choice theory
c. Deflation
d. Keynesian economics

29. In economic models, the _____ time frame assumes no fixed factors of production. Firms can enter or leave the marketplace, and the cost (and availability) of land, labor, raw materials, and capital goods can be assumed to vary. In contrast, in the short-run time frame, certain factors are assumed to be fixed, because there is not sufficient time for them to change.

a. Price/performance ratio
b. Long-run
c. Diseconomies of scale
d. Productivity world

30. _____ describes any movement or theory that proposes a different system of supplying money and financing the economy than the current system.

_____ers may advocate any of the following, among other proposals:

- A return to the gold standard (or silver standard or bimetallism.)

- The issuance of interest-free credit from a government-controlled and fully owned central bank. These interest free but repayable loans would be used for public infrastructure and productive private investment. This proposal seeks to overcome the charge that debt-free money would cause inflation.

a. Silver standard
b. Quantum economics
c. Fiscal theory of the price level
d. Monetary Reform

31. In economics, the concept of the _____ refers to the decision-making time frame of a firm in which at least one factor of production is fixed. Costs which are fixed in the _____ have no impact on a firms decisions. For example a firm can raise output by increasing the amount of labour through overtime.

Chapter 9. The Sticky-Price Income-Expenditure Framework: Consumption and the Multiplier

a. Product Pipeline
b. Productivity model
c. Hicks-neutral technical change
d. Short-run

32. _____ is a broad label that refers to any individuals or households that use goods and services generated within the economy. The concept of a _____ is used in different contexts, so that the usage and significance of the term may vary.

Typically when business people and economists talk of _____s they are talking about person as _____, an aggregated commodity item with little individuality other than that expressed in the buy/not-buy decision.

a. Consumer
b. 130-30 fund
c. 1921 recession
d. 100-year flood

33. In economics, _____ refers to the tendency of people to think of currency in nominal, rather than real, terms. In other words, the numerical/face value (nominal value) of money is mistaken for its purchasing power (real value.) This is a fallacy as modern fiat currencies have no inherent value and their real value is derived from their ability to be exchanged for goods and used for payment of taxes.

a. Representative money
b. Metallism
c. Money changer
d. Money illusion

34. The _____ problem (often 'double _____') is an important category of transaction costs that impose severe limitations on economies lacking money and thus dominated by barter or other in-kind transactions. The problem is caused by the improbability of the wants, needs or events that cause or motivate a transaction occurring at the same time and the same place.

In-kind transactions have several problems, most notably timing constraints.

a. Coincidence of wants
b. RFM
c. Going concern
d. Buy-sell agreement

35. To _____ is to impose a financial charge or other levy upon a taxpayer by a state or the functional equivalent of a state.

_____es are also imposed by many subnational entities. _____es consist of direct _____ or indirect _____, and may be paid in money or as its labour equivalent (often but not always unpaid.)

a. 1921 recession
b. 100-year flood
c. 130-30 fund
d. Tax

36. To tax is to impose a financial charge or other levy upon a taxpayer by a state or the functional equivalent of a state.

_____ are also imposed by many subnational entities. _____ consist of direct tax or indirect tax, and may be paid in money or as its labour equivalent (often but not always unpaid.)

a. 100-year flood
b. 130-30 fund
c. Taxes
d. 1921 recession

37. In economics, the _____ is an empirical metric that quantifies induced consumption, the concept that the increase in personal consumer spending (consumption) that occurs with an increase in disposable income (income after taxes and transfers.) For example, if a household earns one extra dollar of disposable income, and the _____ is 0.65, then of that dollar, the household will spend 65 cents and save 35 cents.

Mathematically, the _____ (MPC) function is expressed as the derivative of the consumption (C) function with respect to disposable income (Y.)

a. Technology shock
b. Marginal propensity to import
c. Supply shock
d. Marginal propensity to consume

38. A _____ product is a product designed for cheapness and short-term convenience rather than medium to long-term durability, with most products only intended for single use. The term is also sometimes used for products that may last several months (ex. _____ air filters) to distinguish from similar products that last indefinitely (ex.

a. Disposable
b. 130-30 fund
c. 1921 recession
d. 100-year flood

39. _____ is gross income minus income tax on that income.

Discretionary income is income after subtracting taxes and normal expenses (such as rent or mortgage, utilities, insurance, medical, transportation, property maintenance, child support, inflation, food and sundries, 'c.) to maintain a certain standard of living.

a. Taxation as theft
b. Stamp Act
c. Disposable personal income
d. Disposable income

40. In economics, an _____ is any good or commodity, transported from one country to another country in a legitimate fashion, typically for use in trade. _____ goods or services are provided to foreign consumers by domestic producers. _____ is an important part of international trade.

a. AD-IA Model
b. Export
c. ACCRA Cost of Living Index
d. ACEA agreement

41. _____ is a concept found in moral, political, and bioethical philosophy. Within these contexts, it refers to the capacity of a rational individual to make an informed, un-coerced decision. In moral and political philosophy, _____ is often used as the basis for determining moral responsibility for one's actions.

a. Autonomy
b. ACCRA Cost of Living Index
c. AD-IA Model
d. ACEA agreement

42. A _____ is an object whose consumption increases the utility of the consumer, for which the quantity demanded exceeds the quantity supplied at zero price. _____s are usually modeled as having diminishing marginal utility. The first individual purchase has high utility; the second has less.

a. Merit good
c. Pie method
b. Composite good
d. Good

43. In microeconomics, the _____ describes the minimum amount of money an individual needs to achieve some level of utility, given a utility function and prices.

Formally, if there is a utility function u that describes preferences over L commodities, the _____

$$e(p, u^*) : \mathbf{R}_+^L \times \mathbf{R} \to \mathbf{R}$$

says what amount of money is needed to achieve a utility u* if prices are set by p. This function is defined by

$$e(p, u^*) = \min_{x \in \geq(u^*)} p \cdot x$$

where

$$\geq (u^*) = \{x \in \mathbf{R}_+^L : u(x) \geq u^*\}$$

is the set of all packages that give utility at least as good as u*.

a. Expenditure minimization problem
c. Indifference curve
b. Income elasticity of demand
d. Expenditure function

44. _____ relates to the composition of GDP. What is produced in a certain country is naturally also sold, but some of the goods produced in a given year may not be sold the same year, but in later years. Conversely, some of the goods sold in a given year might have been produced in an earlier year.

a. Investment decisions
c. Inventory investment
b. Obelisk International
d. Investment theory

45. _____ is the degree of optimism that consumers feel about the overall state of the economy and their personal financial situation. How confident people feel about stability of their incomes determines their spending activity and therefore serves as one of the key indicators for the overall shape of the economy. In essence, if _____ is higher, consumers are making more purchases, boosting the economic expansion.

a. Communal marketing
c. Consumer behavior
b. Rule Developing Experimentation
d. Consumer confidence

Chapter 9. The Sticky-Price Income-Expenditure Framework: Consumption and the Multiplier

46. The _____ is the central banking system of the United States. Created in 1913 by the enactment of the Federal Reserve Act (signed by Woodrow Wilson), it is a quasi-public and quasi-private (government entity with private components) banking system that comprises (1) the presidentially appointed Board of Governors of the _____ in Washington, D.C.; (2) the Federal Open Market Committee; (3) twelve regional Federal Reserve Banks located in major cities throughout the nation acting as fiscal agents for the U.S. Treasury, each with its own nine-member board of directors; (4) numerous other private U.S. member banks, which subscribe to required amounts of non-transferable stock in their regional Federal Reserve Banks; and (5) various advisory councils. Since February 2006, Ben Bernanke has served as the Chairman of the Board of Governors of the _____.

   a. Monetary Policy Report to the Congress
   b. Term auction facility
   c. Federal Reserve System Open Market Account
   d. Federal Reserve System

47. The _____ was a worldwide economic downturn starting in most places in 1929 and ending at different times in the 1930s or early 1940s for different countries. It was the largest and most important economic depression in the 20th century, and is used in the 21st century as an example of how far the world's economy can fall. The _____ originated in the United States; historians most often use as a starting date the stock market crash on October 29, 1929, known as Black Tuesday.

   a. British Empire Economic Conference
   b. Wall Street Crash of 1929
   c. Jarrow March
   d. Great Depression

48. In microeconomics, _____ is quite simply the conversion of inputs into outputs. It is an economic process that uses resources to create a good or service that is suitable for exchange. This can include manufacturing, storing, shipping, and packaging.

   a. Solved
   b. Red Guards
   c. Production
   d. MET

49. A _____ is a reduction in taxes. Economic stimulus via _____s, along with interest rate intervention and deficit spending, are one of the central tenets of Keynesian economics.

   The immediate effects of a _____ are, generally, a decrease in the real income of the government and an increase in the real income of those whose tax rate has been lowered.

   a. Direct taxes
   b. Popiwek
   c. Withholding tax
   d. Tax cut

50. In economics, the multiplier effect or _____ is the idea that an initial amount of spending (usually by the government) leads to increased consumption spending and so results in an increase in national income greater than the initial amount of spending. In other words, an initial change in aggregate demand causes a change in aggregate output for the economy that is a multiple of the initial change.

   The existence of a multiplier effect was initially proposed by Ralph George Hawtrey in 1931.

   a. Spending multiplier
   b. Neo-Keynesian economics
   c. Multiplier effect
   d. Keynesian formula

51. _____ is the a method of technical and economic research of the systems for purpose to optimize a parity between system's consumer functions or properties and expenses to achieve those functions or properties.

120 Chapter 9. The Sticky-Price Income-Expenditure Framework: Consumption and the Multiplier

This methodology for continuous perfection of production, industrial technologies, organizational structures was developed by Juryj Sobolev in 1948 at the 'Perm telephone factory'

- 1948 Juryj Sobolev - the first success in application of a method analysis at the 'Perm telephone factory' .
- 1949 - the first application for the invention as result of use of the new method.

Today in economically developed countries practically each enterprise or the company use methodology of the kind of functional-cost analysis as a practice of the quality management, most full satisfying to principles of standards of series ISO 9000.

- Interest of consumer not in products itself, but the advantage which it will receive from its usage.
- The consumer aspires to reduce his expenses
- Functions needed by consumer can be executed in the various ways, and, hence, with various efficiency and expenses. Among possible alternatives of realization of functions exist such in which the parity of quality and the price is the optimal for the consumer.

The goal of _____ is achievement of the highest consumer satisfaction of production at simultaneous decrease in all kinds of industrial expenses Classical _____ has three English synonyms - Value Engineering, Value Management, Value Analysis.

a. Function cost analysis
c. Staple financing
b. Monopoly wage
d. Willingness to pay

52. The term _____ refers to government debt, expenditures and revenues, or to finance (particularly financial revenue) in general.

- _____ deficit is the budget deficit of federal or local government
- _____ policy is the discretionary spending of governments. Contrasts with monetary policy.
- _____ year and _____ quarter are reporting periods for firms and other agencies.

a. Procter ' Gamble
c. Fiscal
b. Bucket shop
d. Drawdown

53. A _____ is a tax that is a fixed amount no matter what the change in circumstance of the taxed entity. (A lump-sum subsidy or lump-sum redistribution is defined similarly.) It is a regressive tax, such that the lower income is, the higher percentage of income applicable to the tax.

a. Lump-sum tax
c. Grant-in-aid
b. Funding body
d. Budget deficit

54. In economics, the _____ or spending multiplier is the idea that an initial amount of spending (usually by the government) leads to increased consumption spending and so results in an increase in national income greater than the initial amount of spending. In other words, an initial change in aggregate demand causes a change in aggregate output for the economy that is a multiple of the initial change.

The existence of a _____ was initially proposed by Ralph George Hawtrey in 1931.

a. Keynesian cross
b. Multiplier effect
c. Magical triangle
d. Spending multiplier

55. A _____ is a tax imposed so that the tax rate is fixed as the amount subject to taxation increases. In simple terms, it imposes an equal burden (relative to resources) on the rich and poor. 'Proportional' describes a distribution effect on income or expenditure, referring to the way the rate remains consistent (does not progress from 'low to high' or 'high to low' as income or consumption changes), where the marginal tax rate is equal to the average tax rate.

a. 130-30 fund
b. Regressive tax
c. Proportional tax
d. 100-year flood

56. An autarky is an economy that is self-sufficient and does not take part in international trade, or severely limits trade with the outside world. Likewise the term refers to an ecosystem not affected by influences from the outside, which relies entirely on its own resources. In the economic meaning, it is also referred to as a _____.

a. Digital economy
b. Network Economy
c. Transition economy
d. Closed economy

57. An _____ is an economy in which people, including businesses, can trade in goods and services with other people and businesses in the international community at large. This contrasts with a closed economy in which international trade cannot take place.

The act of selling goods or services to a foreign country is called exporting.

a. Attention work
b. Indicative planning
c. Open economy
d. Information economy

Chapter 10. Investment, Net Exports, and Interest Rates: The IS Curve

1. _____ is a concept found in moral, political, and bioethical philosophy. Within these contexts, it refers to the capacity of a rational individual to make an informed, un-coerced decision. In moral and political philosophy, _____ is often used as the basis for determining moral responsibility for one's actions.
   - a. ACEA agreement
   - b. AD-IA Model
   - c. ACCRA Cost of Living Index
   - d. Autonomy

2. The term _____ refers to economy-wide fluctuations in production or economic activity over several months or years. These fluctuations occur around a long-term growth trend, and typically involve shifts over time between periods of relatively rapid economic growth (expansion or boom), and periods of relative stagnation or decline (contraction or recession.)

   These fluctuations are often measured using the growth rate of real gross domestic product.
   - a. Nominal value
   - b. Business cycle
   - c. Tobit model
   - d. Consumer theory

3. The _____ or gross domestic income (GDI), a basic measure of an economy's economic performance, is the market value of all final goods and services produced within the borders of a nation in a year. _____ can be defined in three ways, all of which are conceptually identical. First, it is equal to the total expenditures for all final goods and services produced within the country in a stipulated period of time (usually a 365-day year.)
   - a. Market structure
   - b. Monopolistic competition
   - c. Countercyclical
   - d. Gross domestic product

4. An _____, in economics, is the amount by which the real Gross domestic product exceeds potential GDP. The real GDP is also known as GDP 'adjusted for inflation', 'constant prices' GDP or 'constant dollar' GDP, because it measures the aggregate output in a country's income accounts in a given year, expressed in base-year prices. On the other hand, the potential GDP is the quantity of real GDP when a country's economy is at full-employment.
   - a. AD-IA Model
   - b. ACCRA Cost of Living Index
   - c. ACEA agreement
   - d. Inflationary gap

5. _____ is a fee paid on borrowed assets. It is the price paid for the use of borrowed money , or, money earned by deposited funds . Assets that are sometimes lent with _____ include money, shares, consumer goods through hire purchase, major assets such as aircraft, and even entire factories in finance lease arrangements.
   - a. Asset protection
   - b. Internal debt
   - c. Insolvency
   - d. Interest

6. An _____ is the price a borrower pays for the use of money they do not own, for instance a small company might borrow from a bank to kick start their business, and the return a lender receives for deferring the use of funds, by lending it to the borrower. _____s are normally expressed as a percentage rate over the period of one year.

   _____s targets are also a vital tool of monetary policy and are used to control variables like investment, inflation, and unemployment.
   - a. Enterprise value
   - b. Arrow-Debreu model
   - c. ACCRA Cost of Living Index
   - d. Interest rate

Chapter 10. Investment, Net Exports, and Interest Rates: The IS Curve

7. _____ is a common concept in economics, and gives rise to derived concepts such as consumer debt. Generally _____ is defined by opposition to production. But the precise definition can vary because different schools of economists define production quite differently.
   a. Federal Reserve Bank Notes
   b. Foreclosure data providers
   c. Consumption
   d. Cash or share options

8. In economics, a _____ is a mechanism that allows people to easily buy and sell (trade) financial securities (such as stocks and bonds), commodities (such as precious metals or agricultural goods), and other fungible items of value at low transaction costs and at prices that reflect the efficient-market hypothesis.

   _____s have evolved significantly over several hundred years and are undergoing constant innovation to improve liquidity.

   Both general markets (where many commodities are traded) and specialized markets (where only one commodity is traded) exist.

   a. Convertible arbitrage
   b. Market anomaly
   c. Financial market
   d. Noise trader

9. In economics, the _____ market is a hypothetical market that brings savers and borrowers together, also bringing together the money available in commercial banks and lending institutions available for firms and households to finance expenditures, either investments or consumption. Savers supply the _____; for instance, buying bonds will transfer their money to the institution issuing the bond, which can be a firm or government. In return, borrowers demand _____; when an institution sells a bond, it is demanding _____.
   a. Reservation wage
   b. Spatial inequality
   c. Buffer stock scheme
   d. Loanable funds

10. _____ or economic opportunity loss is the value of the next best alternative foregone as the result of making a decision. _____ analysis is an important part of a company's decision-making processes but is not treated as an actual cost in any financial statement. The next best thing that a person can engage in is referred to as the _____ of doing the best thing and ignoring the next best thing to be done.
    a. Economic
    b. Opportunity cost
    c. Industrial organization
    d. Economic ideology

11. In economics, the term _____ of income or _____ refers to a simple economic model which describes the reciprocal circulation of income between producers and consumers. In the _____ model, the inter-dependent entities of producer and consumer are referred to as 'firms' and 'households' respectively and provide each other with factors in order to facilitate the flow of income. Firms provide consumers with goods and services in exchange for consumer expenditure and 'factors of production' from households.
    a. 100-year flood
    b. 130-30 fund
    c. 1921 recession
    d. Circular flow

12. The '_____' is approximately the nominal interest rate minus the inflation rate Since the inflation rate over the course of a loan is not known initially, volatility in inflation represents a risk to both the lender and the borrower.

In economics and finance, an individual who lends money for repayment at a later point in time expects to be compensated for the time value of money, or not having the use of that money while it is lent.

a. Reflation
b. Core inflation
c. Cost-push inflation
d. Real interest rate

13. In finance, a _____ is a debt security, in which the authorized issuer owes the holders a debt and, depending on the terms of the _____, is obliged to pay interest (the coupon) and/or to repay the principal at a later date, termed maturity. A _____ is a formal contract to repay borrowed money with interest at fixed intervals.

Thus a _____ is like a loan: the issuer is the borrower (debtor), the holder is the lender (creditor), and the coupon is the interest.

a. Prize Bond
b. Callable
c. Zero-coupon
d. Bond

14. The _____ is the central banking system of the United States. Created in 1913 by the enactment of the Federal Reserve Act (signed by Woodrow Wilson), it is a quasi-public and quasi-private (government entity with private components) banking system that comprises (1) the presidentially appointed Board of Governors of the _____ in Washington, D.C.; (2) the Federal Open Market Committee; (3) twelve regional Federal Reserve Banks located in major cities throughout the nation acting as fiscal agents for the U.S. Treasury, each with its own nine-member board of directors; (4) numerous other private U.S. member banks, which subscribe to required amounts of non-transferable stock in their regional Federal Reserve Banks; and (5) various advisory councils. Since February 2006, Ben Bernanke has served as the Chairman of the Board of Governors of the _____.

a. Term auction facility
b. Monetary Policy Report to the Congress
c. Federal Reserve System
d. Federal Reserve System Open Market Account

15. A United States Treasury security is a government debt issued by the United States Department of the Treasury through the Bureau of the Public Debt. Treasury securities are the debt financing instruments of the United States Federal government, and they are often referred to simply as Treasuries. There are four types of marketable treasury securities: _____, Treasury notes, Treasury bonds, and Treasury Inflation Protected Securities (TIPS).

a. Lawcards
b. Debt to Assets
c. Labour battalions
d. Treasury bills

16. _____ in economics and business is the result of an exchange and from that trade we assign a numerical monetary value to a good, service or asset. If Alice trades Bob 4 apples for an orange, the _____ of an orange is 4 apples. Inversely, the _____ of an apple is 1/4 oranges.

a. Premium pricing
b. Price book
c. Price
d. Price war

17. The _____ is a financial market where participants buy and sell debt securities, usually in the form of bonds. As of 2006, the size of the international _____ is an estimated $44.9 trillion, of which the size of the outstanding U.S. _____ debt was $25.2 trillion.

Nearly all of the $923 billion average daily trading volume in the U.S. _____ takes place between broker-dealers and large institutions in a decentralized, over-the-counter market.

a. Bond market
c. Pool factor
b. 130-30 fund
d. 100-year flood

18.   A _____ is the minimum difference a person requires to be willing to take an uncertain bet, between the expected value of the bet and the certain value that he is indifferent to.

The certainty equivalent is the guaranteed payoff at which a person is 'indifferent' between accepting the guaranteed payoff and a higher but uncertain payoff. (It is the amount of the higher payout minus the _____.)

a. Ruin theory
c. Linear model
b. Risk premium
d. Workers compensation

19.   _____ is the risk (variability in value) borne by an interest-bearing asset, such as a loan or a bond, due to variability of interest rates. In general, as rates rise, the price of a fixed rate bond will fall, and vice versa. _____ is commonly measured by the bond's duration.

a. International Fisher effect
c. Official bank rate
b. ACCRA Cost of Living Index
d. Interest rate Risk

20.   In finance and economics _____ or nominal rate of interest refers to the rate of interest before adjustment for inflation (in contrast with the real interest rate); or, for interest rates 'as stated' without adjustment for the full effect of compounding (also referred to as the nominal annual rate.) An interest rate is called nominal if the frequency of compounding (e.g. a month) is not identical to the basic time unit (normally a year.)

The real interest rate includes compensation for the lender's lost value due to inflation, whereas the _____ excludes inflation.

a. London Interbank Offered Rate
c. Fixed interest
b. Nominal interest rate
d. Risk-free interest rate

21.   In finance, _____ is the risk of losses caused by interest rate changes. The prices of most financial instruments, such as stocks and bonds move inversely with interest rates, so investors are subject to capital loss when rates rise.

In the investment world, there are two types of risk rating. One is to manifest company's credit and another to equity securities. The former is represented by the systems of Fitch Ratings, Moody's and Standard ' Poor's whereas the later by that of Comisi>ón Clasificadora de Riesgo, although the two types have some similarities to some extent.

a. Rate Risk
c. Seasonal industry
b. Leontief production function
d. Net pay

22. In economics, an _____ is any good or commodity, transported from one country to another country in a legitimate fashion, typically for use in trade. _____ goods or services are provided to foreign consumers by domestic producers. _____ is an important part of international trade.

a. AD-IA Model
b. ACCRA Cost of Living Index
c. Export
d. ACEA agreement

23. _____ are made by investors and investment managers.

Investors commonly perform investment analysis by making use of fundamental analysis, technical analysis and gut feel.

_____ are often supported by decision tools.

a. Investment strategy
b. Investment decisions
c. Arbitrage betting
d. Inventory investment

24. A _____ is a public market for the trading of company stock and derivatives at an agreed price; these are securities listed on a stock exchange as well as those only traded privately.

The size of the world _____ was estimated at about $36.6 trillion US at the beginning of October 2008 . The total world derivatives market has been estimated at about $791 trillion face or nominal value, 11 times the size of the entire world economy.

a. Adam Smith
b. Stock market
c. Adolf Hitler
d. Adolph Fischer

25. A _____ is a type of economic bubble taking place in stock markets when price of stocks rise and become overvalued by any measure of stock valuation.

The existence of _____s is at odds with the assumptions of efficient market theory which assumes rational investor behaviour. Behavioral finance theory attribute _____s to cognitive biases that lead to groupthink and herd behavior.

a. Growth investing
b. Scrip issue
c. Fill or kill
d. Stock market bubble

26. In finance, the _____s between two currencies specifies how much one currency is worth in terms of the other. It is the value of a foreign natione;s currency in terms of the home natione;s currency. For example an _____ of 102 Japanese yen to the United States dollar means that JPY 102 is worth the same as USD 1.

a. ACEA agreement
b. ACCRA Cost of Living Index
c. Interbank market
d. Exchange rate

Chapter 10. Investment, Net Exports, and Interest Rates: The IS Curve

27. The term _____ refers to government debt, expenditures and revenues, or to finance (particularly financial revenue) in general.

- _____ deficit is the budget deficit of federal or local government
- _____ policy is the discretionary spending of governments. Contrasts with monetary policy.
- _____ year and _____ quarter are reporting periods for firms and other agencies.

   a. Fiscal   b. Drawdown
   c. Procter ' Gamble   d. Bucket shop

28. In economics, _____ is the use of government spending and revenue collection to influence the economy.

_____ can be contrasted with the other main type of economic policy, monetary policy, which attempts to stabilize the economy by controlling interest rates and the supply of money. The two main instruments of _____ are government spending and taxation.

   a. Fiscal policy   b. Sustainable investment rule
   c. 100-year flood   d. Fiscalism

29. _____ or government expenditure is classified by economists into three main types. Government purchases of goods and services for current use are classed as government consumption. Government purchases of goods and services intended to create future benefits, such as infrastructure investment or research spending, are classed as government investment.

   a. 1921 recession   b. 130-30 fund
   c. 100-year flood   d. Government spending

30. In economics, the _____ is the term used to refer to the environment in which bonds are bought and sold between a central bank ' its regulated banks. It is not a free market process.

- To intervene in the 'business cycle', a central bank may choose to go into the _____ and buy or sell government bonds, which is known as _____ operations to increase reserves.

   a. Inside money   b. Outside money
   c. ACCRA Cost of Living Index   d. Open market

31. _____ are the means of implementing monetary policy by which a central bank controls its national money supply by buying and selling government securities, or other financial instruments. Monetary targets, such as interest rates or exchange rates, are used to guide this implementation.

Since most money is now in the form of electronic records, rather than paper records such as banknotes, _____ are conducted simply by electronically increasing or decreasing ('crediting' or 'debiting') the amount of money that a bank has, e.g., in its reserve account at the central bank, in exchange for a bank selling or buying a financial instrument.

a. Open market operations
b. AD-IA Model
c. ACCRA Cost of Living Index
d. ACEA agreement

32. The _____ , a component of the Federal Reserve System, is charged under United States law with overseeing the nation's open market operations. It is the Federal Reserve Committee that makes key decisions about interest rates and the growth jam of the United States money supply. It is the principal organ of United States national monetary policy.
   a. Primary Dealer Credit Facility
   b. Fed Funds Probability
   c. Federal Reserve Transparency Act
   d. Federal Open Market Committee

33. _____, in law and economics, is a form of risk management primarily used to hedge against the risk of a contingent loss. _____ is defined as the equitable transfer of the risk of a loss, from one entity to another, in exchange for a premium, and can be thought of as a guaranteed small loss to prevent a large, possibly devastating loss. An insurer is a company selling the _____; an insured or policyholder is the person or entity buying the _____.
   a. ACCRA Cost of Living Index
   b. ACEA agreement
   c. AD-IA Model
   d. Insurance

34. _____s is the social science that studies the production, distribution, and consumption of goods and services. The term _____s comes from the Ancient Greek oá¼°κονομῖα from oá¼¶κος (oikos, 'house') + vÏŒμος (nomos, 'custom' or 'law'), hence 'rules of the house(hold)'. Current _____ models developed out of the broader field of political economy in the late 19th century, owing to a desire to use an empirical approach more akin to the physical sciences.
   a. Energy economics
   b. Opportunity cost
   c. Economic
   d. Inflation

35. _____ refers to the actions that governments take in the economic field. It covers the systems for setting interest rates and government deficit as well as the labour market, national ownership, and many other areas of government.

Such policies are often influenced by international institutions like the International Monetary Fund or World Bank as well as political beliefs and the consequent policies of parties.

   a. Economic policy
   b. ACCRA Cost of Living Index
   c. AD-IA Model
   d. ACEA agreement

36. _____ is the process by which the government, central bank (ii) availability of money, and (iii) cost of money or rate of interest, in order to attain a set of objectives oriented towards the growth and stability of the economy. Monetary theory provides insight into how to craft optimal _____.

_____ is referred to as either being an expansionary policy where an expansionary policy increases the total supply of money in the economy, and a contractionary policy decreases the total money supply.

   a. 130-30 fund
   b. 1921 recession
   c. 100-year flood
   d. Monetary policy

37. A _____ is a package or set of measures introduced to stabilise a financial system or economy. The term can refer to policies in two distinct sets of circumstances: business cycle stabilization and crisis stabilization.

Stabilization can refer to correcting the normal behavior of the business cycle.

Chapter 10. Investment, Net Exports, and Interest Rates: The IS Curve

a. Stabilization policy
b. Capacity Development
c. Volunteers for Economic Growth Alliance
d. New International Economic Order

38. To _____ is to impose a financial charge or other levy upon a taxpayer by a state or the functional equivalent of a state.

_____es are also imposed by many subnational entities. _____es consist of direct _____ or indirect _____, and may be paid in money or as its labour equivalent (often but not always unpaid.)

a. 1921 recession
b. 130-30 fund
c. 100-year flood
d. Tax

39. A _____ is a reduction in taxes. Economic stimulus via _____s, along with interest rate intervention and deficit spending, are one of the central tenets of Keynesian economics.

The immediate effects of a _____ are, generally, a decrease in the real income of the government and an increase in the real income of those whose tax rate has been lowered.

a. Direct taxes
b. Popiwek
c. Withholding tax
d. Tax cut

40. In economics, _____ refers to the highest level of real Gross Domestic Product output that can be sustained over the long term. The existence of a limit is due to natural and institutional constraints. If actual GDP rises and stays above _____, then (in the absence of wage and price controls) inflation tends to increase as demand exceeds supply.

a. Monetary policy reaction function
b. Monetary conditions index
c. Potential output
d. Fundamental psychological law

41. _____, 1st Baron Keynes was a renowned economist from Britain whose many ideas on economic and political theories as well as on many governments' monetary policies influenced America. He advocated a government that played an active role in the lives of people regarding business, economy, etc. In this role, the government would use fiscal measures to reduce the consequences of recessions, economic depressions and booms.

a. John Maynard Keynes
b. Adam Smith
c. Adolf Hitler
d. Adolph Fischer

42. In economics, a _____ is a monetary-policy rule that stipulates how much the central bank would or should change the nominal interest rate in response to divergences of actual inflation rates from target inflation rates and of actual Gross Domestic Product (GDP) from potential GDP. It was first proposed by the by U.S. economist John B. Taylor in 1993. The rule can be written as follows:

$$i_t = \pi_t + r_t^* + a_\pi(\pi_t - \pi_t^*) + a_y(y_t - \bar{y}_t).$$

In this equation, i_t is the target short-term nominal interest rate (e.g. the federal funds rate in the US), π_t is the rate of inflation as measured by the GDP deflator, π_t^* is the desired rate of inflation, r_t^* is the assumed equilibrium real interest rate, y_t is the logarithm of real GDP, and $\bar{y}_t$ is the logarithm of potential output, as determined by a linear trend.

a. Term Securities Lending Facility
b. Fed Funds Probability
c. Federal Reserve Banks
d. Taylor rule

43. In economics, a _____ is a general slowdown in economic activity over a sustained period of time, or a business cycle contraction. During _____s, many macroeconomic indicators vary in a similar way. Production as measured by Gross Domestic Product (GDP), employment, investment spending, capacity utilization, household incomes and business profits all fall during _____s.
   a. Monetary economics
   b. Treasury View
   c. Recession
   d. Leading indicators

44. A _____ is:

- Rewrite _____, in generative grammar and computer science
- Standardization, a formal and widely-accepted statement, fact, definition, or qualification
- Operation, a determinate _____ for performing a mathematical operation and obtaining a certain result (Mathematics, Logic)
    - Unary operation
    - Binary operation
- _____ of inference, a function from sets of formulae to formulae (Mathematics, Logic)
- _____ of thumb, principle with broad application that is not intended to be strictly accurate or reliable for every situation. Also often simply referred to as a _____
- Moral, an atomic element of a moral code for guiding choices in human behavior
- Heuristic, a quantized '_____' which shows a tendency or probability for successful function
- A regulation, as in sports
- A Production _____, as in computer science
- Procedural law, a _____ set governing the application of laws to cases
    - A law, which may informally be called a '_____'
    - A court ruling, a decision by a court
- In the U.S. Government, a regulation mandated by Congress, but written or expanded upon by the Executive Branch.
- Norm (sociology), an informal but widely accepted _____, concept, truth, definition, or qualification (social norms, legal norms, coding norms)
- Norm (philosophy), a kind of sentence or a reason to act, feel or believe
- 'Rulership' is the concept of governance by a government:
    - Military _____, governance by a military body
    - Monastic _____, a collection of precepts that guides the life of monks or nuns in a religious order where the superior holds the place of Christ
- Slide _____

- '_____,' a song by Ayumi Hamasaki
- '_____,' a song by rapper Nas
- '_____s,' an album by the band The Whitest Boy Alive
- _____s: Pyaar Ka Superhit Formula, a 2003 Bollywood film
- ruler, an instrument for measuring lengths
- _____, a component of an astrolabe, circumferator or similar instrument
- The _____s, a bestselling self-help book
- _____ Project (Run Up-to-date Linux Everywhere), a project that aims to use up-to-date Linux software on old PCs
- _____ engine, a software system that helps managing business _____s
- Ja _____, a hip hop artist
    - R.U.L.E., a 2005 greatest hits album by rapper Ja _____
- '_____s,' a KMFDM song

a. Demand
b. Rule
c. Procter ' Gamble
d. Technocracy

45. _____ is an American economist and was the Chairman of the Federal Reserve of the United States from 1987 to 2006. He currently works as a private advisor and providing consulting for firms through his company, Greenspan Associates LLC.

First appointed Federal Reserve chairman by President Ronald Reagan in August 1987, he was reappointed at successive four-year intervals until retiring on January 31, 2006 after the second-longest tenure in the position.

a. Adolph Fischer
b. Adolf Hitler
c. Adam Smith
d. Alan Greenspan

46. In property law and real estate, a _____ is a legal right to property ownership that does not include the right to present possession or enjoyment of the property. _____s are created on the formation of a defeasible estate; that is, an estate with a condition or event triggering transfer of possessory ownership. A common example is the landlord-tenant relationship.

a. Foreclosure investment
b. Family farm
c. Hedonic regression
d. Future interest

Chapter 11. The Money Market and the LM Curve

1. In finance, a _____ is a debt security, in which the authorized issuer owes the holders a debt and, depending on the terms of the _____, is obliged to pay interest (the coupon) and/or to repay the principal at a later date, termed maturity. A _____ is a formal contract to repay borrowed money with interest at fixed intervals.

Thus a _____ is like a loan: the issuer is the borrower (debtor), the holder is the lender (creditor), and the coupon is the interest.

   a. Prize Bond
   c. Callable
   b. Zero-coupon
   d. Bond

2. The _____ is the central banking system of the United States. Created in 1913 by the enactment of the Federal Reserve Act (signed by Woodrow Wilson), it is a quasi-public and quasi-private (government entity with private components) banking system that comprises (1) the presidentially appointed Board of Governors of the _____ in Washington, D.C.; (2) the Federal Open Market Committee; (3) twelve regional Federal Reserve Banks located in major cities throughout the nation acting as fiscal agents for the U.S. Treasury, each with its own nine-member board of directors; (4) numerous other private U.S. member banks, which subscribe to required amounts of non-transferable stock in their regional Federal Reserve Banks; and (5) various advisory councils. Since February 2006, Ben Bernanke has served as the Chairman of the Board of Governors of the _____.

   a. Federal Reserve System Open Market Account
   c. Monetary Policy Report to the Congress
   b. Term auction facility
   d. Federal Reserve System

3. The _____ is 'the basic residential unit in which economic production, consumption, inheritance, child rearing, and shelter are organized and carried out'; [the _____] 'may or may not be synonymous with family'.

The _____ is the basic unit of analysis in many social, microeconomic and government models. The term refers to all individuals who live in the same dwelling.

   a. Family economics
   c. 130-30 fund
   b. 100-year flood
   d. Household

4. In economics, the term _____ of income or _____ refers to a simple economic model which describes the reciprocal circulation of income between producers and consumers. In the _____ model, the inter-dependent entities of producer and consumer are referred to as 'firms' and 'households' respectively and provide each other with factors in order to facilitate the flow of income. Firms provide consumers with goods and services in exchange for consumer expenditure and 'factors of production' from households.
   a. 100-year flood
   c. Circular flow
   b. 1921 recession
   d. 130-30 fund

5. _____ is a fee paid on borrowed assets. It is the price paid for the use of borrowed money , or, money earned by deposited funds . Assets that are sometimes lent with _____ include money, shares, consumer goods through hire purchase, major assets such as aircraft, and even entire factories in finance lease arrangements.
   a. Insolvency
   c. Asset protection
   b. Interest
   d. Internal debt

6. An _____ is the price a borrower pays for the use of money they do not own, for instance a small company might borrow from a bank to kick start their business, and the return a lender receives for deferring the use of funds, by lending it to the borrower. _____s are normally expressed as a percentage rate over the period of one year.

_____s targets are also a vital tool of monetary policy and are used to control variables like investment, inflation, and unemployment.

a. ACCRA Cost of Living Index
b. Enterprise value
c. Interest rate
d. Arrow-Debreu model

7. In finance, the _____ is the global financial market for short-term borrowing and lending. It provides short-term liquidity funding for the global financial system. The _____ is where short-term obligations such as Treasury bills, commercial paper and bankers' acceptances are bought and sold.

a. Consignment stock
b. Deferred compensation
c. T-Model
d. Money market

8. In economics, _____ is the total amount of money available in an economy at a particular point in time. There are several ways to define 'money', but standard measures usually include currency in circulation and demand deposits.

_____ data are recorded and published, usually by the government or the central bank of the country.

a. Money supply
b. Neutrality of money
c. Velocity of money
d. Veil of money

9. _____ or economic opportunity loss is the value of the next best alternative foregone as the result of making a decision. _____ analysis is an important part of a company's decision-making processes but is not treated as an actual cost in any financial statement. The next best thing that a person can engage in is referred to as the _____ of doing the best thing and ignoring the next best thing to be done.

a. Industrial organization
b. Economic
c. Opportunity cost
d. Economic ideology

10. _____ has several particular meanings:

- in mathematics
    - _____ function
    - Euler _____
    - _____
    - _____ subgroup
    - method of _____s (partial differential equations)
- in physics and engineering
    - any _____ curve that shows the relationship between certain input- and output parameters, e.g.
    - an I-V or current-voltage _____ is the current in a circuit as a function of the applied voltage
    - Receiver-Operator _____
- in fiction
    - in Dungeons ' Dragons, _____ is another name for ability score

Chapter 11. The Money Market and the LM Curve

a. Technocracy
b. Russian financial crisis
c. Demand
d. Characteristic

11. Economics:

   - _____ ,the desire to own something and the ability to pay for it
   - _____ curve,a graphic representation of a _____ schedule
   - _____ deposit, the money in checking accounts
   - _____ pull theory,the theory that inflation occurs when _____ for goods and services exceeds existing supplies
   - _____ schedule,a table that lists the quantity of a good a person will buy it each different price
   - _____ side economics,the school of economics at believes government spending and tax cuts open economy by raising _____

a. Demand
b. Production
c. McKesson ' Robbins scandal
d. Variability

12. In finance and economics _____ or nominal rate of interest refers to the rate of interest before adjustment for inflation (in contrast with the real interest rate); or, for interest rates 'as stated' without adjustment for the full effect of compounding (also referred to as the nominal annual rate.) An interest rate is called nominal if the frequency of compounding (e.g. a month) is not identical to the basic time unit (normally a year.)

The real interest rate includes compensation for the lender's lost value due to inflation, whereas the _____ excludes inflation.

a. London Interbank Offered Rate
b. Fixed interest
c. Risk-free interest rate
d. Nominal interest rate

13. _____ in economics and business is the result of an exchange and from that trade we assign a numerical monetary value to a good, service or asset. If Alice trades Bob 4 apples for an orange, the _____ of an orange is 4 apples. Inversely, the _____ of an apple is 1/4 oranges.

a. Price
b. Price war
c. Premium pricing
d. Price book

14. A _____ is a hypothetical measure of overall prices for some set of goods and services, in a given region during a given interval, normalized relative to some base set. Typically, a _____ is approximated with a price index.

The classical dichotomy is the assumption that there is a relatively clean distinction between overall increases or decreases in prices and underlying, e;reale; economic variables.

a. Discouraged worker
b. Discretionary spending
c. Price elasticity of supply
d. Price level

15. In economics, economic equilibrium is simply a state of the world where economic forces are balanced and in the absence of external influences the (equilibrium) values of economic variables will not change. It is the point at which quantity demanded and quantity supplied are equal. _____, for example, refers to a condition where a market price is established through competition such that the amount of goods or services sought by buyers is equal to the amount of goods or services produced by sellers.
   a. Regulated market
   b. Marketization
   c. Market Equilibrium
   d. Product-Market Growth Matrix

16. In economics, the _____ of money is a theory emphasizing the positive relationship of overall prices or the nominal value of expenditures to the quantity of money.

   It is the mainstream economic theory of the price level. Alternative theories include the real bills doctrine and the more recent fiscal theory of the price level.

   a. Romer Model
   b. Real business cycle
   c. Dishoarding
   d. Quantity theory

17. In economics, the _____ is a theory emphasizing the positive relationship of overall prices or the nominal value of expenditures to the quantity of money.

   It is the mainstream economic theory of the price level. Alternative theories include the real bills doctrine and the more recent fiscal theory of the price level.

   a. Consumer spending
   b. Microsimulation
   c. Quantity theory of money
   d. Fundamental psychological law

18. In economics, the _____ can be defined as the graph depicting the relationship between the price of a certain commodity, and the amount of it that consumers are willing and able to purchase at that given price. It is a graphic representation of a demand schedule. The _____ for all consumers together follows from the _____ of every individual consumer: the individual demands at each price are added together.
   a. Cost curve
   b. Kuznets curve
   c. Wage curve
   d. Demand curve

19. In economics, _____ is the total demand for final goods and services in the economy (Y) at a given time and price level. It is the amount of goods and services in the economy that will be purchased at all possible price levels. This is the demand for the gross domestic product of a country when inventory levels are static.
   a. Aggregate supply
   b. Aggregate expenditure
   c. Aggregation problem
   d. Aggregate demand

20. _____s is the social science that studies the production, distribution, and consumption of goods and services. The term _____s comes from the Ancient Greek oá¼°κονομία from oá¼¶κος (oikos, 'house') + vÏŒμος (nomos, 'custom' or 'law'), hence 'rules of the house(hold)'. Current _____ models developed out of the broader field of political economy in the late 19th century, owing to a desire to use an empirical approach more akin to the physical sciences.
   a. Energy economics
   b. Opportunity cost
   c. Economic
   d. Inflation

Chapter 11. The Money Market and the LM Curve

21. _____ are usually numerical time-series, i.e., sets of data (covering periods of time) for part or all of a single economy or the international economy. When they are time-series the data sets are usually monthly but can be quarterly and annual. The data may be adjusted in various ways (for ease of further analysis), most commonly adjusted or unadjusted for seasonal fluctuations.
   a. AD-IA Model
   b. ACEA agreement
   c. ACCRA Cost of Living Index
   d. Economic data

22. _____ and Keynesian Theory) is a macroeconomic theory based on the ideas of 20th-century British economist John Maynard Keynes. _____ argues that private sector decisions sometimes lead to inefficient macroeconomic outcomes and therefore advocates active policy responses by the public sector, including monetary policy actions by the central bank and fiscal policy actions by the government to stabilize output over the business cycle.

The theories forming the basis of _____ were first presented in The General Theory of Employment, Interest and Money, published in 1936.

   a. Rational choice theory
   b. Market failure
   c. Deflation
   d. Keynesian economics

23. The '_____' is approximately the nominal interest rate minus the inflation rate Since the inflation rate over the course of a loan is not known initially, volatility in inflation represents a risk to both the lender and the borrower.

In economics and finance, an individual who lends money for repayment at a later point in time expects to be compensated for the time value of money, or not having the use of that money while it is lent.

   a. Cost-push inflation
   b. Core inflation
   c. Reflation
   d. Real interest rate

24. _____ is a concept found in moral, political, and bioethical philosophy. Within these contexts, it refers to the capacity of a rational individual to make an informed, un-coerced decision. In moral and political philosophy, _____ is often used as the basis for determining moral responsibility for one's actions.
   a. ACCRA Cost of Living Index
   b. Autonomy
   c. AD-IA Model
   d. ACEA agreement

25. To _____ is to impose a financial charge or other levy upon a taxpayer by a state or the functional equivalent of a state.

_____es are also imposed by many subnational entities. _____es consist of direct _____ or indirect _____, and may be paid in money or as its labour equivalent (often but not always unpaid.)

   a. Tax
   b. 100-year flood
   c. 1921 recession
   d. 130-30 fund

26. _____ is a common concept in economics, and gives rise to derived concepts such as consumer debt. Generally _____ is defined by opposition to production. But the precise definition can vary because different schools of economists define production quite differently.

a. Foreclosure data providers
b. Cash or share options
c. Consumption
d. Federal Reserve Bank Notes

27. In economics, _____ is the total supply of goods and services produced by a national economy during a specific time period. It is the total amount of goods and services in the economy available at all possible price levels.
    a. Aggregate supply
    b. Aggregate expenditure
    c. Aggregation problem
    d. Aggregate demand

28. The _____ or gross domestic income (GDI), a basic measure of an economy's economic performance, is the market value of all final goods and services produced within the borders of a nation in a year. _____ can be defined in three ways, all of which are conceptually identical. First, it is equal to the total expenditures for all final goods and services produced within the country in a stipulated period of time (usually a 365-day year.)
    a. Gross domestic product
    b. Countercyclical
    c. Market structure
    d. Monopolistic competition

29. An _____, in economics, is the amount by which the real Gross domestic product exceeds potential GDP. The real GDP is also known as GDP 'adjusted for inflation', 'constant prices' GDP or 'constant dollar' GDP, because it measures the aggregate output in a country's income accounts in a given year, expressed in base-year prices. On the other hand, the potential GDP is the quantity of real GDP when a country's economy is at full-employment.
    a. ACEA agreement
    b. AD-IA Model
    c. ACCRA Cost of Living Index
    d. Inflationary gap

30. The term _____ refers to economy-wide fluctuations in production or economic activity over several months or years. These fluctuations occur around a long-term growth trend, and typically involve shifts over time between periods of relatively rapid economic growth (expansion or boom), and periods of relative stagnation or decline (contraction or recession.)

These fluctuations are often measured using the growth rate of real gross domestic product.

    a. Nominal value
    b. Consumer theory
    c. Tobit model
    d. Business cycle

31. In statistics, a _____ is a value that allows data to be measured over time in terms of some base period ussually through a price index in order to distinguish between changes in the money value of GNP which result from a change in prices and those which result from a change in physical output. It is the measure of the price level for some quantity. A _____ serves as a price index in which the effects of inflation are nulled.
    a. Market microstructure
    b. Deflator
    c. Blanket order
    d. Contingent employment

32. In economics, _____ is a rise in the general level of prices of goods and services in an economy over a period of time. When the general price level rises, each unit of currency buys fewer goods and services; consequently, _____ is also a decline in the real value of money--a loss of purchasing power in the medium of exchange which is also the monetary unit of account in the economy. A chief measure of general price-level _____ is the general _____ rate, which is the percentage change in a general price index (normally the Consumer Price Index) over time.

a. Economic
b. Energy economics
c. Inflation
d. Opportunity cost

33. In economics, the _____ is a measure of inflation, the rate of increase of a price index (for example, a consumer price index.)It is the percentage rate of change in price level over time. The rate of decrease in the purchasing power of money is approximately equal.

It's used to calculate the real interest rate, as well as real increases in wages, and official measurements of this rate act as input variables to COLA adjustments and Inflation derivatives prices.

a. Inflation rate
b. Interest rate option
c. Edgeworth paradox
d. Equity value

34. In economics, _____ refers to the highest level of real Gross Domestic Product output that can be sustained over the long term. The existence of a limit is due to natural and institutional constraints. If actual GDP rises and stays above _____, then (in the absence of wage and price controls) inflation tends to increase as demand exceeds supply.

a. Potential output
b. Fundamental psychological law
c. Monetary policy reaction function
d. Monetary conditions index

35. _____, 1st Baron Keynes was a renowned economist from Britain whose many ideas on economic and political theories as well as on many governments' monetary policies influenced America. He advocated a government that played an active role in the lives of people regarding business, economy, etc. In this role, the government would use fiscal measures to reduce the consequences of recessions, economic depressions and booms.

a. Adolph Fischer
b. John Maynard Keynes
c. Adam Smith
d. Adolf Hitler

36. _____ is monetary policy that seeks to increase the size of the money supply. In most nations, monetary policy is controlled by either a central bank or a finance ministry

Neoclassical and Keynesian economics significantly differ on the effects and effectiveness of monetary policy on influencing the real economy; there is no clear consensus on how monetary policy affects real economic variables (aggregate output or income, employment.) Both economic schools accept that monetary policy affects monetary variables (price levels, interest rates.)

a. Expansionary monetary policy
b. ACCRA Cost of Living Index
c. AD-IA Model
d. ACEA agreement

37. The _____ was a worldwide economic downturn starting in most places in 1929 and ending at different times in the 1930s or early 1940s for different countries. It was the largest and most important economic depression in the 20th century, and is used in the 21st century as an example of how far the world's economy can fall. The _____ originated in the United States; historians most often use as a starting date the stock market crash on October 29, 1929, known as Black Tuesday.

a. British Empire Economic Conference
b. Great Depression
c. Jarrow March
d. Wall Street Crash of 1929

Chapter 11. The Money Market and the LM Curve

38. _____ is an American economist and was the Chairman of the Federal Reserve of the United States from 1987 to 2006. He currently works as a private advisor and providing consulting for firms through his company, Greenspan Associates LLC.

First appointed Federal Reserve chairman by President Ronald Reagan in August 1987, he was reappointed at successive four-year intervals until retiring on January 31, 2006 after the second-longest tenure in the position.

a. Adam Smith
b. Adolf Hitler
c. Adolph Fischer
d. Alan Greenspan

39. _____ is the process by which the government, central bank (ii) availability of money, and (iii) cost of money or rate of interest, in order to attain a set of objectives oriented towards the growth and stability of the economy. Monetary theory provides insight into how to craft optimal _____.

_____ is referred to as either being an expansionary policy where an expansionary policy increases the total supply of money in the economy, and a contractionary policy decreases the total money supply.

a. 100-year flood
b. 1921 recession
c. 130-30 fund
d. Monetary policy

40. A _____ is a package or set of measures introduced to stabilise a financial system or economy. The term can refer to policies in two distinct sets of circumstances: business cycle stabilization and crisis stabilization.

Stabilization can refer to correcting the normal behavior of the business cycle.

a. New International Economic Order
b. Stabilization policy
c. Volunteers for Economic Growth Alliance
d. Capacity Development

41. A _____ is a public market for the trading of company stock and derivatives at an agreed price; these are securities listed on a stock exchange as well as those only traded privately.

The size of the world _____ was estimated at about $36.6 trillion US at the beginning of October 2008 . The total world derivatives market has been estimated at about $791 trillion face or nominal value, 11 times the size of the entire world economy.

a. Adolph Fischer
b. Adolf Hitler
c. Stock market
d. Adam Smith

42. A _____ is a type of economic bubble taking place in stock markets when price of stocks rise and become overvalued by any measure of stock valuation.

The existence of _____s is at odds with the assumptions of efficient market theory which assumes rational investor behaviour. Behavioral finance theory attribute _____s to cognitive biases that lead to groupthink and herd behavior.

| a. Growth investing | b. Fill or kill |
| c. Scrip issue | d. Stock market bubble |

43. _____ is an economic situation in which inflation and economic stagnation occur simultaneously and remain unchecked for a period of time. The portmanteau _____ is generally attributed to British politician Iain Macleod, who coined the term in a speech to Parliament in 1965. The concept is notable partly because, in postwar macroeconomic theory, inflation and recession were regarded as mutually exclusive, and also because _____ has generally proven to be difficult and costly to eradicate once it gets started.

| a. Chronic inflation | b. Price/wage spiral |
| c. Stagflation | d. Real interest rate |

44. A _____ is a reduction in taxes. Economic stimulus via _____s, along with interest rate intervention and deficit spending, are one of the central tenets of Keynesian economics.

The immediate effects of a _____ are, generally, a decrease in the real income of the government and an increase in the real income of those whose tax rate has been lowered.

| a. Direct taxes | b. Withholding tax |
| c. Popiwek | d. Tax cut |

Chapter 12. The Phillips Curve, Expectations, and Monetary Policy

1. In economics, _____ is the total supply of goods and services produced by a national economy during a specific time period. It is the total amount of goods and services in the economy available at all possible price levels.

   a. Aggregation problem
   b. Aggregate supply
   c. Aggregate expenditure
   d. Aggregate demand

2. The _____ is the central banking system of the United States. Created in 1913 by the enactment of the Federal Reserve Act (signed by Woodrow Wilson), it is a quasi-public and quasi-private (government entity with private components) banking system that comprises (1) the presidentially appointed Board of Governors of the _____ in Washington, D.C.; (2) the Federal Open Market Committee; (3) twelve regional Federal Reserve Banks located in major cities throughout the nation acting as fiscal agents for the U.S. Treasury, each with its own nine-member board of directors; (4) numerous other private U.S. member banks, which subscribe to required amounts of non-transferable stock in their regional Federal Reserve Banks; and (5) various advisory councils. Since February 2006, Ben Bernanke has served as the Chairman of the Board of Governors of the _____.

   a. Federal Reserve System Open Market Account
   b. Federal Reserve System
   c. Monetary Policy Report to the Congress
   d. Term auction facility

3. _____ and Keynesian Theory) is a macroeconomic theory based on the ideas of 20th-century British economist John Maynard Keynes. _____ argues that private sector decisions sometimes lead to inefficient macroeconomic outcomes and therefore advocates active policy responses by the public sector, including monetary policy actions by the central bank and fiscal policy actions by the government to stabilize output over the business cycle.

   The theories forming the basis of _____ were first presented in The General Theory of Employment, Interest and Money, published in 1936.

   a. Deflation
   b. Rational choice theory
   c. Keynesian economics
   d. Market failure

4. _____ is the process by which the government, central bank (ii) availability of money, and (iii) cost of money or rate of interest, in order to attain a set of objectives oriented towards the growth and stability of the economy. Monetary theory provides insight into how to craft optimal _____.

   _____ is referred to as either being an expansionary policy where an expansionary policy increases the total supply of money in the economy, and a contractionary policy decreases the total money supply.

   a. Monetary policy
   b. 130-30 fund
   c. 1921 recession
   d. 100-year flood

5. The _____ is the upward-sloping relationship between the inflation rate and the unemployment rate. When the inflation rate rises, a central bank wishing to fight inflation will raise interest rates to reduce output and thus increase the unemployment rate. The _____ is a function of the Taylor Rule, the Investment-Spending Curve (IS Curve) and Okun's Law

   The _____ has the equation:

   $u = u_0 + \Phi(\pi - \pi t)$

Where Φ is a parameter that tells us how much unemployment rises when the central bank raises the real interest rate r because it thinks that inflation is too high and needs to be reduced.

a. Secular basis
b. Marginal propensity to import
c. Value added
d. Monetary policy reaction function

6. The _____ is a concept of economic activity developed in particular by Milton Friedman and Edmund Phelps in the 1960s, both recipients of the Nobel prize in economics. In both cases, the development of the concept is cited as a main motivation behind the prize. It represents the hypothetical unemployment rate consistent with aggregate production being at the 'long-run' level.

a. Real Business Cycle Theory
b. Robertson lag
c. Natural rate of unemployment
d. Romer Model

7. In economics, the _____ is a historical inverse relation between the rate of unemployment and the rate of inflation in an economy. Stated simply, the lower the unemployment in an economy, the higher the rate of increase in nominal wages in the economy. Rate of Change of Wages against Unemployment, United Kingdom 1913-1948 from Phillips (1958)

William Phillips, a New Zealand born economist, wrote a paper in 1958 titled The Relationship between Unemployment and the Rate of Change of Money Wages in the United Kingdom 1861-1957, which was published in the quarterly journal Economica.

a. Demand curve
b. Lorenz curve
c. Cost curve
d. Phillips curve

8. _____ in economics and business is the result of an exchange and from that trade we assign a numerical monetary value to a good, service or asset. If Alice trades Bob 4 apples for an orange, the _____ of an orange is 4 apples. Inversely, the _____ of an apple is 1/4 oranges.

a. Price war
b. Price book
c. Premium pricing
d. Price

9. _____ is an assumption used in many contemporary macroeconomic models, and also in other areas of contemporary economics and game theory and in other applications of rational choice theory.

Since most macroeconomic models today study decisions over many periods, the expectations of workers, consumers, and firms about future economic conditions are an essential part of the model. How to model these expectations has long been controversial, and it is well known that the macroeconomic predictions of the model may differ depending on the assumptions made about expectations

a. Minimum wage
b. Balanced-growth equilibrium
c. Rational expectations
d. Potential output

10. The GDP gap or the _____ is the difference between potential GDP and actual GDP or actual output. The calculation for the _____ is Y-Y* where Y* is potential output and Y is actual output. If this calculation yields a positive number it is called an expansionary gap and indicates an economy in expansion; if the calculation yields a negative number it is called a recessionary gap and indicates an economy in recession.

a. Output gap
b. ACEA agreement
c. ACCRA Cost of Living Index
d. AD-IA Model

11. Unemployment occurs when a person is available to work and seeking work but currently without work. The prevalence of unemployment is usually measured using the _____, which is defined as the percentage of those in the labor force who are unemployed. The _____ is also used in economic studies and economic indexes such as the United States' Conference Board's Index of Leading Indicators as a measure of the state of the macroeconomics.
   a. ACEA agreement
   b. AD-IA Model
   c. ACCRA Cost of Living Index
   d. Unemployment rate

12. The _____ or gross domestic income (GDI), a basic measure of an economy's economic performance, is the market value of all final goods and services produced within the borders of a nation in a year. _____ can be defined in three ways, all of which are conceptually identical. First, it is equal to the total expenditures for all final goods and services produced within the country in a stipulated period of time (usually a 365-day year.)
   a. Monopolistic competition
   b. Countercyclical
   c. Gross domestic product
   d. Market structure

13. _____, 1st Baron Keynes was a renowned economist from Britain whose many ideas on economic and political theories as well as on many governments' monetary policies influenced America. He advocated a government that played an active role in the lives of people regarding business, economy, etc. In this role, the government would use fiscal measures to reduce the consequences of recessions, economic depressions and booms.
   a. John Maynard Keynes
   b. Adolf Hitler
   c. Adam Smith
   d. Adolph Fischer

14. A _____ is a hypothetical measure of overall prices for some set of goods and services, in a given region during a given interval, normalized relative to some base set. Typically, a _____ is approximated with a price index.

The classical dichotomy is the assumption that there is a relatively clean distinction between overall increases or decreases in prices and underlying, e;reale; economic variables.

   a. Discretionary spending
   b. Price level
   c. Price elasticity of supply
   d. Discouraged worker

15. An _____, in economics, is the amount by which the real Gross domestic product exceeds potential GDP. The real GDP is also known as GDP 'adjusted for inflation', 'constant prices' GDP or 'constant dollar' GDP, because it measures the aggregate output in a country's income accounts in a given year, expressed in base-year prices. On the other hand, the potential GDP is the quantity of real GDP when a country's economy is at full-employment.
   a. ACEA agreement
   b. AD-IA Model
   c. Inflationary gap
   d. ACCRA Cost of Living Index

16. In economics, a _____ is a general slowdown in economic activity over a sustained period of time, or a business cycle contraction. During _____s, many macroeconomic indicators vary in a similar way. Production as measured by Gross Domestic Product (GDP), employment, investment spending, capacity utilization, household incomes and business profits all fall during _____s.

a. Recession
b. Monetary economics
c. Treasury View
d. Leading indicators

17. _____ has several particular meanings:

- in mathematics
    - _____ function
    - Euler _____
    - _____
    - _____ subgroup
    - method of _____s (partial differential equations)
- in physics and engineering
    - any _____ curve that shows the relationship between certain input- and output parameters, e.g.
    - an I-V or current-voltage _____ is the current in a circuit as a function of the applied voltage
    - Receiver-Operator _____
- in fiction
    - in Dungeons ' Dragons, _____ is another name for ability score

a. Russian financial crisis
b. Technocracy
c. Demand
d. Characteristic

18. In economics, _____ refers to the highest level of real Gross Domestic Product output that can be sustained over the long term. The existence of a limit is due to natural and institutional constraints. If actual GDP rises and stays above _____, then (in the absence of wage and price controls) inflation tends to increase as demand exceeds supply.
a. Monetary policy reaction function
b. Fundamental psychological law
c. Potential output
d. Monetary conditions index

19. _____s is the social science that studies the production, distribution, and consumption of goods and services. The term _____s comes from the Ancient Greek oá¼°κονομῖα from oá¼¶κος (oikos, 'house') + vÏŒμος (nomos, 'custom' or 'law'), hence 'rules of the house(hold)'. Current _____ models developed out of the broader field of political economy in the late 19th century, owing to a desire to use an empirical approach more akin to the physical sciences.
a. Energy economics
b. Opportunity cost
c. Inflation
d. Economic

20. In economics, _____ is a rise in the general level of prices of goods and services in an economy over a period of time. When the general price level rises, each unit of currency buys fewer goods and services; consequently, _____ is also a decline in the real value of money--a loss of purchasing power in the medium of exchange which is also the monetary unit of account in the economy. A chief measure of general price-level _____ is the general _____ rate, which is the percentage change in a general price index (normally the Consumer Price Index) over time.
a. Opportunity cost
b. Economic
c. Energy economics
d. Inflation

21. A _____ is an event that suddenly changes the price of a commodity or service. It may be caused by a sudden increase or decrease in the supply of a particular good. This sudden change affects the equilibrium price.

a. Friedman rule
c. Supply shock
b. Demand shock
d. SIMIC

22. In economics, a _____ is a monetary-policy rule that stipulates how much the central bank would or should change the nominal interest rate in response to divergences of actual inflation rates from target inflation rates and of actual Gross Domestic Product (GDP) from potential GDP. It was first proposed by the by U.S. economist John B. Taylor in 1993. The rule can be written as follows:

$$i_t = \pi_t + r_t^* + a_\pi(\pi_t - \pi_t^*) + a_y(y_t - \bar{y}_t).$$

In this equation, i_t is the target short-term nominal interest rate (e.g. the federal funds rate in the US), π_t is the rate of inflation as measured by the GDP deflator, π_t^* is the desired rate of inflation, r_t^* is the assumed equilibrium real interest rate, y_t is the logarithm of real GDP, and $\bar{y}_t$ is the logarithm of potential output, as determined by a linear trend.

a. Fed Funds Probability
c. Term Securities Lending Facility
b. Federal Reserve Banks
d. Taylor rule

23. _____ is a fee paid on borrowed assets. It is the price paid for the use of borrowed money, or, money earned by deposited funds. Assets that are sometimes lent with _____ include money, shares, consumer goods through hire purchase, major assets such as aircraft, and even entire factories in finance lease arrangements.

a. Asset protection
c. Internal debt
b. Insolvency
d. Interest

Chapter 12. The Phillips Curve, Expectations, and Monetary Policy 147

24. A _____ is:

- Rewrite _____, in generative grammar and computer science
- Standardization, a formal and widely-accepted statement, fact, definition, or qualification
- Operation, a determinate _____ for performing a mathematical operation and obtaining a certain result (Mathematics, Logic)
    - Unary operation
    - Binary operation
- _____ of inference, a function from sets of formulae to formulae (Mathematics, Logic)
- _____ of thumb, principle with broad application that is not intended to be strictly accurate or reliable for every situation. Also often simply referred to as a _____
- Moral, an atomic element of a moral code for guiding choices in human behavior
- Heuristic, a quantized '_____' which shows a tendency or probability for successful function
- A regulation, as in sports
- A Production _____, as in computer science
- Procedural law, a _____ set governing the application of laws to cases
    - A law, which may informally be called a '_____'
    - A court ruling, a decision by a court
- In the U.S. Government, a regulation mandated by Congress, but written or expanded upon by the Executive Branch.
- Norm (sociology), an informal but widely accepted _____, concept, truth, definition, or qualification (social norms, legal norms, coding norms)
- Norm (philosophy), a kind of sentence or a reason to act, feel or believe
- 'Rulership' is the concept of governance by a government:
    - Military _____, governance by a military body
    - Monastic _____, a collection of precepts that guides the life of monks or nuns in a religious order where the superior holds the place of Christ
- Slide _____

- '_____,' a song by Ayumi Hamasaki
- '_____,' a song by rapper Nas
- '_____s,' an album by the band The Whitest Boy Alive
- _____s: Pyaar Ka Superhit Formula, a 2003 Bollywood film
- ruler, an instrument for measuring lengths
- _____, a component of an astrolabe, circumferator or similar instrument
- The _____s, a bestselling self-help book
- _____ Project (Run Up-to-date Linux Everywhere), a project that aims to use up-to-date Linux software on old PCs
- _____ engine, a software system that helps managing business _____s
- Ja _____, a hip hop artist
    - R.U.L.E., a 2005 greatest hits album by rapper Ja _____
- '_____s,' a KMFDM song

a. Rule   b. Procter ' Gamble
c. Technocracy   d. Demand

25. _____ is the a method of technical and economic research of the systems for purpose to optimize a parity between system's consumer functions or properties and expenses to achieve those functions or properties.

This methodology for continuous perfection of production, industrial technologies, organizational structures was developed by Juryj Sobolev in 1948 at the 'Perm telephone factory'

- 1948 Juryj Sobolev - the first success in application of a method analysis at the 'Perm telephone factory' .
- 1949 - the first application for the invention as result of use of the new method.

Today in economically developed countries practically each enterprise or the company use methodology of the kind of functional-cost analysis as a practice of the quality management, most full satisfying to principles of standards of series ISO 9000.

- Interest of consumer not in products itself, but the advantage which it will receive from its usage.
- The consumer aspires to reduce his expenses
- Functions needed by consumer can be executed in the various ways, and, hence, with various efficiency and expenses. Among possible alternatives of realization of functions exist such in which the parity of quality and the price is the optimal for the consumer.

The goal of _____ is achievement of the highest consumer satisfaction of production at simultaneous decrease in all kinds of industrial expenses Classical _____ has three English synonyms - Value Engineering, Value Management, Value Analysis.

a. Willingness to pay
b. Monopoly wage
c. Staple financing
d. Function cost analysis

26. In economics, the _____ functional form of production functions is widely used to represent the relationship of an output to inputs. It was proposed by Knut Wicksell (1851-1926), and tested against statistical evidence by Charles Cobb and Paul Douglas in 1900-1928.

For production, the function is

$$Y = AL^{\alpha}K^{\beta},$$

where:

- Y = total production (the monetary value of all goods produced in a year)
- L = labor input
- K = capital input
- A = total factor productivity
- α and β are the output elasticities of labor and capital, respectively. These values are constants determined by available technology.

Output elasticity measures the responsiveness of output to a change in levels of either labor or capital used in production, ceteris paribus. For example if α = 0.15, a 1% increase in labor would lead to approximately a 0.15% increase in output.

- a. Social savings
- b. Growth accounting
- c. Demand-pull theory
- d. Cobb-Douglas

27. In microeconomics, _____ is quite simply the conversion of inputs into outputs. It is an economic process that uses resources to create a good or service that is suitable for exchange. This can include manufacturing, storing, shipping, and packaging.
- a. MET
- b. Solved
- c. Production
- d. Red Guards

28. In economics, a _____ is a function that specifies the output of a firm, an industry, or an entire economy for all combinations of inputs. A meta-_____ compares the practice of the existing entities converting inputs X into output y to determine the most efficient practice _____ of the existing entities, whether the most efficient feasible practice production or the most efficient actual practice production. In either case, the maximum output of a technologically-determined production process is a mathematical function of input factors of production.
- a. Constant elasticity of substitution
- b. Production function
- c. Post-Fordism
- d. Short-run

29. In mathematics, a _____ is a constant multiplicative factor of a certain object. For example, in the expression $9x^2$, the _____ of x^2 is 9.

The object can be such things as a variable, a vector, a function, etc.

- a. 130-30 fund
- b. 100-year flood
- c. 1921 recession
- d. Coefficient

30. _____ refers to the actions that governments take in the economic field. It covers the systems for setting interest rates and government deficit as well as the labour market, national ownership, and many other areas of government.

Such policies are often influenced by international institutions like the International Monetary Fund or World Bank as well as political beliefs and the consequent policies of parties.

- a. ACEA agreement
- b. Economic policy
- c. ACCRA Cost of Living Index
- d. AD-IA Model

31. In economics, an _____ is any good or commodity, transported from one country to another country in a legitimate fashion, typically for use in trade. _____ goods or services are provided to foreign consumers by domestic producers. _____ is an important part of international trade.
- a. ACEA agreement
- b. ACCRA Cost of Living Index
- c. AD-IA Model
- d. Export

Chapter 12. The Phillips Curve, Expectations, and Monetary Policy

32. _____ is a concept found in moral, political, and bioethical philosophy. Within these contexts, it refers to the capacity of a rational individual to make an informed, un-coerced decision. In moral and political philosophy, _____ is often used as the basis for determining moral responsibility for one's actions.

   a. Autonomy
   b. AD-IA Model
   c. ACCRA Cost of Living Index
   d. ACEA agreement

33. _____ is a common concept in economics, and gives rise to derived concepts such as consumer debt. Generally _____ is defined by opposition to production. But the precise definition can vary because different schools of economists define production quite differently.

   a. Consumption
   b. Cash or share options
   c. Foreclosure data providers
   d. Federal Reserve Bank Notes

34. In economics, _____ is the total demand for final goods and services in the economy (Y) at a given time and price level. It is the amount of goods and services in the economy that will be purchased at all possible price levels. This is the demand for the gross domestic product of a country when inventory levels are static.

   a. Aggregate expenditure
   b. Aggregation problem
   c. Aggregate supply
   d. Aggregate demand

35. The term _____ refers to economy-wide fluctuations in production or economic activity over several months or years. These fluctuations occur around a long-term growth trend, and typically involve shifts over time between periods of relatively rapid economic growth (expansion or boom), and periods of relative stagnation or decline (contraction or recession.) These fluctuations are often measured using the growth rate of real gross domestic product.

   a. Consumer theory
   b. Nominal value
   c. Tobit model
   d. Business cycle

36. Economics:

- _____ ,the desire to own something and the ability to pay for it
- _____ curve,a graphic representation of a _____ schedule
- _____ deposit, the money in checking accounts
- _____ pull theory,the theory that inflation occurs when _____ for goods and services exceeds existing supplies
- _____ schedule,a table that lists the quantity of a good a person will buy it each different price
- _____ side economics,the school of economics at believes government spending and tax cuts open economy by raising _____

   a. McKesson ' Robbins scandal
   b. Variability
   c. Production
   d. Demand

Chapter 12. The Phillips Curve, Expectations, and Monetary Policy

37. _____ data refers to selected population characteristics as used in government, marketing or opinion research, or the _____ profiles used in such research. Note the distinction from the term 'demography' Commonly-used _____s include race, age, income, disabilities, mobility (in terms of travel time to work or number of vehicles available), educational attainment, home ownership, employment status, and even location.
- a. Generation Z
- b. Demographic warfare
- c. Demographic
- d. NEET

38. _____ is a system of training a new generation of practitioners of a skill. Apprentices (or in early modern usage 'prentices') or protégés build their careers from _____s. Most of their training is done on the job while working for an employer who helps the apprentices learn their trade, in exchange for their continuing labour for an agreed period after they become skilled.
- a. ACEA agreement
- b. ACCRA Cost of Living Index
- c. Apprenticeship
- d. AD-IA Model

39. A trade union or _____ is an organization of workers who have banded together to achieve common goals in key areas and working conditions. The trade union, through its leadership, bargains with the employer on behalf of union members (rank and file members) and negotiates labor contracts (Collective bargaining) with employers. This may include the negotiation of wages, work rules, complaint procedures, rules governing hiring, firing and promotion of workers, benefits, workplace safety and policies.
- a. Basis of futures
- b. Business valuation standards
- c. Labor union
- d. Demand-side technologies

40. _____ in economics refers to metrics and measures of output from production processes, per unit of input. Labor _____, for example, is typically measured as a ratio of output per labor-hour, an input. _____ may be conceived of as a metrics of the technical or engineering efficiency of production.
- a. Productivity
- b. Piece work
- c. Fordism
- d. Production-possibility frontier

41. The term _____s refers to wages that have been adjusted for inflation. This term is used in contrast to nominal wages or unadjusted wages.

The use of adjusted figures is in undertaking some form of economic analysis.

- a. Profit sharing
- b. Federal Wage System
- c. Living wage
- d. Real wage

42. The term _____ refers to government debt, expenditures and revenues, or to finance (particularly financial revenue) in general.

- _____ deficit is the budget deficit of federal or local government
- _____ policy is the discretionary spending of governments. Contrasts with monetary policy.
- _____ year and _____ quarter are reporting periods for firms and other agencies.

Chapter 12. The Phillips Curve, Expectations, and Monetary Policy

a. Procter ' Gamble
b. Drawdown
c. Fiscal
d. Bucket shop

43. In economics, _____ is the use of government spending and revenue collection to influence the economy.

_____ can be contrasted with the other main type of economic policy, monetary policy, which attempts to stabilize the economy by controlling interest rates and the supply of money. The two main instruments of _____ are government spending and taxation.

a. Fiscalism
b. Fiscal policy
c. Sustainable investment rule
d. 100-year flood

44. A _____ or labor union is an organization of workers who have banded together to achieve common goals in key areas and working conditions. The _____, through its leadership, bargains with the employer on behalf of union members (rank and file members) and negotiates labor contracts (Collective bargaining) with employers. This may include the negotiation of wages, work rules, complaint procedures, rules governing hiring, firing and promotion of workers, benefits, workplace safety and policies.

a. Case-Shiller Home Price Indices
b. Consumer goods
c. Guaranteed investment contracts
d. Trade union

45. _____ was a survey conducted by the U.S. Department of Justice to gauge the prevalence of alcohol and illegal drug use among prior arrestees. It was a reformulation of the prior Drug Use Forecasting (DUF) program, focused on five drugs in particular: cocaine, marijuana, methamphetamine, opiates, and PCP.

Participants were randomly selected from arrest records in major metropolitan areas; because no personally identifying information is taken from each record chosen, the resulting data can be correlated to arrest rates, but not to the total population of persons charged.

a. ACCRA Cost of Living Index
b. Arrestee Drug Abuse Monitoring
c. AD-IA Model
d. ACEA agreement

46. In economics, _____ means that people form their expectations about what will happen in the future based on what has happened in the past. For example, if inflation has been higher than expected in the past, people would revise expectations for the future.

One simple version of _____ is stated in the following equation, where p^e is the next year's rate of inflation that is currently expected; p^e_{-1} is this year's rate of inflation that was expected last year; and p is this year's actual rate of inflation:

$$p^e = p^e_{-1} + \lambda(p_{-1} - p^e_{-1})$$

With λ is between 0 and 1, this says that current expectations of future inflation reflect past expectations and an 'error-adjustment' term, in which current expectations are raised (or lowered) according to the gap between actual inflation and previous expectations.

a. Investment-specific technological progress b. Adaptive expectations
c. Economic interdependence d. AD-IA Model

47. _____ is a decrease in the rate of inflation. This phase of the business cycle, in which retailers can no longer pass on higher prices to their customers, often occurs during a recession. In contrast, deflation occurs when prices are actually dropping.
   a. Mundell-Tobin effect b. Stealth inflation
   c. Disinflation d. Reflation

48. A _____ is a package or set of measures introduced to stabilise a financial system or economy. The term can refer to policies in two distinct sets of circumstances: business cycle stabilization and crisis stabilization.

Stabilization can refer to correcting the normal behavior of the business cycle.

   a. Volunteers for Economic Growth Alliance b. Capacity Development
   c. New International Economic Order d. Stabilization policy

49. In economic models, the _____ time frame assumes no fixed factors of production. Firms can enter or leave the marketplace, and the cost (and availability) of land, labor, raw materials, and capital goods can be assumed to vary. In contrast, in the short-run time frame, certain factors are assumed to be fixed, because there is not sufficient time for them to change.
   a. Long-run b. Diseconomies of scale
   c. Productivity world d. Price/performance ratio

50. _____ is monetary policy that seeks to reduce the size of the money supply. They are fiscal policies, like lower spending and higher taxes, that reduce economic growth. In most nations, monetary policy is controlled by either a central bank or a finance ministry.
   a. Shadow Open Market Committee b. Monetary policy of Sweden
   c. Money creation d. Contractionary monetary policy

51. _____ is monetary policy that seeks to increase the size of the money supply. In most nations, monetary policy is controlled by either a central bank or a finance ministry

Neoclassical and Keynesian economics significantly differ on the effects and effectiveness of monetary policy on influencing the real economy; there is no clear consensus on how monetary policy affects real economic variables (aggregate output or income, employment.) Both economic schools accept that monetary policy affects monetary variables (price levels, interest rates.)

   a. ACCRA Cost of Living Index b. Expansionary monetary policy
   c. AD-IA Model d. ACEA agreement

Chapter 13. Stabilization Policy

1. _____s is the social science that studies the production, distribution, and consumption of goods and services. The term _____s comes from the Ancient Greek οἰκονομία from οἶκος (oikos, 'house') + νόμος (nomos, 'custom' or 'law'), hence 'rules of the house(hold)'. Current _____ models developed out of the broader field of political economy in the late 19th century, owing to a desire to use an empirical approach more akin to the physical sciences.

   a. Inflation
   b. Energy economics
   c. Economic
   d. Opportunity cost

2. _____ refers to the actions that governments take in the economic field. It covers the systems for setting interest rates and government deficit as well as the labour market, national ownership, and many other areas of government.

   Such policies are often influenced by international institutions like the International Monetary Fund or World Bank as well as political beliefs and the consequent policies of parties.

   a. Economic policy
   b. ACEA agreement
   c. ACCRA Cost of Living Index
   d. AD-IA Model

3. The _____ is the central banking system of the United States. Created in 1913 by the enactment of the Federal Reserve Act (signed by Woodrow Wilson), it is a quasi-public and quasi-private (government entity with private components) banking system that comprises (1) the presidentially appointed Board of Governors of the _____ in Washington, D.C.; (2) the Federal Open Market Committee; (3) twelve regional Federal Reserve Banks located in major cities throughout the nation acting as fiscal agents for the U.S. Treasury, each with its own nine-member board of directors; (4) numerous other private U.S. member banks, which subscribe to required amounts of non-transferable stock in their regional Federal Reserve Banks; and (5) various advisory councils. Since February 2006, Ben Bernanke has served as the Chairman of the Board of Governors of the _____.

   a. Term auction facility
   b. Federal Reserve System Open Market Account
   c. Monetary Policy Report to the Congress
   d. Federal Reserve System

4. The term _____ refers to government debt, expenditures and revenues, or to finance (particularly financial revenue) in general.

   - _____ deficit is the budget deficit of federal or local government
   - _____ policy is the discretionary spending of governments. Contrasts with monetary policy.
   - _____ year and _____ quarter are reporting periods for firms and other agencies.

   a. Drawdown
   b. Bucket shop
   c. Fiscal
   d. Procter ' Gamble

5. In economics, _____ is the use of government spending and revenue collection to influence the economy.

   _____ can be contrasted with the other main type of economic policy, monetary policy, which attempts to stabilize the economy by controlling interest rates and the supply of money. The two main instruments of _____ are government spending and taxation.

Chapter 13. Stabilization Policy

a. 100-year flood
b. Fiscalism
c. Sustainable investment rule
d. Fiscal policy

6. _____ is the process by which the government, central bank (ii) availability of money, and (iii) cost of money or rate of interest, in order to attain a set of objectives oriented towards the growth and stability of the economy. Monetary theory provides insight into how to craft optimal _____.

_____ is referred to as either being an expansionary policy where an expansionary policy increases the total supply of money in the economy, and a contractionary policy decreases the total money supply.

a. 130-30 fund
b. 100-year flood
c. 1921 recession
d. Monetary policy

7. The _____ is the upward-sloping relationship between the inflation rate and the unemployment rate. When the inflation rate rises, a central bank wishing to fight inflation will raise interest rates to reduce output and thus increase the unemployment rate. The _____ is a function of the Taylor Rule, the Investment-Spending Curve (IS Curve) and Okun's Law

The _____ has the equation:

$u = u_0 + \Phi(\pi - \pi t)$

Where Φ is a parameter that tells us how much unemployment rises when the central bank raises the real interest rate r because it thinks that inflation is too high and needs to be reduced.

a. Value added
b. Secular basis
c. Marginal propensity to import
d. Monetary policy reaction function

8. _____ in economics and business is the result of an exchange and from that trade we assign a numerical monetary value to a good, service or asset. If Alice trades Bob 4 apples for an orange, the _____ of an orange is 4 apples. Inversely, the _____ of an apple is 1/4 oranges.
a. Price
b. Price book
c. Premium pricing
d. Price war

9. The _____, a component of the Federal Reserve System, is charged under United States law with overseeing the nation's open market operations. It is the Federal Reserve Committee that makes key decisions about interest rates and the growth jam of the United States money supply. It is the principal organ of United States national monetary policy.
a. Fed Funds Probability
b. Primary Dealer Credit Facility
c. Federal Reserve Transparency Act
d. Federal Open Market Committee

10. The _____ was a worldwide economic downturn starting in most places in 1929 and ending at different times in the 1930s or early 1940s for different countries. It was the largest and most important economic depression in the 20th century, and is used in the 21st century as an example of how far the world's economy can fall. The _____ originated in the United States; historians most often use as a starting date the stock market crash on October 29, 1929, known as Black Tuesday.

a. Wall Street Crash of 1929
b. British Empire Economic Conference
c. Jarrow March
d. Great Depression

11.   In economics, the _____ is the term used to refer to the environment in which bonds are bought and sold between a central bank ' its regulated banks. It is not a free market process.

- To intervene in the 'business cycle', a central bank may choose to go into the _____ and buy or sell government bonds, which is known as _____ operations to increase reserves.

a. Inside money
b. ACCRA Cost of Living Index
c. Outside money
d. Open Market

12.   The Federal Reserve System (also the Federal Reserve; informally The Fed) is the central banking system of the United States. Created in 1913 by the enactment of the Federal Reserve Act (signed by Woodrow Wilson), it is a quasi-public and quasi-private (government entity with private components) banking system that comprises (1) the presidentially appointed Board of Governors of the Federal Reserve System in Washington, D.C.; (2) the Federal Open Market Committee; (3) twelve regional _____ located in major cities throughout the nation acting as fiscal agents for the U.S. Treasury, each with its own nine-member board of directors; (4) numerous other private U.S. member banks, which subscribe to required amounts of non-transferable stock in their regional _____; and (5) various advisory councils. Since February 2006, Ben Bernanke has served as the Chairman of the Board of Governors of the Federal Reserve System.

a. Federal Open Market Committee
b. Fed Funds Probability
c. Federal funds
d. Federal Reserve banks

13.   _____ is an American economist and was the Chairman of the Federal Reserve of the United States from 1987 to 2006. He currently works as a private advisor and providing consulting for firms through his company, Greenspan Associates LLC.

First appointed Federal Reserve chairman by President Ronald Reagan in August 1987, he was reappointed at successive four-year intervals until retiring on January 31, 2006 after the second-longest tenure in the position.

a. Adolph Fischer
b. Adolf Hitler
c. Adam Smith
d. Alan Greenspan

14.   _____ are the means of implementing monetary policy by which a central bank controls its national money supply by buying and selling government securities, or other financial instruments. Monetary targets, such as interest rates or exchange rates, are used to guide this implementation.

Since most money is now in the form of electronic records, rather than paper records such as banknotes, _____ are conducted simply by electronically increasing or decreasing ('crediting' or 'debiting') the amount of money that a bank has, e.g., in its reserve account at the central bank, in exchange for a bank selling or buying a financial instrument.

a. ACEA agreement
b. ACCRA Cost of Living Index
c. Open market operations
d. AD-IA Model

Chapter 13. Stabilization Policy 157

15. The '_____' is approximately the nominal interest rate minus the inflation rate Since the inflation rate over the course of a loan is not known initially, volatility in inflation represents a risk to both the lender and the borrower.

In economics and finance, an individual who lends money for repayment at a later point in time expects to be compensated for the time value of money, or not having the use of that money while it is lent.

a. Cost-push inflation
b. Core inflation
c. Reflation
d. Real interest rate

16. The _____ is a bank regulation that sets the minimum reserves each bank must hold to customer deposits and notes. It would normally be in the form of fiat currency stored in a bank vault (vault cash), or with a central bank.

The reserve ratio is sometimes used as a tool in the monetary policy, influencing the country's economy, borrowing, and interest rates.

a. Reserve requirement
b. Probability of default
c. Fractional-reserve banking
d. Private money

17. In economics, _____ is a rise in the general level of prices of goods and services in an economy over a period of time. When the general price level rises, each unit of currency buys fewer goods and services; consequently, _____ is also a decline in the real value of money--a loss of purchasing power in the medium of exchange which is also the monetary unit of account in the economy. A chief measure of general price-level _____ is the general _____ rate, which is the percentage change in a general price index (normally the Consumer Price Index) over time.

a. Energy economics
b. Opportunity cost
c. Economic
d. Inflation

18. In economics, the _____ is a measure of inflation, the rate of increase of a price index (for example, a consumer price index.)It is the percentage rate of change in price level over time. The rate of decrease in the purchasing power of money is approximately equal.

It's used to calculate the real interest rate, as well as real increases in wages, and official measurements of this rate act as input variables to COLA adjustments and Inflation derivatives prices.

a. Equity value
b. Interest rate option
c. Inflation rate
d. Edgeworth paradox

19. _____ is a fee paid on borrowed assets. It is the price paid for the use of borrowed money , or, money earned by deposited funds . Assets that are sometimes lent with _____ include money, shares, consumer goods through hire purchase, major assets such as aircraft, and even entire factories in finance lease arrangements.

a. Asset protection
b. Internal debt
c. Insolvency
d. Interest

20. An _____ is the price a borrower pays for the use of money they do not own, for instance a small company might borrow from a bank to kick start their business, and the return a lender receives for deferring the use of funds, by lending it to the borrower. _____s are normally expressed as a percentage rate over the period of one year.

_____s targets are also a vital tool of monetary policy and are used to control variables like investment, inflation, and unemployment.

a. Enterprise value
b. Arrow-Debreu model
c. ACCRA Cost of Living Index
d. Interest rate

21. In economics, _____ is a sustained decrease in the general price level of goods and services. _____ occurs when the annual inflation rate falls below zero percent, resulting in an increase in the real value of money -- a negative inflation rate. This should not be confused with disinflation, a slow-down in the inflation rate (i.e. when the inflation decreases, but still remains positive.)

a. Literacy rate
b. Price revolution
c. Tobit model
d. Deflation

22. Market _____ is a business, economics or investment term that refers to an asset's ability to be easily converted through an act of buying or selling without causing a significant movement in the price and with minimum loss of value. Money, or cash on hand, is the most liquid asset. An act of exchange of a less liquid asset with a more liquid asset is called liquidation.

a. 1921 recession
b. 130-30 fund
c. 100-year flood
d. Liquidity

23. The term _____ is used in macroeconomics to refer to a situation where a country's nominal interest rate has been lowered nearly to or equal to zero to avoid a recession, but the liquidity in the market created by these low interest rates does not stimulate the economy to full employment. In this situation, any further increase in the money supply will not stimulate the economy any further. This is because any further injection of liquidity will no longer lower the nominal interest rate, as the nominal interest rate cannot drop below zero.

a. Minimum wage
b. Robertson lag
c. Macroeconomic models
d. Liquidity trap

24. A _____ is a legal document that is often passed by the legislature, and approved by the chief executive-or president. For example, only certain types of revenue may be imposed and collected. Property tax is frequently the basis for municipal and county revenues, while sales tax and/or income tax are the basis for state revenues, and income tax and corporate tax are the basis for national revenues.

a. Right-financing
b. Lump-sum tax
c. Structural deficit
d. Government budget

25. A _____ is a package or set of measures introduced to stabilise a financial system or economy. The term can refer to policies in two distinct sets of circumstances: business cycle stabilization and crisis stabilization.

Stabilization can refer to correcting the normal behavior of the business cycle.

a. Stabilization policy
b. Capacity Development
c. New International Economic Order
d. Volunteers for Economic Growth Alliance

26. A _____ occurs when a government discontinues providing services that are not considered 'essential.' Typically, essential services include police, fire fighting, armed forces, and corrections.

Chapter 13. Stabilization Policy

A shutdown can occur when a legislative body (including the legislative power of veto by the executive) cannot agree on a budget financing its government programs for a pending fiscal year. In the absence of appropriated funds, the government discontinues providing non-essential services at the beginning of the affected fiscal year.

a. 1921 recession
b. 130-30 fund
c. 100-year flood
d. Government shutdown

27. In economics, an _____ is the amount of time it takes for a government or a central bank to respond to a shock in the economy.It is a delay in implementing monetary policy. Its converse is outside lag (the amount of time before an action by a government or a central bank affects an economy.) _____ comprises recognition lag, the time taken to recognize the shock, and decision lag (or implementation lag), the time taken to decide a response.

a. Inside lag
b. Overnight trade
c. Ostrich strategy
d. Employee experience management

28. _____ is a spending category about which government planners can make choices. See Government spending.It refers to spending set on a yearly basis by decision of Congress and is part of fiscal policy. This spending is optional, in contrast to entitlement programs for which funding is mandatory.

a. Financial system
b. Dynamic efficiency
c. Lean consumption
d. Discretionary spending

29. The term financial crisis is applied broadly to a variety of situations in which some financial institutions or assets suddenly lose a large part of their value. In the 19th and early 20th centuries, many _____ were associated with banking panics, and many recessions coincided with these panics. Other situations that are often called _____ include stock market crashes and the bursting of other financial bubbles, currency crises, and sovereign defaults.

a. Georgism
b. Microeconomics
c. General equilibrium
d. Financial crises

30. _____ or government expenditure is classified by economists into three main types. Government purchases of goods and services for current use are classed as government consumption. Government purchases of goods and services intended to create future benefits, such as infrastructure investment or research spending, are classed as government investment.

a. Government spending
b. 100-year flood
c. 1921 recession
d. 130-30 fund

31. _____ is a common concept in economics, and gives rise to derived concepts such as consumer debt. Generally _____ is defined by opposition to production. But the precise definition can vary because different schools of economists define production quite differently.

a. Foreclosure data providers
b. Federal Reserve Bank Notes
c. Cash or share options
d. Consumption

32. The term _____ refers to economy-wide fluctuations in production or economic activity over several months or years. These fluctuations occur around a long-term growth trend, and typically involve shifts over time between periods of relatively rapid economic growth (expansion or boom), and periods of relative stagnation or decline (contraction or recession).

These fluctuations are often measured using the growth rate of real gross domestic product.

a. Nominal value
b. Business Cycle
c. Tobit model
d. Consumer theory

33. _____, 1st Baron Keynes was a renowned economist from Britain whose many ideas on economic and political theories as well as on many governments' monetary policies influenced America. He advocated a government that played an active role in the lives of people regarding business, economy, etc. In this role, the government would use fiscal measures to reduce the consequences of recessions, economic depressions and booms.

a. Adam Smith
b. Adolph Fischer
c. Adolf Hitler
d. John Maynard Keynes

34. _____ and Keynesian Theory) is a macroeconomic theory based on the ideas of 20th-century British economist John Maynard Keynes. _____ argues that private sector decisions sometimes lead to inefficient macroeconomic outcomes and therefore advocates active policy responses by the public sector, including monetary policy actions by the central bank and fiscal policy actions by the government to stabilize output over the business cycle.

The theories forming the basis of _____ were first presented in The General Theory of Employment, Interest and Money, published in 1936.

a. Rational choice theory
b. Keynesian economics
c. Market failure
d. Deflation

35. The _____ was a fundamental reworking of economic theory concerning the factors determining employment levels in the overall economy. The revolution was set against the orthodox classical economic framework, which based on Say's Law argued that unless special conditions prevailed the free market would naturally establish full employment equilibrium with no need for government intervention. Employers will be able to make a profit by employing all available workers as long as workers drop their wages below the value of the total output they are able to produce - and classical economics assumed that in a free market workers would be willing to lower their wage demands accordingly , because they are rational agents who would rather work for less than face unemployment.

a. Speculative demand
b. Military Keynesianism
c. Neo-Keynesian economics
d. Keynesian revolution

36. In economics, the _____ is a historical inverse relation between the rate of unemployment and the rate of inflation in an economy. Stated simply, the lower the unemployment in an economy, the higher the rate of increase in nominal wages in the economy. Rate of Change of Wages against Unemployment, United Kingdom 1913-1948 from Phillips (1958)

William Phillips, a New Zealand born economist, wrote a paper in 1958 titled The Relationship between Unemployment and the Rate of Change of Money Wages in the United Kingdom 1861-1957, which was published in the quarterly journal Economica.

a. Demand curve
b. Cost curve
c. Lorenz curve
d. Phillips curve

37. _____ originally was the term for studying production, buying and selling, and their relations with law, custom, and government. _____ originated in moral philosophy. It developed in the 18th century as the study of the economies of states -- polities, hence _____.
   a. Productive and unproductive labour
   b. Political Economy
   c. Dirigisme
   d. Geoeconomics

38. In economics, a _____ is a general slowdown in economic activity over a sustained period of time, or a business cycle contraction. During _____s, many macroeconomic indicators vary in a similar way. Production as measured by Gross Domestic Product (GDP), employment, investment spending, capacity utilization, household incomes and business profits all fall during _____s.
   a. Treasury View
   b. Recession
   c. Leading indicators
   d. Monetary economics

39. In economics, a _____ is a monetary-policy rule that stipulates how much the central bank would or should change the nominal interest rate in response to divergences of actual inflation rates from target inflation rates and of actual Gross Domestic Product (GDP) from potential GDP. It was first proposed by the by U.S. economist John B. Taylor in 1993. The rule can be written as follows:

$$i_t = \pi_t + r_t^* + a_\pi(\pi_t - \pi_t^*) + a_y(y_t - \bar{y}_t).$$

In this equation, i_t is the target short-term nominal interest rate (e.g. the federal funds rate in the US), π_t is the rate of inflation as measured by the GDP deflator, π_t^* is the desired rate of inflation, r_t^* is the assumed equilibrium real interest rate, y_t is the logarithm of real GDP, and $\bar{y}_t$ is the logarithm of potential output, as determined by a linear trend.

   a. Federal Reserve Banks
   b. Term Securities Lending Facility
   c. Fed Funds Probability
   d. Taylor rule

162   *Chapter 13. Stabilization Policy*

40. A _____ is:

- Rewrite _____, in generative grammar and computer science
- Standardization, a formal and widely-accepted statement, fact, definition, or qualification
- Operation, a determinate _____ for performing a mathematical operation and obtaining a certain result (Mathematics, Logic)
    - Unary operation
    - Binary operation
- _____ of inference, a function from sets of formulae to formulae (Mathematics, Logic)
- _____ of thumb, principle with broad application that is not intended to be strictly accurate or reliable for every situation. Also often simply referred to as a _____
- Moral, an atomic element of a moral code for guiding choices in human behavior
- Heuristic, a quantized '_____' which shows a tendency or probability for successful function
- A regulation, as in sports
- A Production _____, as in computer science
- Procedural law, a _____ set governing the application of laws to cases
    - A law, which may informally be called a '_____'
    - A court ruling, a decision by a court
- In the U.S. Government, a regulation mandated by Congress, but written or expanded upon by the Executive Branch.
- Norm (sociology), an informal but widely accepted _____, concept, truth, definition, or qualification (social norms, legal norms, coding norms)
- Norm (philosophy), a kind of sentence or a reason to act, feel or believe
- 'Rulership' is the concept of governance by a government:
    - Military _____, governance by a military body
    - Monastic _____, a collection of precepts that guides the life of monks or nuns in a religious order where the superior holds the place of Christ
- Slide _____

- '_____,' a song by Ayumi Hamasaki
- '_____,' a song by rapper Nas
- '_____s,' an album by the band The Whitest Boy Alive
- _____s: Pyaar Ka Superhit Formula, a 2003 Bollywood film
- ruler, an instrument for measuring lengths
- _____, a component of an astrolabe, circumferator or similar instrument
- The _____s, a bestselling self-help book
- _____ Project (Run Up-to-date Linux Everywhere), a project that aims to use up-to-date Linux software on old PCs
- _____ engine, a software system that helps managing business _____s
- Ja _____, a hip hop artist
    - R.U.L.E., a 2005 greatest hits album by rapper Ja _____
- '_____s,' a KMFDM song

a. Technocracy   b. Procter ' Gamble
c. Demand   d. Rule

Chapter 13. Stabilization Policy

41. The _____ is the average frequency with which a unit of money is spent in a specific period of time. Velocity associates the amount of economic activity associated with a given money supply. When the period is understood, the velocity may be present as a pure number; otherwise it should be given as a pure number over time.

a. Money supply
c. Chartalism

b. Neutrality of money
d. Velocity of money

42. The _____ says that it is naïve to try to predict the effects of a change in economic policy entirely on the basis of relationships observed in historical data, especially highly aggregated historical data.

The basic idea pre-dates Lucas's contribution, but in a 1976 paper he drove home the point that this simple notion invalidated policy advice based on conclusions drawn from estimated system of equation models. Because the parameters of those models were not structural - that is, not policy-invariant - they would necessarily change whenever policy - the rules of the game - was changed.

a. Demand management
c. Peak-load pricing

b. Dahrendorf hypothesis
d. Lucas critique

43. _____ is an assumption used in many contemporary macroeconomic models, and also in other areas of contemporary economics and game theory and in other applications of rational choice theory.

Since most macroeconomic models today study decisions over many periods, the expectations of workers, consumers, and firms about future economic conditions are an essential part of the model. How to model these expectations has long been controversial, and it is well known that the macroeconomic predictions of the model may differ depending on the assumptions made about expectations

a. Minimum wage
c. Potential output

b. Balanced-growth equilibrium
d. Rational expectations

44. In economics, _____ are key economic variables that economists used to predict a new phase of the business cycle. A leading indicator is one that changes before the economy does; a lagging indicator is one that changes after the economy has changed. Examples of _____ include stock prices, which often improve or worsen before a similar change in the economy.

a. Medium of exchange
c. Gross domestic product

b. Macroeconomics
d. Leading indicators

45. A _____ is a public market for the trading of company stock and derivatives at an agreed price; these are securities listed on a stock exchange as well as those only traded privately.

The size of the world _____ was estimated at about $36.6 trillion US at the beginning of October 2008 . The total world derivatives market has been estimated at about $791 trillion face or nominal value, 11 times the size of the entire world economy.

a. Adolph Fischer
c. Adam Smith

b. Adolf Hitler
d. Stock market

46. A _____ is a type of economic bubble taking place in stock markets when price of stocks rise and become overvalued by any measure of stock valuation.

The existence of _____s is at odds with the assumptions of efficient market theory which assumes rational investor behaviour. Behavioral finance theory attribute _____s to cognitive biases that lead to groupthink and herd behavior.

   a. Fill or kill
   b. Scrip issue
   c. Growth investing
   d. Stock market bubble

47. The _____ is an American economic index intended to estimate future economic activity. It is calculated by The Conference Board, a non-governmental organization, which determines the value of the index from the values of ten key variables. These variables have historically turned downward before a recession and upward before an expansion.
   a. Atkinson index
   b. Index of Leading indicators
   c. Index of dissimilarity
   d. Index of diversity

48. In economics, _____ is the total amount of money available in an economy at a particular point in time. There are several ways to define 'money', but standard measures usually include currency in circulation and demand deposits.

_____ data are recorded and published, usually by the government or the central bank of the country.

   a. Money supply
   b. Velocity of money
   c. Veil of money
   d. Neutrality of money

49. The most common mechanism used to measure this increase in the money supply is typically called the _____. It calculates the maximum amount of money that an initial deposit can be expanded to with a given reserve ratio - such a factor is called a multiplier.

The _____, m, is the inverse of the reserve requirement, R:

$$m = \frac{1}{R}$$

This formula stems from the fact that the sum of the 'amount loaned out' column above can be expressed mathematically as a geometric series with a common ratio of 1 − R.

   a. Fixed-income arbitrage
   b. Flow to Equity-Approach
   c. Kibbutz volunteers
   d. Money multiplier

50. In economics, the _____ is a term relating to the money supply, the amount of money in the economy. The _____ comprises only coins, paper money, and commercial banks' reserves with the central bank. Broader measures of the money supply include the public's bank deposits.
   a. Quantum economics
   b. Chartalism
   c. Monetary economy
   d. Monetary base

Chapter 13. Stabilization Policy

51. In banking, _____ are bank reserves in excess of the reserve requirement set by a central bank (in the United States, the Federal Reserve System, called the Fed; in Canada, the Bank of Canada.) They are reserves of cash more than the required amounts. Holding _____ is generally considered costly and uneconomical as no interest is earned on the excess amount.

    a. Annual percentage rate
    b. Origination fee
    c. Excess reserves
    d. Universal bank

52. _____, in law and economics, is a form of risk management primarily used to hedge against the risk of a contingent loss. _____ is defined as the equitable transfer of the risk of a loss, from one entity to another, in exchange for a premium, and can be thought of as a guaranteed small loss to prevent a large, possibly devastating loss. An insurer is a company selling the _____; an insured or policyholder is the person or entity buying the _____.

    a. ACCRA Cost of Living Index
    b. AD-IA Model
    c. ACEA agreement
    d. Insurance

53. A _____ is an expression that compares quantities relative to each other. The most common examples involve two quantities, but any number of quantities can be compared. _____s are represented mathematically by separating each quantity with a colon, for example the _____ 2:3, which is read as the _____ 'two to three'.

    a. Ratio
    b. 130-30 fund
    c. Y-intercept
    d. 100-year flood

54. To _____ is to impose a financial charge or other levy upon a taxpayer by a state or the functional equivalent of a state.

_____es are also imposed by many subnational entities. _____es consist of direct _____ or indirect _____, and may be paid in money or as its labour equivalent (often but not always unpaid.)

    a. 1921 recession
    b. 130-30 fund
    c. 100-year flood
    d. Tax

55. A _____ is a reduction in taxes. Economic stimulus via _____s, along with interest rate intervention and deficit spending, are one of the central tenets of Keynesian economics.

The immediate effects of a _____ are, generally, a decrease in the real income of the government and an increase in the real income of those whose tax rate has been lowered.

    a. Direct taxes
    b. Tax cut
    c. Withholding tax
    d. Popiwek

56. Unemployment occurs when a person is available to work and seeking work but currently without work. The prevalence of unemployment is usually measured using the _____, which is defined as the percentage of those in the labor force who are unemployed. The _____ is also used in economic studies and economic indexes such as the United States' Conference Board's Index of Leading Indicators as a measure of the state of the macroeconomics.

    a. ACCRA Cost of Living Index
    b. ACEA agreement
    c. AD-IA Model
    d. Unemployment rate

57. In economics, a _____ is a mechanism that allows people to easily buy and sell (trade) financial securities (such as stocks and bonds), commodities (such as precious metals or agricultural goods), and other fungible items of value at low transaction costs and at prices that reflect the efficient-market hypothesis.

_____s have evolved significantly over several hundred years and are undergoing constant innovation to improve liquidity.

Both general markets (where many commodities are traded) and specialized markets (where only one commodity is traded) exist.

   a. Noise trader
   c. Market anomaly
   b. Convertible arbitrage
   d. Financial market

58. In economics, the term _____ of income or _____ refers to a simple economic model which describes the reciprocal circulation of income between producers and consumers. In the _____ model, the inter-dependent entities of producer and consumer are referred to as 'firms' and 'households' respectively and provide each other with factors in order to facilitate the flow of income. Firms provide consumers with goods and services in exchange for consumer expenditure and 'factors of production' from households.
   a. 1921 recession
   c. Circular flow
   b. 130-30 fund
   d. 100-year flood

59. _____ refers to the objective and subjective components of the believability of a source or message.

Traditionally, _____ has two key components: trustworthiness and expertise, which both have objective and subjective components. Trustworthiness is a based more on subjective factors, but can include objective measurements such as established reliability.

   a. 130-30 fund
   c. 100-year flood
   b. 1921 recession
   d. Credibility

60. _____ is monetary policy that seeks to increase the size of the money supply. In most nations, monetary policy is controlled by either a central bank or a finance ministry

Neoclassical and Keynesian economics significantly differ on the effects and effectiveness of monetary policy on influencing the real economy; there is no clear consensus on how monetary policy affects real economic variables (aggregate output or income, employment.) Both economic schools accept that monetary policy affects monetary variables (price levels, interest rates.)

   a. Expansionary monetary policy
   c. ACEA agreement
   b. ACCRA Cost of Living Index
   d. AD-IA Model

61. A _____, reserve bank, or monetary authority is the entity responsible for the monetary policy of a country or of a group of member states. It is a bank that can lend money to other banks in times of need. Its primary responsibility is to maintain the stability of the national currency and money supply, but more active duties include controlling subsidized-loan interest rates, and acting as a lender of last resort to the banking sector during times of financial crisis (private banks often being integral to the national financial system.)

Chapter 13. Stabilization Policy

a. 1921 recession
b. 130-30 fund
c. 100-year flood
d. Central bank

62. In economics, _____ describes a situation where a decision-maker's preferences change over time, such that what is preferred at one point in time is inconsistent with what is preferred at another point in time. It is often easiest to think about preferences over time in this context by thinking of decision-makers as being made up of many different 'selves', with each self representing the decision-maker at a different point in time. So, for example, there is my today self, my tomorrow self, my next Tuesday self, my year from now self, etc.
   a. Graph continuous
   b. Dynamic inconsistency
   c. Bondareva-Shapley theorem
   d. Cheap talk

63. The _____ or gross domestic income (GDI), a basic measure of an economy's economic performance, is the market value of all final goods and services produced within the borders of a nation in a year. _____ can be defined in three ways, all of which are conceptually identical. First, it is equal to the total expenditures for all final goods and services produced within the country in a stipulated period of time (usually a 365-day year.)
   a. Monopolistic competition
   b. Countercyclical
   c. Gross domestic product
   d. Market structure

64. In economics, _____ refers to the highest level of real Gross Domestic Product output that can be sustained over the long term. The existence of a limit is due to natural and institutional constraints. If actual GDP rises and stays above _____, then (in the absence of wage and price controls) inflation tends to increase as demand exceeds supply.
   a. Fundamental psychological law
   b. Potential output
   c. Monetary policy reaction function
   d. Monetary conditions index

65. An _____, in economics, is the amount by which the real Gross domestic product exceeds potential GDP. The real GDP is also known as GDP 'adjusted for inflation', 'constant prices' GDP or 'constant dollar' GDP, because it measures the aggregate output in a country's income accounts in a given year, expressed in base-year prices. On the other hand, the potential GDP is the quantity of real GDP when a country's economy is at full-employment.
   a. AD-IA Model
   b. ACEA agreement
   c. ACCRA Cost of Living Index
   d. Inflationary gap

66. In business and accounting, _____ are everything of value that is owned by a person or company. It is a claim on the property your income of a borrower. The balance sheet of a firm records the monetary value of the _____ owned by the firm.
   a. Assets
   b. ACEA agreement
   c. Amortization schedule
   d. ACCRA Cost of Living Index

67. _____ is the increase in the amount of the goods and services produced by an economy over time. It is conventionally measured as the percent rate of increase in real gross domestic product, or real GDP. Growth is usually calculated in real terms, i.e. inflation-adjusted terms, in order to net out the effect of inflation on the price of the goods and services produced.
   a. ACCRA Cost of Living Index
   b. AD-IA Model
   c. ACEA agreement
   d. Economic growth

68. The term _____ is applied broadly to a variety of situations in which some financial institutions or assets suddenly lose a large part of their value. In the 19th and early 20th centuries, many financial crises were associated with banking panics, and many recessions coincided with these panics. Other situations that are often called financial crises include stock market crashes and the bursting of other financial bubbles, currency crises, and sovereign defaults.

   a. Co-operative economics
   b. Macroeconomics
   c. Financial crisis
   d. Market failure

69. A _____ is an institution willing to extend credit when no one else will.

Originally the term referred to a reserve financial institution that secured other banks or eligible institutions, as a last resort; most often the central bank of a country. The purpose of this loan and lender is to prevent the collapse of institutions that are experiencing financial difficulty, most often near collapse.

   a. Transactional account
   b. Time deposit
   c. Capital requirement
   d. Lender of last resort

70. A _____ occurs when a bank is unable to meet its obligations to its depositors or other creditors. More specifically, a bank fails economically when the market value of its assets declines to a value that is less than the market value of its liabilities. As such, the bank is unable to fulfill the demands of all of its depositors on time.

   a. Lombard Club
   b. Transactional account
   c. Concentration account
   d. Bank failure

71. The _____ consists of a number of economic theories which describe the nature of the firm, company including its existence, its behaviour, and its relationship with the market.

In simplified terms, the _____ aims to answer these questions:

   1. Existence - why do firms emerge, why are not all transactions in the economy mediated over the market?
   2. Boundaries - why the boundary between firms and the market is located exactly there? Which transactions are performed internally and which are negotiated on the market?
   3. Organization - why are firms structured in such specific way? What is the interplay of formal and informal relationships?

Despite looking simple, these questions are not answered by the established economic theory, which usually views firms as given, and treats them as black boxes without any internal structure.

The First World War period saw a change of emphasis in economic theory away from industry-level analysis which mainly included analysing markets to analysis at the level of the firm, as it became increasingly clear that perfect competition was no longer an adequate model of how firms behaved. Economic theory till then had focussed on trying to understand markets alone and there had been little study on understanding why firms or organisations exist.

   a. Policy Ineffectiveness Proposition
   b. Technology gap
   c. Khazzoom-Brookes postulate
   d. Theory of the firm

72. The _____ is a United States government corporation created by the Glass-Steagall Act of 1933. It provides deposit insurance, which guarantees the safety of deposits in member banks, currently up to $250,000 per depositor per bank. Funds in non-interest bearing transaction accounts are fully insured, with no limit, under the temporary Transaction Account Guarantee Program.
   a. Federal Deposit Insurance Corporation
   b. Foreign direct investment
   c. Great Leap Forward
   d. Luxembourg Income Study

73. _____ is the prospect that a party insulated from risk may behave differently from the way it would behave if it were fully exposed to the risk. In insurance, _____ that occurs without conscious or malicious action is called morale hazard.

   _____ is related to information asymmetry, a situation in which one party in a transaction has more information than another.

   a. 1921 recession
   b. 130-30 fund
   c. 100-year flood
   d. Moral hazard

74. _____, often referred to by his initials _____, was the 32nd President of the United States. He was a central figure of the 20th century during a time of worldwide economic crisis and world war. Elected to four terms in office, he served from 1933 to 1945 and is the only U.S. president to have served more than two terms.
   a. Adolph Fischer
   b. Adolf Hitler
   c. Franklin Delano Roosevelt
   d. Adam Smith

Chapter 14. Budget Balance, National Debt, and Investment

1. The term _____ refers to government debt, expenditures and revenues, or to finance (particularly financial revenue) in general.

    - _____ deficit is the budget deficit of federal or local government
    - _____ policy is the discretionary spending of governments. Contrasts with monetary policy.
    - _____ year and _____ quarter are reporting periods for firms and other agencies.

    a. Drawdown
    b. Bucket shop
    c. Procter ' Gamble
    d. Fiscal

2. In economics, _____ is the use of government spending and revenue collection to influence the economy.

    _____ can be contrasted with the other main type of economic policy, monetary policy, which attempts to stabilize the economy by controlling interest rates and the supply of money. The two main instruments of _____ are government spending and taxation.

    a. 100-year flood
    b. Fiscal policy
    c. Sustainable investment rule
    d. Fiscalism

3. If the government intervenes by implementing, for example, a tax or a subsidy, then the graph of supply and demand becomes more complicated and will also include an area that represents _____.

    Combined, the consumer surplus, the producer surplus, and the _____ make up the social surplus or the total surplus. Total surplus is the primary measure used in welfare economics to evaluate the efficiency of a proposed policy.

    a. Marginal revenue
    b. Long term
    c. Customer equity
    d. Government surplus

4. _____ is the process by which the government, central bank (ii) availability of money, and (iii) cost of money or rate of interest, in order to attain a set of objectives oriented towards the growth and stability of the economy. Monetary theory provides insight into how to craft optimal _____.

    _____ is referred to as either being an expansionary policy where an expansionary policy increases the total supply of money in the economy, and a contractionary policy decreases the total money supply.

    a. 1921 recession
    b. 130-30 fund
    c. 100-year flood
    d. Monetary policy

5. The _____ is the upward-sloping relationship between the inflation rate and the unemployment rate. When the inflation rate rises, a central bank wishing to fight inflation will raise interest rates to reduce output and thus increase the unemployment rate. The _____ is a function of the Taylor Rule, the Investment-Spending Curve (IS Curve) and Okun's Law

    The _____ has the equation:

Chapter 14. Budget Balance, National Debt, and Investment

$u = u_0 + \Phi(\pi - \pi t)$

Where Φ is a parameter that tells us how much unemployment rises when the central bank raises the real interest rate r because it thinks that inflation is too high and needs to be reduced.

a. Secular basis
b. Marginal propensity to import
c. Value added
d. Monetary policy reaction function

6. _____, is an economic theory that suggests consumers internalise the government's budget constraint and thus the timing of any tax change does not affect their change in spending. Consequently, _____ suggests that it does not matter whether a government finances its spending with debt or a tax increase, the effect on total level of demand in an economy will be the same. It was proposed, and then rejected, by the 19th-century economist David Ricardo.

a. Ricardian equivalence
b. Municipalization
c. Quasi-market
d. Social discount rate

7. A _____ is a package or set of measures introduced to stabilise a financial system or economy. The term can refer to policies in two distinct sets of circumstances: business cycle stabilization and crisis stabilization.

Stabilization can refer to correcting the normal behavior of the business cycle.

a. Volunteers for Economic Growth Alliance
b. New International Economic Order
c. Stabilization policy
d. Capacity Development

8. _____ is that which is owed; usually referencing assets owed, but the term can also cover moral obligations and other interactions not requiring money. In the case of assets, _____ is a means of using future purchasing power in the present before a summation has been earned. Some companies and corporations use _____ as a part of their overall corporate finance strategy.

a. Hard money loan
b. Debenture
c. Collateral Management
d. Debt

9. The term financial crisis is applied broadly to a variety of situations in which some financial institutions or assets suddenly lose a large part of their value. In the 19th and early 20th centuries, many _____ were associated with banking panics, and many recessions coincided with these panics. Other situations that are often called _____ include stock market crashes and the bursting of other financial bubbles, currency crises, and sovereign defaults.

a. General equilibrium
b. Georgism
c. Microeconomics
d. Financial crises

10. _____ is a fee paid on borrowed assets. It is the price paid for the use of borrowed money, or, money earned by deposited funds. Assets that are sometimes lent with _____ include money, shares, consumer goods through hire purchase, major assets such as aircraft, and even entire factories in finance lease arrangements.

a. Insolvency
b. Internal debt
c. Asset protection
d. Interest

11. In economics, _____ is the total demand for final goods and services in the economy (Y) at a given time and price level. It is the amount of goods and services in the economy that will be purchased at all possible price levels. This is the demand for the gross domestic product of a country when inventory levels are static.
   a. Aggregate expenditure
   b. Aggregate supply
   c. Aggregation problem
   d. Aggregate demand

12. _____ is a broad label that refers to any individuals or households that use goods and services generated within the economy. The concept of a _____ is used in different contexts, so that the usage and significance of the term may vary.

Typically when business people and economists talk of _____s they are talking about person as _____, an aggregated commodity item with little individuality other than that expressed in the buy/not-buy decision.

   a. Consumer
   b. 100-year flood
   c. 1921 recession
   d. 130-30 fund

13. _____ is the degree of optimism that consumers feel about the overall state of the economy and their personal financial situation. How confident people feel about stability of their incomes determines their spending activity and therefore serves as one of the key indicators for the overall shape of the economy. In essence, if _____ is higher, consumers are making more purchases, boosting the economic expansion.
   a. Consumer behavior
   b. Communal marketing
   c. Rule Developing Experimentation
   d. Consumer confidence

14. The _____ is the central banking system of the United States. Created in 1913 by the enactment of the Federal Reserve Act (signed by Woodrow Wilson), it is a quasi-public and quasi-private (government entity with private components) banking system that comprises (1) the presidentially appointed Board of Governors of the _____ in Washington, D.C.; (2) the Federal Open Market Committee; (3) twelve regional Federal Reserve Banks located in major cities throughout the nation acting as fiscal agents for the U.S. Treasury, each with its own nine-member board of directors; (4) numerous other private U.S. member banks, which subscribe to required amounts of non-transferable stock in their regional Federal Reserve Banks; and (5) various advisory councils. Since February 2006, Ben Bernanke has served as the Chairman of the Board of Governors of the _____.
   a. Federal Reserve System Open Market Account
   b. Term auction facility
   c. Monetary Policy Report to the Congress
   d. Federal Reserve System

15. A _____ is a legal document that is often passed by the legislature, and approved by the chief executive-or president. For example, only certain types of revenue may be imposed and collected. Property tax is frequently the basis for municipal and county revenues, while sales tax and/or income tax are the basis for state revenues, and income tax and corporate tax are the basis for national revenues.
   a. Right-financing
   b. Structural deficit
   c. Government budget
   d. Lump-sum tax

Chapter 14. Budget Balance, National Debt, and Investment

16. The _____ was a worldwide economic downturn starting in most places in 1929 and ending at different times in the 1930s or early 1940s for different countries. It was the largest and most important economic depression in the 20th century, and is used in the 21st century as an example of how far the world's economy can fall. The _____ originated in the United States; historians most often use as a starting date the stock market crash on October 29, 1929, known as Black Tuesday.

a. Jarrow March
b. Wall Street Crash of 1929
c. British Empire Economic Conference
d. Great Depression

17. In economics, an _____ is the amount of time it takes for a government or a central bank to respond to a shock in the economy. It is a delay in implementing monetary policy. Its converse is outside lag (the amount of time before an action by a government or a central bank affects an economy.) _____ comprises recognition lag, the time taken to recognize the shock, and decision lag (or implementation lag), the time taken to decide a response.

a. Inside lag
b. Ostrich strategy
c. Overnight trade
d. Employee experience management

18. The term _____ refers to economy-wide fluctuations in production or economic activity over several months or years. These fluctuations occur around a long-term growth trend, and typically involve shifts over time between periods of relatively rapid economic growth (expansion or boom), and periods of relative stagnation or decline (contraction or recession.)

These fluctuations are often measured using the growth rate of real gross domestic product.

a. Nominal value
b. Consumer theory
c. Tobit model
d. Business cycle

19. Economics:

- _____, the desire to own something and the ability to pay for it
- _____ curve, a graphic representation of a _____ schedule
- _____ deposit, the money in checking accounts
- _____ pull theory, the theory that inflation occurs when _____ for goods and services exceeds existing supplies
- _____ schedule, a table that lists the quantity of a good a person will buy it each different price
- _____ side economics, the school of economics at believes government spending and tax cuts open economy by raising _____

a. Production
b. Variability
c. McKesson ' Robbins scandal
d. Demand

20. _____s is the social science that studies the production, distribution, and consumption of goods and services. The term _____s comes from the Ancient Greek oá¼°κονομῖα from oá¼¶κος (oikos, 'house') + vῐΌέμος (nomos, 'custom' or 'law'), hence 'rules of the house(hold)'. Current _____ models developed out of the broader field of political economy in the late 19th century, owing to a desire to use an empirical approach more akin to the physical sciences.

a. Economic
b. Energy economics
c. Inflation
d. Opportunity cost

21. _____ refers to the actions that governments take in the economic field. It covers the systems for setting interest rates and government deficit as well as the labour market, national ownership, and many other areas of government.

Such policies are often influenced by international institutions like the International Monetary Fund or World Bank as well as political beliefs and the consequent policies of parties.

a. AD-IA Model
b. Economic policy
c. ACEA agreement
d. ACCRA Cost of Living Index

22. The _____ or gross domestic income (GDI), a basic measure of an economy's economic performance, is the market value of all final goods and services produced within the borders of a nation in a year. _____ can be defined in three ways, all of which are conceptually identical. First, it is equal to the total expenditures for all final goods and services produced within the country in a stipulated period of time (usually a 365-day year.)

a. Market structure
b. Gross domestic product
c. Countercyclical
d. Monopolistic competition

23. An _____, in economics, is the amount by which the real Gross domestic product exceeds potential GDP. The real GDP is also known as GDP 'adjusted for inflation', 'constant prices' GDP or 'constant dollar' GDP, because it measures the aggregate output in a country's income accounts in a given year, expressed in base-year prices. On the other hand, the potential GDP is the quantity of real GDP when a country's economy is at full-employment.

a. ACEA agreement
b. ACCRA Cost of Living Index
c. AD-IA Model
d. Inflationary gap

24. _____, 1st Baron Keynes was a renowned economist from Britain whose many ideas on economic and political theories as well as on many governments' monetary policies influenced America. He advocated a government that played an active role in the lives of people regarding business, economy, etc. In this role, the government would use fiscal measures to reduce the consequences of recessions, economic depressions and booms.

a. John Maynard Keynes
b. Adolf Hitler
c. Adam Smith
d. Adolph Fischer

25. In economics, _____ is a rise in the general level of prices of goods and services in an economy over a period of time. When the general price level rises, each unit of currency buys fewer goods and services; consequently, _____ is also a decline in the real value of money--a loss of purchasing power in the medium of exchange which is also the monetary unit of account in the economy. A chief measure of general price-level _____ is the general _____ rate, which is the percentage change in a general price index (normally the Consumer Price Index) over time.

a. Opportunity cost
b. Inflation
c. Energy economics
d. Economic

Chapter 14. Budget Balance, National Debt, and Investment

26. _____ or amortisation is the process of increasing an amount over a period of time. The word comes from Middle English amortisen to kill, alienate in mortmain, from Anglo-French amorteser, alteration of amortir, from Vulgar Latin admortire to kill, from Latin ad- + mort-, mors death. Particular instances of the term include:

- _____, the allocation of a lump sum amount to different time periods, particularly for loans and other forms of finance, including related interest or other finance charges.
  - _____ schedule, a table detailing each periodic payment on a loan (typically a mortgage), as generated by an _____ calculator.
  - Negative _____, an _____ schedule where the loan amount actually increases through not paying the full interest
- Amortized analysis, analyzing the execution cost of algorithms over a sequence of operations.
- _____ of capital expenditures of certain assets under accounting rules, particularly intangible assets, in a manner analogous to depreciation.
- _____ (tax law)

_____ is also used in the context of zoning regulations and describes the time in which a property owner has to relocate when the property's use constitutes a preexisting nonconforming use under zoning regulations.

a. Amortization
b. Augmentation
c. Economic miracle
d. Oslo Agreements

27. _____ is the planning process used to determine whether a firm's long term investments such as new machinery, replacement machinery, new plants, new products, and research development projects are worth pursuing. It is budget for major capital, or investment, expenditures.

Many formal methods are used in _____, including the techniques such as

- Net present value
- Profitability index
- Internal rate of return
- Modified Internal Rate of Return
- Equivalent annuity

These methods use the incremental cash flows from each potential investment, or project. Techniques based on accounting earnings and accounting rules are sometimes used - though economists consider this to be improper - such as the accounting rate of return, and 'return on investment.' Simplified and hybrid methods are used as well, such as payback period and discounted payback period.

a. Preferred stock
b. Capital budgeting
c. Voting interest
d. Participating preferred stock

28. _____ is a method of accounting for redistribution of lifetime tax burdens across generations from social insurance, including social security and social health insurance. It goes beyond conventional government budget measures, such the national debt and budget deficits, by accounting for projected lifetime taxes per capita net of transfers, which may not be reflected in a pay-as-you-go system of social-insurance accounting. The latter includes only current taxes for retirees less current outlays.

Chapter 14. Budget Balance, National Debt, and Investment

a. 1921 recession
b. Generational accounting
c. 100-year flood
d. 130-30 fund

29. _____ is a common concept in economics, and gives rise to derived concepts such as consumer debt. Generally _____ is defined by opposition to production. But the precise definition can vary because different schools of economists define production quite differently.
   a. Cash or share options
   b. Federal Reserve Bank Notes
   c. Foreclosure data providers
   d. Consumption

30. The accounting equation relates assets, _____, and owner's equity:

   Assets = _____ + Owner's Equity

The accounting equation is the mathematical structure of the balance sheet.

The Australian Accounting Research Foundation defines _____ as: 'future sacrifice of economic benefits that the entity is presently obliged to make to other entities as a result of past transactions and other past events.'

Probably the most accepted accounting definition of liability is the one used by the International Accounting Standards Board (IASB.) The following is a quotation from IFRS Framework:

A liability is a present obligation of the enterprise arising from past events, the settlement of which is expected to result in an outflow from the enterprise of resources embodying economic benefits

-

Regulations as to the recognition of _____ are different all over the world, but are roughly similar to those of the IASB.

   a. Community property
   b. Liabilities
   c. Coase theorem
   d. Competition law theory

31. From a Keynesian point of view, a _____ in the public sector is achieved when the government equates the revenues with expenditure over the business cycles. In other words, a government's budget is balanced if its income is equal to its expenditure. It is a budget in which revenues are equal to spending.
   a. Balanced budget
   b. Budget support
   c. Budget crisis
   d. Budget theory

32. In economic models, the _____ time frame assumes no fixed factors of production. Firms can enter or leave the marketplace, and the cost (and availability) of land, labor, raw materials, and capital goods can be assumed to vary. In contrast, in the short-run time frame, certain factors are assumed to be fixed, because there is not sufficient time for them to change.
   a. Diseconomies of scale
   b. Price/performance ratio
   c. Productivity world
   d. Long-run

Chapter 14. Budget Balance, National Debt, and Investment

33. _____, in general terms, is the ability to maintain balance of a certain process or state in any system. It is now most frequently used in connection with biological and human systems. In an ecological context, _____ can be defined as the ability of an ecosystem to maintain ecological processes, functions, biodiversity and productivity into the future.
   a. Adam Smith
   b. Adolph Fischer
   c. Sustainability
   d. Adolf Hitler

34. In statistics, a _____ is a value that allows data to be measured over time in terms of some base period ussually through a price index in order to distinguish between changes in the money value of GNP which result from a change in prices and those which result from a change in physical output. It is the measure of the price level for some quantity. A _____ serves as a price index in which the effects of inflation are nulled.
   a. Deflator
   b. Blanket order
   c. Contingent employment
   d. Market microstructure

35. In economics, particularly macroeconomics, various _____ can be calculated. The most commonly used ratio is the Government debt divided by the Gross Domestic Product (GDP), which reflects the government's finances, while another common ratio is the total debt to GDP, which reflects the nation as a whole's finance.

It is generally expressed as a percentage, but properly, has units of years, as below.

   a. 130-30 fund
   b. 1921 recession
   c. 100-year flood
   d. Debt-to-GDP ratio

36. A _____ is an expression that compares quantities relative to each other. The most common examples involve two quantities, but any number of quantities can be compared. _____s are represented mathematically by separating each quantity with a colon, for example the _____ 2:3, which is read as the _____ 'two to three'.
   a. Y-intercept
   b. 130-30 fund
   c. 100-year flood
   d. Ratio

37. In economics, _____ is the transfer of income, wealth or property from some individuals to others.

One premise of _____ is that money should be distributed to benefit the poorer members of society, and that the rich have an obligation to assist the poor, thus creating a more financially egalitarian society. Another argument is that the rich exploit the poor or otherwise gain unfair benefits.

   a. 100-year flood
   b. Redistribution
   c. 1921 recession
   d. 130-30 fund

38. _____ is the increase in the amount of the goods and services produced by an economy over time. It is conventionally measured as the percent rate of increase in real gross domestic product, or real GDP. Growth is usually calculated in real terms, i.e. inflation-adjusted terms, in order to net out the effect of inflation on the price of the goods and services produced.
   a. Economic growth
   b. AD-IA Model
   c. ACCRA Cost of Living Index
   d. ACEA agreement

Chapter 14. Budget Balance, National Debt, and Investment

39. _____ was the first United States Secretary of the Treasury, a Founding Father, economist, and political philosopher. He led calls for the Philadelphia Convention, was one of America's first Constitutional lawyers, and cowrote the Federalist Papers, a primary source for Constitutional interpretation.

Born on the British West Indian island of Nevis, Hamilton was educated in the Thirteen Colonies.

a. Economic impact of immigration
b. American exceptionalism
c. Adam Smith
d. Alexander Hamilton

40. A _____ is:

- Rewrite _____, in generative grammar and computer science
- Standardization, a formal and widely-accepted statement, fact, definition, or qualification
- Operation, a determinate _____ for performing a mathematical operation and obtaining a certain result (Mathematics, Logic)
    - Unary operation
    - Binary operation
- _____ of inference, a function from sets of formulae to formulae (Mathematics, Logic)
- _____ of thumb, principle with broad application that is not intended to be strictly accurate or reliable for every situation. Also often simply referred to as a _____
- Moral, an atomic element of a moral code for guiding choices in human behavior
- Heuristic, a quantized '_____' which shows a tendency or probability for successful function
- A regulation, as in sports
- A Production _____, as in computer science
- Procedural law, a _____ set governing the application of laws to cases
    - A law, which may informally be called a '_____'
    - A court ruling, a decision by a court
- In the U.S. Government, a regulation mandated by Congress, but written or expanded upon by the Executive Branch.
- Norm (sociology), an informal but widely accepted _____, concept, truth, definition, or qualification (social norms, legal norms, coding norms)
- Norm (philosophy), a kind of sentence or a reason to act, feel or believe
- 'Rulership' is the concept of governance by a government:
    - Military _____, governance by a military body
    - Monastic _____, a collection of precepts that guides the life of monks or nuns in a religious order where the superior holds the place of Christ
- Slide _____

- '_____,' a song by Ayumi Hamasaki
- '_____,' a song by rapper Nas
- '_____s,' an album by the band The Whitest Boy Alive
- _____s: Pyaar Ka Superhit Formula, a 2003 Bollywood film
- ruler, an instrument for measuring lengths
- _____, a component of an astrolabe, circumferator or similar instrument
- The _____s, a bestselling self-help book
- _____ Project (Run Up-to-date Linux Everywhere), a project that aims to use up-to-date Linux software on old PCs
- _____ engine, a software system that helps managing business _____s
- Ja _____, a hip hop artist
    - R.U.L.E., a 2005 greatest hits album by rapper Ja _____
- '_____s,' a KMFDM song

a. Rule
b. Procter ' Gamble
c. Technocracy
d. Demand

Chapter 14. Budget Balance, National Debt, and Investment

41. _____ is a term used in accounting relating to the increase in value of an asset. In this sense it is the reverse of depreciation, which measures the fall in value of assets over their normal life-time.

_____ is a rise of a currency in a floating exchange rate.

a. ACCRA Cost of Living Index
b. Appreciation
c. AD-IA Model
d. ACEA agreement

42. An economic and _____ is a single market with a common currency. It is to be distinguished from a mere currency union, which does not involve a single market. This is the fifth stage of economic integration.

a. Free trade zone
b. Commercial invoice
c. Customs union
d. Monetary union

43. In economics, a _____ is a monetary-policy rule that stipulates how much the central bank would or should change the nominal interest rate in response to divergences of actual inflation rates from target inflation rates and of actual Gross Domestic Product (GDP) from potential GDP. It was first proposed by the by U.S. economist John B. Taylor in 1993. The rule can be written as follows:

$$i_t = \pi_t + r_t^* + a_\pi(\pi_t - \pi_t^*) + a_y(y_t - \bar{y}_t).$$

In this equation, i_t is the target short-term nominal interest rate (e.g. the federal funds rate in the US), π_t is the rate of inflation as measured by the GDP deflator, π_t^* is the desired rate of inflation, r_t^* is the assumed equilibrium real interest rate, y_t is the logarithm of real GDP, and $\bar{y}_t$ is the logarithm of potential output, as determined by a linear trend.

a. Taylor rule
b. Federal Reserve Banks
c. Fed Funds Probability
d. Term Securities Lending Facility

44. The balance of trade (or net exports, sometimes symbolized as NX) is the difference between the monetary value of exports and imports in an economy over a certain period of time. It is the relationship between a nation's imports and exports. A favorable balance of trade is known as a trade surplus and consists of exporting more than is imported; an unfavorable balance of trade is known as a _____ or, informally, a trade gap.

a. Computational economic
b. Complementary asset
c. Demographics of India
d. Trade deficit

45. An _____ is the price a borrower pays for the use of money they do not own, for instance a small company might borrow from a bank to kick start their business, and the return a lender receives for deferring the use of funds, by lending it to the borrower. _____s are normally expressed as a percentage rate over the period of one year.

_____s targets are also a vital tool of monetary policy and are used to control variables like investment, inflation, and unemployment.

a. Arrow-Debreu model
b. Enterprise value
c. ACCRA Cost of Living Index
d. Interest rate

Chapter 14. Budget Balance, National Debt, and Investment

46. _____ and Keynesian Theory) is a macroeconomic theory based on the ideas of 20th-century British economist John Maynard Keynes. _____ argues that private sector decisions sometimes lead to inefficient macroeconomic outcomes and therefore advocates active policy responses by the public sector, including monetary policy actions by the central bank and fiscal policy actions by the government to stabilize output over the business cycle.

The theories forming the basis of _____ were first presented in The General Theory of Employment, Interest and Money, published in 1936.

- a. Deflation
- b. Rational choice theory
- c. Market failure
- d. Keynesian economics

47. To _____ is to impose a financial charge or other levy upon a taxpayer by a state or the functional equivalent of a state.

_____es are also imposed by many subnational entities. _____es consist of direct _____ or indirect _____, and may be paid in money or as its labour equivalent (often but not always unpaid.)

- a. 130-30 fund
- b. 100-year flood
- c. 1921 recession
- d. Tax

48. A _____ is a set of exclusive rights granted by a state to an inventor or his assignee for a limited period of time in exchange for a disclosure of an invention.

The procedure for granting _____s, the requirements placed on the _____ee and the extent of the exclusive rights vary widely between countries according to national laws and international agreements. Typically, however, a _____ application must include one or more claims defining the invention which must be new, inventive, and useful or industrially applicable.

- a. Long service leave
- b. Patent
- c. Bank regulation
- d. Bona fide occupational qualification

49. _____ is a macroeconomic measure of the size of an economy adjusted for price changes and inflation. It measures in constant prices the output of final goods and services and incomes within an economy. The formula for its definition is [(Nominal GDP)/(GDP deflator)] x 100, however, it is not calculated in this way.

- a. Real Gross Domestic Product
- b. Gross world product
- c. Bureau of Labor Statistics
- d. TED spread

50. A _____ is a reduction in taxes. Economic stimulus via _____s, along with interest rate intervention and deficit spending, are one of the central tenets of Keynesian economics.

The immediate effects of a _____ are, generally, a decrease in the real income of the government and an increase in the real income of those whose tax rate has been lowered.

- a. Direct taxes
- b. Tax cut
- c. Withholding tax
- d. Popiwek

Chapter 15. International Economic Policy

1. The _____ of monetary management established the rules for commercial and financial relations among the world's major industrial states in the mid 20th Century. The _____ was the first example of a fully negotiated monetary order intended to govern monetary relations among independent nation-states.

Preparing to rebuild the international economic system as World War II was still raging, 730 delegates from all 44 Allied nations gathered at the Mount Washington Hotel in Bretton Woods, New Hampshire, United States, for the United Nations Monetary and Financial Conference.

   a. 130-30 fund
   b. 1921 recession
   c. Bretton Woods system
   d. 100-year flood

2. A _____, sometimes called a pegged exchange rate, is a type of exchange rate regime wherein a currency's value is matched to the value of another single currency or to a basket of other currencies such as gold.

A _____ is usually used to stabilize the value of a currency, vis-a-vis the currency it is pegged to. This facilitates trade and investments between the two countries, and is especially useful for small economies where external trade forms a large part of their GDP.

   a. Fixed exchange rate
   b. Law of supply
   c. Monetary economics
   d. Leading indicators

3. A _____ or a flexible exchange rate is a type of exchange rate regime wherein a currency's value is allowed to fluctuate according to the foreign exchange market. A currency that uses a _____ is known as a floating currency. The opposite of a _____ is a fixed exchange rate.
   a. Trade Weighted US dollar Index
   b. Floating currency
   c. Foreign exchange market
   d. Floating exchange rate

4. The _____ is a monetary system in which a region's common medium of exchange are paper notes that are normally freely convertible into pre-set, fixed quantities of gold. The _____ is not currently used by any government, having been replaced completely by fiat currency. Gold certificates were used as paper currency in the United States from 1882 to 1933, these certificates were freely convertable into gold coins.

In the 1790s Britain suffered a massive shortage of silver coinage and ceased to mint larger silver coins.

   a. 1921 recession
   b. 130-30 fund
   c. 100-year flood
   d. Gold standard

5. _____ is exchange of capital, goods, and services across international borders or territories. In most countries, it represents a significant share of gross domestic product (GDP.) While _____ has been present throughout much of history , its economic, social, and political importance has been on the rise in recent centuries.
   a. Import license
   b. Intra-industry trade
   c. Incoterms
   d. International trade

6. In finance, the _____s between two currencies specifies how much one currency is worth in terms of the other. It is the value of a foreign natione;s currency in terms of the home natione;s currency. For example an _____ of 102 Japanese yen to the United States dollar means that JPY 102 is worth the same as USD 1.

Chapter 15. International Economic Policy

a. Interbank market
c. ACEA agreement
b. Exchange rate
d. ACCRA Cost of Living Index

7. _____ is a term used in accounting relating to the increase in value of an asset. In this sense it is the reverse of depreciation, which measures the fall in value of assets over their normal life-time.

_____ is a rise of a currency in a floating exchange rate.

a. ACEA agreement
c. AD-IA Model
b. ACCRA Cost of Living Index
d. Appreciation

8. In economics and finance, _____ is the practice of taking advantage of a price differential between two or more markets: striking a combination of matching deals that capitalize upon the imbalance, the profit being the difference between the market prices. When used by academics, an _____ is a transaction that involves no negative cash flow at any probabilistic or temporal state and a positive cash flow in at least one state; in simple terms, a risk-free profit. A person who engages in _____ is called an arbitrageur--such as a bank or brokerage firm.

a. Options Price Reporting Authority
c. Alternext
b. Electronic trading
d. Arbitrage

9. _____ is money accepted for exchange of goods in an economy. The prevalence of one money over another arises, usually, when a government designates through decrees that the government shall accept only particular notes and coins in payment for taxes. Typically, money of _____ consists of stamped coins and minted paper bills.

a. Security thread
c. Totnes pound
b. Local currency
d. Currency

10. _____ is a term used in accounting, economics and finance to spread the cost of an asset over the span of several years.

In simple words we can say that _____ is the reduction in the value of an asset due to usage, passage of time, wear and tear, technological outdating or obsolescence, depletion, inadequacy, rot, rust, decay or other such factors.

In accounting, _____ is a term used to describe any method of attributing the historical or purchase cost of an asset across its useful life, roughly corresponding to normal wear and tear.

a. Salvage value
c. Net income per employee
b. Historical cost
d. Depreciation

11. The _____ is where currency trading takes place. It is where banks and other official institutions facilitate the buying and selling of foreign currencies. FX transactions typically involve one party purchasing a quantity of one currency in exchange for paying a quantity of another.

a. Covered interest arbitrage
c. Currency swap
b. Floating currency
d. Foreign exchange market

12. _____ is monetary policy that seeks to reduce the size of the money supply. They are fiscal policies, like lower spending and higher taxes, that reduce economic growth. In most nations, monetary policy is controlled by either a central bank or a finance ministry.

   a. Money creation
   b. Contractionary monetary policy
   c. Monetary policy of Sweden
   d. Shadow Open Market Committee

13. _____ is a reduction in the value of a currency with respect to other monetary units. In common modern usage, it specifically implies an official lowering of the value of a country's currency within a fixed exchange rate system, by which the monetary authority formally sets a new fixed rate with respect to a foreign reference currency. In contrast, (currency) depreciation is used for the unofficial decrease in the exchange rate in a floating exchange rate system.

   a. Texas redbacks
   b. Petrodollar recycling
   c. Devaluation
   d. Reserve currency

14. The _____ is the central banking system of the United States. Created in 1913 by the enactment of the Federal Reserve Act (signed by Woodrow Wilson), it is a quasi-public and quasi-private (government entity with private components) banking system that comprises (1) the presidentially appointed Board of Governors of the _____ in Washington, D.C.; (2) the Federal Open Market Committee; (3) twelve regional Federal Reserve Banks located in major cities throughout the nation acting as fiscal agents for the U.S. Treasury, each with its own nine-member board of directors; (4) numerous other private U.S. member banks, which subscribe to required amounts of non-transferable stock in their regional Federal Reserve Banks; and (5) various advisory councils. Since February 2006, Ben Bernanke has served as the Chairman of the Board of Governors of the _____.

   a. Federal Reserve System Open Market Account
   b. Monetary Policy Report to the Congress
   c. Term auction facility
   d. Federal Reserve System

15. _____ in a strict sense are only the foreign currency deposits and bonds held by central banks and monetary authorities. However, the term in popular usage commonly includes foreign exchange and gold, SDRs and IMF reserve positions. This broader figure is more readily available, but it is more accurately termed official international reserves or international reserves.

   a. Foreign exchange trading
   b. Foreign exchange market
   c. Currency swap
   d. Foreign exchange reserves

16. _____ is the process by which the government, central bank (ii) availability of money, and (iii) cost of money or rate of interest, in order to attain a set of objectives oriented towards the growth and stability of the economy. Monetary theory provides insight into how to craft optimal _____.

_____ is referred to as either being an expansionary policy where an expansionary policy increases the total supply of money in the economy, and a contractionary policy decreases the total money supply.

   a. Monetary policy
   b. 100-year flood
   c. 1921 recession
   d. 130-30 fund

17. In economics, an _____ is any good or commodity, transported from one country to another country in a legitimate fashion, typically for use in trade. _____ goods or services are provided to foreign consumers by domestic producers. _____ is an important part of international trade.

a. ACCRA Cost of Living Index
c. AD-IA Model
b. ACEA agreement
d. Export

18. The _____ was a worldwide economic downturn starting in most places in 1929 and ending at different times in the 1930s or early 1940s for different countries. It was the largest and most important economic depression in the 20th century, and is used in the 21st century as an example of how far the world's economy can fall. The _____ originated in the United States; historians most often use as a starting date the stock market crash on October 29, 1929, known as Black Tuesday.
   a. Jarrow March
   c. Great Depression
   b. Wall Street Crash of 1929
   d. British Empire Economic Conference

19. In economics, a _____ is a general slowdown in economic activity over a sustained period of time, or a business cycle contraction. During _____s, many macroeconomic indicators vary in a similar way. Production as measured by Gross Domestic Product (GDP), employment, investment spending, capacity utilization, household incomes and business profits all fall during _____s.
   a. Leading indicators
   c. Treasury View
   b. Recession
   d. Monetary economics

20. The _____ is an international organization that oversees the global financial system by following the macroeconomic policies of its member countries, in particular those with an impact on exchange rates and the balance of payments. It is an organization formed to stabilize international exchange rates and facilitate development. It also offers financial and technical assistance to its members, making it an international lender of last resort.
   a. Office of Thrift Supervision
   c. ACCRA Cost of Living Index
   b. ACEA agreement
   d. International Monetary Fund

21. _____, 1st Baron Keynes was a renowned economist from Britain whose many ideas on economic and political theories as well as on many governments' monetary policies influenced America. He advocated a government that played an active role in the lives of people regarding business, economy, etc. In this role, the government would use fiscal measures to reduce the consequences of recessions, economic depressions and booms.
   a. Adam Smith
   c. Adolph Fischer
   b. Adolf Hitler
   d. John Maynard Keynes

22. _____ means a rise of a price of goods or products. This term is specially used as _____ of a currency, where it means a rise of currency to the relation with a foreign currency in a fixed exchange rate. In floating exchange rate correct term would be appreciation.
   a. Death spiral financing
   c. Revaluation
   b. Legal monopoly
   d. Deglobalization

23. In economics, _____ is a rise in the general level of prices of goods and services in an economy over a period of time. When the general price level rises, each unit of currency buys fewer goods and services; consequently, _____ is also a decline in the real value of money--a loss of purchasing power in the medium of exchange which is also the monetary unit of account in the economy. A chief measure of general price-level _____ is the general _____ rate, which is the percentage change in a general price index (normally the Consumer Price Index) over time.
   a. Economic
   c. Energy economics
   b. Inflation
   d. Opportunity cost

24. A _____ secures the proper functioning of money by regulating economic agents, transaction types, and money supply.

_____s are traditionally formed by the policy decisions of individual governments and administrated as a domestic economic issue.

The current trend, however, is to use international trade and investment to alter the policy and legislation of individual governments.

    a. Netting
    b. Financial rand
    c. Consumer basket
    d. Monetary system

25. _____ is a phrase that may take on different meanings in different contexts.

In the language of crime, _____ refers to stolen currency that can easily be traced back to the crime, such as marked bills or new currency with consecutive serial numbers. It is also known as bait money.

    a. Comparative advantage
    b. Gravity model of trade
    c. Small open economy
    d. Hot money

26. The term _____ refers to economy-wide fluctuations in production or economic activity over several months or years. These fluctuations occur around a long-term growth trend, and typically involve shifts over time between periods of relatively rapid economic growth (expansion or boom), and periods of relative stagnation or decline (contraction or recession.)

These fluctuations are often measured using the growth rate of real gross domestic product.

    a. Tobit model
    b. Consumer theory
    c. Business cycle
    d. Nominal value

27. A _____, reserve bank, or monetary authority is the entity responsible for the monetary policy of a country or of a group of member states. It is a bank that can lend money to other banks in times of need. Its primary responsibility is to maintain the stability of the national currency and money supply, but more active duties include controlling subsidized-loan interest rates, and acting as a lender of last resort to the banking sector during times of financial crisis (private banks often being integral to the national financial system.)

    a. Central bank
    b. 100-year flood
    c. 1921 recession
    d. 130-30 fund

28. _____ is a fee paid on borrowed assets. It is the price paid for the use of borrowed money , or, money earned by deposited funds . Assets that are sometimes lent with _____ include money, shares, consumer goods through hire purchase, major assets such as aircraft, and even entire factories in finance lease arrangements.

    a. Internal debt
    b. Asset protection
    c. Interest
    d. Insolvency

29. An _____ is the price a borrower pays for the use of money they do not own, for instance a small company might borrow from a bank to kick start their business, and the return a lender receives for deferring the use of funds, by lending it to the borrower. _____s are normally expressed as a percentage rate over the period of one year.

_____s targets are also a vital tool of monetary policy and are used to control variables like investment, inflation, and unemployment.

    a. Interest rate
    b. ACCRA Cost of Living Index
    c. Enterprise value
    d. Arrow-Debreu model

30. In finance, _____ is a financial action that does not promise safety of the initial investment along with the return on the principal sum. _____ typically involves the lending of money or the purchase of assets, equity or debt but in a manner that has not been given thorough analysis or is deemed to have low margin of safety or a significant risk of the loss of the principal investment. The term, '_____,' which is formally defined as above in Graham and Dodd's 1934 text, Security Analysis, contrasts with the term 'investment,' which is a financial operation that, upon thorough analysis, promises safety of principal and a satisfactory return.

    a. Global Financial Centres Index
    b. Hybrid market
    c. Speculation
    d. Municipal Bond Arbitrage

31. The _____ is the upward-sloping relationship between the inflation rate and the unemployment rate. When the inflation rate rises, a central bank wishing to fight inflation will raise interest rates to reduce output and thus increase the unemployment rate. The _____ is a function of the Taylor Rule, the Investment-Spending Curve (IS Curve) and Okun's Law

The _____ has the equation:

$$u = u_0 + \Phi(\pi - \pi t)$$

Where Φ is a parameter that tells us how much unemployment rises when the central bank raises the real interest rate r because it thinks that inflation is too high and needs to be reduced.

    a. Marginal propensity to import
    b. Value added
    c. Secular basis
    d. Monetary policy reaction function

32. A _____ is a package or set of measures introduced to stabilise a financial system or economy. The term can refer to policies in two distinct sets of circumstances: business cycle stabilization and crisis stabilization.

Stabilization can refer to correcting the normal behavior of the business cycle.

    a. Volunteers for Economic Growth Alliance
    b. New International Economic Order
    c. Capacity Development
    d. Stabilization policy

33. The term financial crisis is applied broadly to a variety of situations in which some financial institutions or assets suddenly lose a large part of their value. In the 19th and early 20th centuries, many _____ were associated with banking panics, and many recessions coincided with these panics. Other situations that are often called _____ include stock market crashes and the bursting of other financial bubbles, currency crises, and sovereign defaults.
   a. General equilibrium
   b. Georgism
   c. Microeconomics
   d. Financial crises

34. The _____ is an economic and political union of 27 member states, located primarily in Europe. It was established by the Treaty of Maastricht on 1 November 1993, upon the foundations of the pre-existing European Economic Community. With a population of almost 500 million, the _____ generates an estimated 30% share (US$18.4 trillion in 2008) of the nominal gross world product.
   a. European Union
   b. ACEA agreement
   c. European Court of Justice
   d. ACCRA Cost of Living Index

35. The European _____, was a system introduced by the European Community in March 1979, as part of the European Monetary System (EMS), to reduce exchange rate variability and achieve monetary stability in Europe, in preparation for Economic and Monetary Union and the introduction of a single currency, the euro, which took place on 1 January 1999. Subsequent exchange rate agreements made with countries wishing to join the Eurozone are known as _____ II.

The _____ is based on the concept of fixed currency exchange rate margins, but with exchange rates variable within those margins.

   a. European Monetary Union
   b. Exchange Rate Mechanism
   c. European Monetary System
   d. Euro Interbank Offered Rate

36. _____ in economics is a state in which a country maintains full employment and price level stability. It is a function of a country's total output,

   $II = C (Yf - T) + I + G + CA (E \times P^*/P, Yf\text{-}T; Yf^* - T^*)$

   _____ = Consumption [determined by disposable income] + Investment + Government Spending + Current Account (determined by the real exchange rate, disposable income of home country and disposable income of the foreign country.)

External balance signifies a condition in which the country's current account, its exports minus imports, is neither too far in surplus nor in deficit.

   a. Energy intensity
   b. Autonomous consumption
   c. Uneconomic growth
   d. Internal balance

37. _____ and Keynesian Theory) is a macroeconomic theory based on the ideas of 20th-century British economist John Maynard Keynes. _____ argues that private sector decisions sometimes lead to inefficient macroeconomic outcomes and therefore advocates active policy responses by the public sector, including monetary policy actions by the central bank and fiscal policy actions by the government to stabilize output over the business cycle.

The theories forming the basis of _____ were first presented in The General Theory of Employment, Interest and Money, published in 1936.

a. Deflation
b. Keynesian economics
c. Rational choice theory
d. Market failure

38. An economic and _____ is a single market with a common currency. It is to be distinguished from a mere currency union , which does not involve a single market. This is the fifth stage of economic integration.

a. Free trade zone
b. Customs union
c. Monetary union
d. Commercial invoice

39. The _____ is the official currency of 16 of the 27 member states of the European Union (EU.) The states, known collectively as the Eurozone, are Austria, Belgium, Cyprus, Finland, France, Germany, Greece, Ireland, Italy, Luxembourg, Malta, the Netherlands, Portugal, Slovakia, Slovenia, and Spain. The currency is also used in a further five European countries, with and without formal agreements and is consequently used daily by some 327 million Europeans.

a. Import and Export Price Indices
b. Euro
c. Equity capital market
d. IRS Code 3401

40. _____ is a common concept in economics, and gives rise to derived concepts such as consumer debt. Generally _____ is defined by opposition to production. But the precise definition can vary because different schools of economists define production quite differently.

a. Federal Reserve Bank Notes
b. Foreclosure data providers
c. Cash or share options
d. Consumption

41. The term _____ refers to government debt, expenditures and revenues, or to finance (particularly financial revenue) in general.

- _____ deficit is the budget deficit of federal or local government
- _____ policy is the discretionary spending of governments. Contrasts with monetary policy.
- _____ year and _____ quarter are reporting periods for firms and other agencies.

a. Bucket shop
b. Drawdown
c. Procter ' Gamble
d. Fiscal

42. In economics, _____ is the use of government spending and revenue collection to influence the economy.

_____ can be contrasted with the other main type of economic policy, monetary policy, which attempts to stabilize the economy by controlling interest rates and the supply of money. The two main instruments of _____ are government spending and taxation.

a. Sustainable investment rule
b. Fiscalism
c. Fiscal policy
d. 100-year flood

43. The term _____ is applied broadly to a variety of situations in which some financial institutions or assets suddenly lose a large part of their value. In the 19th and early 20th centuries, many financial crises were associated with banking panics, and many recessions coincided with these panics. Other situations that are often called financial crises include stock market crashes and the bursting of other financial bubbles, currency crises, and sovereign defaults.

   a. Market failure
   b. Macroeconomics
   c. Co-operative economics
   d. Financial crisis

44. A _____, which is also called a balance-of-payments crisis, occurs when the value of a currency changes quickly, undermining its ability to serve as a medium of exchange or a store of value. It is a type of financial crisis and is often associated with a real economic crisis. Currency crises can be especially destructive to small open economies or bigger, but not sufficiently stable ones.

   a. 130-30 fund
   b. Speculative attack
   c. 100-year flood
   d. Currency crisis

45. _____ is sometimes referred to as _____, actually it means Economic Monetary Union.

First ideas of an economic and monetary union in Europe were raised well before establishing the European Communities. For example, already in the League of Nations, Gustav Stresemann asked in 1929 for a European currency (Link) against the background of an increased economic division due to a number of new nation states in Europe after WWI.

   a. Exchange rate mechanism
   b. European Monetary System
   c. Euro Interbank Offered Rate
   d. European Monetary Union

46. A _____ is the massive selling of a country's currency assets by both domestic and foreign investors. Countries that utilize a fixed exchange rate are more susceptible to a _____ than countries utilizing a floating exchange rate. This is because of the large amount of reserves necessary to hold the fixed exchange rate in place at that fixed level.

   a. Speculative attack
   b. 100-year flood
   c. Currency crisis
   d. 130-30 fund

47. The _____ is an emergency reserve fund of the United States Treasury Department, normally used for foreign exchange intervention. This arrangement (as opposed to having the central bank intervene directly) allows the US government to influence currency exchange rates without affecting domestic money supply.

As of June, 2008, the fund held assets worth $51.2 billion.

   a. ACEA agreement
   b. ACCRA Cost of Living Index
   c. Exchange Stabilization Fund
   d. AD-IA Model

48. The _____ or gross domestic income (GDI), a basic measure of an economy's economic performance, is the market value of all final goods and services produced within the borders of a nation in a year. _____ can be defined in three ways, all of which are conceptually identical. First, it is equal to the total expenditures for all final goods and services produced within the country in a stipulated period of time (usually a 365-day year.)

   a. Market structure
   b. Countercyclical
   c. Gross domestic product
   d. Monopolistic competition

Chapter 15. International Economic Policy

49. An _____, in economics, is the amount by which the real Gross domestic product exceeds potential GDP. The real GDP is also known as GDP 'adjusted for inflation', 'constant prices' GDP or 'constant dollar' GDP, because it measures the aggregate output in a country's income accounts in a given year, expressed in base-year prices. On the other hand, the potential GDP is the quantity of real GDP when a country's economy is at full-employment.
- a. ACCRA Cost of Living Index
- b. ACEA agreement
- c. Inflationary gap
- d. AD-IA Model

50. _____s is the social science that studies the production, distribution, and consumption of goods and services. The term _____s comes from the Ancient Greek oá¼°κονομῖα from oá¼¶κος (oikos, 'house') + vĭŒµος (nomos, 'custom' or 'law'), hence 'rules of the house(hold)'. Current _____ models developed out of the broader field of political economy in the late 19th century, owing to a desire to use an empirical approach more akin to the physical sciences.
- a. Energy economics
- b. Inflation
- c. Opportunity cost
- d. Economic

51. _____ is the increase in the amount of the goods and services produced by an economy over time. It is conventionally measured as the percent rate of increase in real gross domestic product, or real GDP. Growth is usually calculated in real terms, i.e. inflation-adjusted terms, in order to net out the effect of inflation on the price of the goods and services produced.
- a. AD-IA Model
- b. ACEA agreement
- c. Economic growth
- d. ACCRA Cost of Living Index

52. In economics, the _____ is one of the two primary components of the balance of payments, the other being the capital account. It is the sum of the balance of trade (exports minus imports of goods and services), net factor income (such as interest and dividends) and net transfer payments (such as foreign aid.)

$$\text{Current account} = \text{Balance of trade} \\ + \text{Net factor income from abroad} \\ + \text{Net unilateral transfers from abroad}$$

The _____ balance is one of two major metrics of the nature of a country's foreign trade (the other being the net capital outflow.)

- a. Compensation of employees
- b. Current account
- c. National Income and Product Accounts
- d. Gross private domestic investment

53. In economics, _____ is a sustained decrease in the general price level of goods and services. _____ occurs when the annual inflation rate falls below zero percent, resulting in an increase in the real value of money -- a negative inflation rate. This should not be confused with disinflation, a slow-down in the inflation rate (i.e. when the inflation decreases, but still remains positive.)
- a. Tobit model
- b. Literacy rate
- c. Price revolution
- d. Deflation

54. The balance of trade (or net exports, sometimes symbolized as NX) is the difference between the monetary value of exports and imports in an economy over a certain period of time. It is the relationship between a nation's imports and exports. A favorable balance of trade is known as a trade surplus and consists of exporting more than is imported; an unfavorable balance of trade is known as a _____ or, informally, a trade gap.

a. Demographics of India
b. Computational economic
c. Complementary asset
d. Trade deficit

55. In economics, a _____ is a mechanism that allows people to easily buy and sell (trade) financial securities (such as stocks and bonds), commodities (such as precious metals or agricultural goods), and other fungible items of value at low transaction costs and at prices that reflect the efficient-market hypothesis.

_____s have evolved significantly over several hundred years and are undergoing constant innovation to improve liquidity.

Both general markets (where many commodities are traded) and specialized markets (where only one commodity is traded) exist.

a. Financial market
b. Noise trader
c. Market anomaly
d. Convertible arbitrage

56. In economics, the term _____ of income or _____ refers to a simple economic model which describes the reciprocal circulation of income between producers and consumers. In the _____ model, the inter-dependent entities of producer and consumer are referred to as 'firms' and 'households' respectively and provide each other with factors in order to facilitate the flow of income. Firms provide consumers with goods and services in exchange for consumer expenditure and 'factors of production' from households.

a. Circular flow
b. 130-30 fund
c. 1921 recession
d. 100-year flood

57. In economics, _____ is the monetary policy device that a country's government (i.e., sovereign power) uses to regulate the flows into and out of a country's capital account, i.e., the flows of investment-oriented money into and out of a country or currency. _____s have become more prominent in the years since the Clinton administration blessed the efforts of the world community to create the World Trade Organization (WTO), primarily because globalization has increased the acceleration of currency domain strength, in other words, giving some currencies utility far beyond their physical geographic boundaries.

One characteristic of developed economies is liquid debt markets.

a. Shadow Open Market Committee
b. Second-round effect
c. Money creation
d. Capital control

58. _____ refers to the actions that governments take in the economic field. It covers the systems for setting interest rates and government deficit as well as the labour market, national ownership, and many other areas of government.

Such policies are often influenced by international institutions like the International Monetary Fund or World Bank as well as political beliefs and the consequent policies of parties.

a. ACCRA Cost of Living Index
b. AD-IA Model
c. ACEA agreement
d. Economic policy

Chapter 15. International Economic Policy

59. _____, in economics, occurs when assets and/or money rapidly flow out of a country, due to an economic event that disturbs investors and causes them to lower their valuation of the assets in that country, or otherwise to lose confidence in its economic strength. This leads to a disappearance of wealth and is usually accompanied by a sharp drop in the exchange rate of the affected country (depreciation in a variable exchange rate regime, or a forced devaluation in a fixed exchange rate regime.)

This fall is particularly damaging when the capital belongs to the people of the affected country, because not only are the citizens now burdened by the loss of faith in the economy and devaluation of their currency, but probably also their assets have lost much of their nominal value.

a. Liquid capital
b. Capital formation
c. Firm-specific infrastructure
d. Capital flight

60. A _____ is a monetary authority which is required to maintain a fixed exchange rate with a foreign currency. This policy objective requires the conventional objectives of a central bank to be subordinated to the exchange rate target.

The main qualities of an orthodox _____ are:

- A _____'s foreign currency reserves must be sufficient to ensure that all holders of its notes and coins (and all banks creditor of a Reserve Account at the _____) can convert them into the reserve currency (usually 110-115% of the monetary base M0.)
- A _____ maintains absolute, unlimited convertibility between its notes and coins and the currency against which they are pegged (the anchor currency), at a fixed rate of exchange, with no restrictions on current-account or capital-account transactions.
- A _____ only earns profit from interests on foreign reserves (less the expense of note-issuing), and does not engage in forward-exchange transactions. These foreign reserves exist (1) because local notes have been issued in exchange, or (2) because commercial banks must by regulation deposit a minimum reserve at the _____. (1) generates a seignorage revenue. (2) is the revenue on minimum reserves (revenue of investment activities less cost of minimum reserves remuneration)
- A _____ has no discretionary powers to effect monetary policy and does not lend to the government. Governments cannot print money, and can only tax or borrow to meet their spending commitments.
- A _____ does not act as a lender of last resort to commercial banks, and does not regulate reserve requirements.
- A _____ does not attempt to manipulate interest rates by establishing a discount rate like a central bank. The peg with the foreign currency tends to keep interest rates and inflation very closely aligned to those in the country against whose currency the peg is fixed.

The _____ in question will no longer issue fiat money but instead will only issue one unit of local currency for each unit (or decided amount) of foreign currency it has in its vault (often a hard currency such as the U.S. dollar or the euro.) The surplus on the balance of payments of that country is reflected by higher deposits local banks hold at the central bank as well as (initially) higher deposits of the (net) exporting firms at their local banks.

a. Currency competition
b. Petrodollar
c. Reserve currency
d. Currency board

61. _____ is that which is owed; usually referencing assets owed, but the term can also cover moral obligations and other interactions not requiring money. In the case of assets, _____ is a means of using future purchasing power in the present before a summation has been earned. Some companies and corporations use _____ as a part of their overall corporate finance strategy.
   a. Debenture
   b. Collateral Management
   c. Hard money loan
   d. Debt

62. _____ is a type of trade policy that allows traders to act and transact without interference from government. Thus, the policy permits trading partners mutual gains from trade, with goods and services produced according to the theory of comparative advantage.

Under a _____ policy, prices are a reflection of true supply and demand, and are the sole determinant of resource allocation.

   a. 130-30 fund
   b. 1921 recession
   c. 100-year flood
   d. Free Trade

63. The _____ is a trilateral trade bloc in North America created by the governments of the United States, Canada, and Mexico. The agreement creating the trade bloc came into force on January 1, 1994. It superseded the Canada-United States Free Trade Agreement between the U.S. and Canada.
   a. Federal Reserve Bank Notes
   b. Case-Shiller Home Price Indices
   c. Demand-side technologies
   d. North American Free Trade Agreement

Chapter 16. Changes in the Macroeconomy and Changes in Macroeconomic Policy

1. In finance, the _____ is the system that allows the transfer of money between savers and borrowers.

    Put another way: the _____ is a set of complex and closely interconnected financial institutions, markets, instruments, services, practices, and transactions.

    a. Hedonimetry
    b. Lean consumption
    c. Foreign investment
    d. Financial system

2. In economics, the people in the _____ are the suppliers of labor. The _____ is all the nonmilitary people who are employed or unemployed. In 2005, the worldwide _____ was over 3 billion people.
    a. Distributed workforce
    b. Departmentalization
    c. Grenelle agreements
    d. Labor force

3. A _____ is a package or set of measures introduced to stabilise a financial system or economy. The term can refer to policies in two distinct sets of circumstances: business cycle stabilization and crisis stabilization.

    Stabilization can refer to correcting the normal behavior of the business cycle.

    a. New International Economic Order
    b. Capacity Development
    c. Stabilization policy
    d. Volunteers for Economic Growth Alliance

4. _____ of an economy refers to a long-term widespread change of the fundamental structure, rather than microscale or short-term output and employment. For example, a subsistence economy is transformed into a manufacturing economy, or a regulated mixed economy is liberalized. A current _____ in the world economy is globalization.
    a. Fiscal adjustment
    b. Structural change
    c. Robertson lag
    d. Dishoarding

5. _____, in law and economics, is a form of risk management primarily used to hedge against the risk of a contingent loss. _____ is defined as the equitable transfer of the risk of a loss, from one entity to another, in exchange for a premium, and can be thought of as a guaranteed small loss to prevent a large, possibly devastating loss. An insurer is a company selling the _____; an insured or policyholder is the person or entity buying the _____.
    a. ACCRA Cost of Living Index
    b. ACEA agreement
    c. AD-IA Model
    d. Insurance

6. A _____ is a set of exclusive rights granted by a state to an inventor or his assignee for a limited period of time in exchange for a disclosure of an invention.

    The procedure for granting _____s, the requirements placed on the _____ee and the extent of the exclusive rights vary widely between countries according to national laws and international agreements. Typically, however, a _____ application must include one or more claims defining the invention which must be new, inventive, and useful or industrially applicable.

    a. Long service leave
    b. Bona fide occupational qualification
    c. Patent
    d. Bank regulation

Chapter 16. Changes in the Macroeconomy and Changes in Macroeconomic Policy

7. _____ is a common concept in economics, and gives rise to derived concepts such as consumer debt. Generally _____ is defined by opposition to production. But the precise definition can vary because different schools of economists define production quite differently.
   - a. Foreclosure data providers
   - b. Cash or share options
   - c. Federal Reserve Bank Notes
   - d. Consumption

8. _____ is a term used in economics to describe an economy where capital per worker is increasing. A process of increasing the amount of capital per worker. It is an increase in the capital intensity.
   - a. Capital formation
   - b. Firm-specific infrastructure
   - c. Capital expenditure
   - d. Capital deepening

9. _____s is the social science that studies the production, distribution, and consumption of goods and services. The term _____s comes from the Ancient Greek oá¼°κονομῖα from oá¼¶κος (oikos, 'house') + vÏŒμος (nomos, 'custom' or 'law'), hence 'rules of the house(hold)'. Current _____ models developed out of the broader field of political economy in the late 19th century, owing to a desire to use an empirical approach more akin to the physical sciences.
   - a. Opportunity cost
   - b. Inflation
   - c. Energy economics
   - d. Economic

10. The phrase _____, according to the Organization for Economic Co-operation and Development, refers to 'creative work undertaken on a systematic basis in order to increase the stock of knowledge, including knowledge of man, culture and society, and the use of this stock of knowledge to devise new applications [sic]'

    New product design and development is more than often a crucial factor in the survival of a company. In an industry that is fast changing, firms must continually revise their design and range of products. This is necessary due to continuous technology change and development as well as other competitors and the changing preference of customers.

    - a. Research and development
    - b. 1921 recession
    - c. 100-year flood
    - d. 130-30 fund

11. In economics, the term _____ of income or _____ refers to a simple economic model which describes the reciprocal circulation of income between producers and consumers. In the _____ model, the inter-dependent entities of producer and consumer are referred to as 'firms' and 'households' respectively and provide each other with factors in order to facilitate the flow of income. Firms provide consumers with goods and services in exchange for consumer expenditure and 'factors of production' from households.
    - a. 100-year flood
    - b. 1921 recession
    - c. 130-30 fund
    - d. Circular flow

12. The _____ is a monetary system in which a region's common medium of exchange are paper notes that are normally freely convertible into pre-set, fixed quantities of gold. The _____ is not currently used by any government, having been replaced completely by fiat currency. Gold certificates were used as paper currency in the United States from 1882 to 1933, these certificates were freely convertable into gold coins.

    In the 1790s Britain suffered a massive shortage of silver coinage and ceased to mint larger silver coins.

Chapter 16. Changes in the Macroeconomy and Changes in Macroeconomic Policy

a. 1921 recession
b. 100-year flood
c. 130-30 fund
d. Gold standard

13. _____ in economics refers to metrics and measures of output from production processes, per unit of input. Labor _____, for example, is typically measured as a ratio of output per labor-hour, an input. _____ may be conceived of as a metrics of the technical or engineering efficiency of production.

a. Piece work
b. Fordism
c. Production-possibility frontier
d. Productivity

14. A _____ refers to any type debt instrument, such as a loan, bond, mortgage that does not have a fixed rate of interest over the life of the instrument. Such debt typically uses an index or other base rate for establishing the interest rate for each relevant period. One of the most common rates to use as the basis for applying interest rates is the London Inter-bank Offered Rate, or LIBOR

a. Money market
b. Floating interest rate
c. Disposal tax effect
d. Moneylender

15. In economics, a _____ is a mechanism that allows people to easily buy and sell (trade) financial securities (such as stocks and bonds), commodities (such as precious metals or agricultural goods), and other fungible items of value at low transaction costs and at prices that reflect the efficient-market hypothesis.

_____s have evolved significantly over several hundred years and are undergoing constant innovation to improve liquidity.

Both general markets (where many commodities are traded) and specialized markets (where only one commodity is traded) exist.

a. Convertible arbitrage
b. Noise trader
c. Financial market
d. Market anomaly

16. The _____ is 'the basic residential unit in which economic production, consumption, inheritance, child rearing, and shelter are organized and carried out'; [the _____] 'may or may not be synonymous with family'.

The _____ is the basic unit of analysis in many social, microeconomic and government models. The term refers to all individuals who live in the same dwelling.

a. Family economics
b. 100-year flood
c. 130-30 fund
d. Household

17. _____ and Keynesian Theory) is a macroeconomic theory based on the ideas of 20th-century British economist John Maynard Keynes. _____ argues that private sector decisions sometimes lead to inefficient macroeconomic outcomes and therefore advocates active policy responses by the public sector, including monetary policy actions by the central bank and fiscal policy actions by the government to stabilize output over the business cycle.

The theories forming the basis of _____ were first presented in The General Theory of Employment, Interest and Money, published in 1936.

a. Keynesian economics
c. Market failure
b. Rational choice theory
d. Deflation

18. Market _____ is a business, economics or investment term that refers to an asset's ability to be easily converted through an act of buying or selling without causing a significant movement in the price and with minimum loss of value. Money, or cash on hand, is the most liquid asset. An act of exchange of a less liquid asset with a more liquid asset is called liquidation.

   a. 130-30 fund
   c. 1921 recession
   b. 100-year flood
   d. Liquidity

19. The term _____ refers to economy-wide fluctuations in production or economic activity over several months or years. These fluctuations occur around a long-term growth trend, and typically involve shifts over time between periods of relatively rapid economic growth (expansion or boom), and periods of relative stagnation or decline (contraction or recession.)

These fluctuations are often measured using the growth rate of real gross domestic product.

   a. Tobit model
   c. Consumer theory
   b. Nominal value
   d. Business cycle

20. _____ in its literal sense is the process of transformation of local or regional phenomena into global ones. It can be described as a process by which the people of the world are unified into a single society and function together.

This process is a combination of economic, technological, sociocultural and political forces.

   a. Global Cosmopolitanism
   c. Globalization
   b. Helsinki Process on Globalisation and Democracy
   d. Globally Integrated Enterprise

21. In economics, the _____ is an empirical metric that quantifies induced consumption, the concept that the increase in personal consumer spending (consumption) that occurs with an increase in disposable income (income after taxes and transfers.) For example, if a household earns one extra dollar of disposable income, and the _____ is 0.65, then of that dollar, the household will spend 65 cents and save 35 cents.

Mathematically, the _____ (MPC) function is expressed as the derivative of the consumption (C) function with respect to disposable income (Y.)

   a. Marginal propensity to import
   c. Marginal propensity to consume
   b. Supply shock
   d. Technology shock

22. A _____ product is a product designed for cheapness and short-term convenience rather than medium to long-term durability, with most products only intended for single use. The term is also sometimes used for products that may last several months (ex. _____ air filters) to distinguish from similar products that last indefinitely (ex.

   a. 130-30 fund
   c. Disposable
   b. 1921 recession
   d. 100-year flood

23. _____ is gross income minus income tax on that income.

Chapter 16. Changes in the Macroeconomy and Changes in Macroeconomic Policy

Discretionary income is income after subtracting taxes and normal expenses (such as rent or mortgage, utilities, insurance, medical, transportation, property maintenance, child support, inflation, food and sundries, 'c.) to maintain a certain standard of living.

- a. Disposable personal income
- b. Stamp Act
- c. Taxation as theft
- d. Disposable income

24. A _____ is an object whose consumption increases the utility of the consumer, for which the quantity demanded exceeds the quantity supplied at zero price. _____s are usually modeled as having diminishing marginal utility. The first individual purchase has high utility; the second has less.
- a. Good
- b. Pie method
- c. Merit good
- d. Composite good

25. In economics, an _____ is any good (e.g. a commodity) or service brought into one country from another country in a legitimate fashion, typically for use in trade. It is a good that is brought in from another country for sale. _____ goods or services are provided to domestic consumers by foreign producers. An _____ in the receiving country is an export to the sending country.
- a. Economic integration
- b. Incoterms
- c. Import quota
- d. Import

26. _____ is a branch of economics that deals with the performance, structure, and behavior of a national or regional economy as a whole. Along with microeconomics, _____ is one of the two most general fields in economics. It is the study of the behavior and decision-making of entire economies.
- a. New Trade Theory
- b. Nominal value
- c. Tobit model
- d. Macroeconomics

27. _____ is the increase in the amount of the goods and services produced by an economy over time. It is conventionally measured as the percent rate of increase in real gross domestic product, or real GDP. Growth is usually calculated in real terms, i.e. inflation-adjusted terms, in order to net out the effect of inflation on the price of the goods and services produced.
- a. ACEA agreement
- b. Economic growth
- c. AD-IA Model
- d. ACCRA Cost of Living Index

28. The term _____ is applied broadly to a variety of situations in which some financial institutions or assets suddenly lose a large part of their value. In the 19th and early 20th centuries, many financial crises were associated with banking panics, and many recessions coincided with these panics. Other situations that are often called financial crises include stock market crashes and the bursting of other financial bubbles, currency crises, and sovereign defaults.
- a. Macroeconomics
- b. Financial crisis
- c. Co-operative economics
- d. Market failure

Chapter 16. Changes in the Macroeconomy and Changes in Macroeconomic Policy

29. The _____ is the central banking system of the United States. Created in 1913 by the enactment of the Federal Reserve Act (signed by Woodrow Wilson), it is a quasi-public and quasi-private (government entity with private components) banking system that comprises (1) the presidentially appointed Board of Governors of the _____ in Washington, D.C.; (2) the Federal Open Market Committee; (3) twelve regional Federal Reserve Banks located in major cities throughout the nation acting as fiscal agents for the U.S. Treasury, each with its own nine-member board of directors; (4) numerous other private U.S. member banks, which subscribe to required amounts of non-transferable stock in their regional Federal Reserve Banks; and (5) various advisory councils. Since February 2006, Ben Bernanke has served as the Chairman of the Board of Governors of the _____.

   a. Monetary Policy Report to the Congress   b. Term auction facility
   c. Federal Reserve System   d. Federal Reserve System Open Market Account

30. The _____ or gross domestic income (GDI), a basic measure of an economy's economic performance, is the market value of all final goods and services produced within the borders of a nation in a year. _____ can be defined in three ways, all of which are conceptually identical. First, it is equal to the total expenditures for all final goods and services produced within the country in a stipulated period of time (usually a 365-day year.)

   a. Monopolistic competition   b. Countercyclical
   c. Market structure   d. Gross domestic product

31. In economics, the _____ is the term used to refer to the environment in which bonds are bought and sold between a central bank ' its regulated banks. It is not a free market process.

- To intervene in the 'business cycle', a central bank may choose to go into the _____ and buy or sell government bonds, which is known as _____ operations to increase reserves.

   a. Outside money   b. Inside money
   c. ACCRA Cost of Living Index   d. Open market

32. _____ are the means of implementing monetary policy by which a central bank controls its national money supply by buying and selling government securities, or other financial instruments. Monetary targets, such as interest rates or exchange rates, are used to guide this implementation.

Since most money is now in the form of electronic records, rather than paper records such as banknotes, _____ are conducted simply by electronically increasing or decreasing ('crediting' or 'debiting') the amount of money that a bank has, e.g., in its reserve account at the central bank, in exchange for a bank selling or buying a financial instrument.

   a. ACEA agreement   b. ACCRA Cost of Living Index
   c. AD-IA Model   d. Open market operations

33. _____ is the process by which the government, central bank (ii) availability of money, and (iii) cost of money or rate of interest, in order to attain a set of objectives oriented towards the growth and stability of the economy. Monetary theory provides insight into how to craft optimal _____.

_____ is referred to as either being an expansionary policy where an expansionary policy increases the total supply of money in the economy, and a contractionary policy decreases the total money supply.

Chapter 16. Changes in the Macroeconomy and Changes in Macroeconomic Policy

a. Monetary policy
c. 100-year flood
b. 1921 recession
d. 130-30 fund

34. The _____ is the upward-sloping relationship between the inflation rate and the unemployment rate. When the inflation rate rises, a central bank wishing to fight inflation will raise interest rates to reduce output and thus increase the unemployment rate. The _____ is a function of the Taylor Rule, the Investment-Spending Curve (IS Curve) and Okun's Law

The _____ has the equation:

$u = u_0 + \Phi(\pi - \pi t)$

Where Φ is a parameter that tells us how much unemployment rises when the central bank raises the real interest rate r because it thinks that inflation is too high and needs to be reduced.

a. Marginal propensity to import
c. Secular basis
b. Value added
d. Monetary policy reaction function

35. A _____ is a situation that involves losing one quality or aspect of something in return for gaining another quality or aspect. It implies a decision to be made with full comprehension of both the upside and downside of a particular choice.

In economics the term is expressed as opportunity cost, referring the most preferred alternative given up.

a. Nonmarket
c. Friedman-Savage utility function
b. Whitemail
d. Trade-off

36. The _____, a unit of the United States Department of Labor, is the principal fact-finding agency for the U.S. government in the broad field of labor economics and statistics. The BLS is an independent national statistical agency that collects, processes, analyzes, and disseminates essential statistical data to the American public, the U.S. Congress, other Federal agencies, State and local governments, business, and labor representatives. The BLS also serves as a statistical resource to the Department of Labor.

a. Bureau of Labor Statistics
c. Gross Regional Product
b. Gross world product
d. Gross national product

37. The _____ was a worldwide economic downturn starting in most places in 1929 and ending at different times in the 1930s or early 1940s for different countries. It was the largest and most important economic depression in the 20th century, and is used in the 21st century as an example of how far the world's economy can fall. The _____ originated in the United States; historians most often use as a starting date the stock market crash on October 29, 1929, known as Black Tuesday.

a. Wall Street Crash of 1929
c. British Empire Economic Conference
b. Great Depression
d. Jarrow March

38. An _____, in economics, is the amount by which the real Gross domestic product exceeds potential GDP. The real GDP is also known as GDP 'adjusted for inflation', 'constant prices' GDP or 'constant dollar' GDP, because it measures the aggregate output in a country's income accounts in a given year, expressed in base-year prices. On the other hand, the potential GDP is the quantity of real GDP when a country's economy is at full-employment.

Chapter 16. Changes in the Macroeconomy and Changes in Macroeconomic Policy

a. ACCRA Cost of Living Index
c. AD-IA Model
b. Inflationary gap
d. ACEA agreement

39. In economics, a _____ is a general slowdown in economic activity over a sustained period of time, or a business cycle contraction. During _____s, many macroeconomic indicators vary in a similar way. Production as measured by Gross Domestic Product (GDP), employment, investment spending, capacity utilization, household incomes and business profits all fall during _____s.
    a. Monetary economics
    c. Leading indicators
    b. Treasury View
    d. Recession

40. In statistics, a _____ is a value that allows data to be measured over time in terms of some base period ussually through a price index in order to distinguish between changes in the money value of GNP which result from a change in prices and those which result from a change in physical output. It is the measure of the price level for some quantity. A _____ serves as a price index in which the effects of inflation are nulled.
    a. Market microstructure
    c. Contingent employment
    b. Blanket order
    d. Deflator

41. In microeconomics, _____ is quite simply the conversion of inputs into outputs. It is an economic process that uses resources to create a good or service that is suitable for exchange. This can include manufacturing, storing, shipping, and packaging.
    a. Solved
    c. MET
    b. Production
    d. Red Guards

42. In economics, _____ is the total demand for final goods and services in the economy (Y) at a given time and price level. It is the amount of goods and services in the economy that will be purchased at all possible price levels. This is the demand for the gross domestic product of a country when inventory levels are static.
    a. Aggregate expenditure
    c. Aggregate demand
    b. Aggregate supply
    d. Aggregation problem

43. _____ is a term used in economics to describe how an economic quantity is related to economic fluctuations. It is the opposite of procyclical. However, it has more than one meaning.
    a. Price revolution
    c. Countercyclical
    b. Mathematical economics
    d. Law of comparative advantage

44. _____ refers to the actions that governments take in the economic field. It covers the systems for setting interest rates and government deficit as well as the labour market, national ownership, and many other areas of government.

    Such policies are often influenced by international institutions like the International Monetary Fund or World Bank as well as political beliefs and the consequent policies of parties.

    a. ACCRA Cost of Living Index
    c. ACEA agreement
    b. AD-IA Model
    d. Economic policy

45. An _____ is a tax levied on the financial income of people, corporations, or other legal entities. Various _____ systems exist, with varying degrees of tax incidence. Income taxation can be progressive, proportional, or regressive.

Chapter 16. Changes in the Macroeconomy and Changes in Macroeconomic Policy   203

a. AD-IA Model
c. ACCRA Cost of Living Index
b. ACEA agreement
d. Income tax

46. The _____ says that it is naïve to try to predict the effects of a change in economic policy entirely on the basis of relationships observed in historical data, especially highly aggregated historical data.

The basic idea pre-dates Lucas's contribution, but in a 1976 paper he drove home the point that this simple notion invalidated policy advice based on conclusions drawn from estimated system of equation models. Because the parameters of those models were not structural - that is, not policy-invariant - they would necessarily change whenever policy - the rules of the game - was changed.

a. Lucas critique
c. Dahrendorf hypothesis
b. Peak-load pricing
d. Demand management

47. Economics:

- _____, the desire to own something and the ability to pay for it
- _____ curve, a graphic representation of a _____ schedule
- _____ deposit, the money in checking accounts
- _____ pull theory, the theory that inflation occurs when _____ for goods and services exceeds existing supplies
- _____ schedule, a table that lists the quantity of a good a person will buy it each different price
- _____ side economics, the school of economics at believes government spending and tax cuts open economy by raising _____

a. McKesson ' Robbins scandal
c. Demand
b. Variability
d. Production

48. In economics, _____ is the art or science of controlling economic demand to avoid a recession. In natural resources management and environmental policy more generally, it refers to policies to control consumer demand for environmentally sensitive or harmful goods such as water and energy. Within manufacturing firms the term is used to describe the activities of demand forecasting, planning and order fulfillment.

a. Cobra effect
c. Peak-load pricing
b. Fiscal imbalance
d. Demand management

49. The term _____ refers to government debt, expenditures and revenues, or to finance (particularly financial revenue) in general.

- _____ deficit is the budget deficit of federal or local government
- _____ policy is the discretionary spending of governments. Contrasts with monetary policy.
- _____ year and _____ quarter are reporting periods for firms and other agencies.

Chapter 16. Changes in the Macroeconomy and Changes in Macroeconomic Policy

a. Fiscal
c. Procter ' Gamble
b. Drawdown
d. Bucket shop

50. In economics, _____ is the use of government spending and revenue collection to influence the economy.

_____ can be contrasted with the other main type of economic policy, monetary policy, which attempts to stabilize the economy by controlling interest rates and the supply of money. The two main instruments of _____ are government spending and taxation.

a. Sustainable investment rule
c. 100-year flood
b. Fiscal policy
d. Fiscalism

51. _____ in economics and business is the result of an exchange and from that trade we assign a numerical monetary value to a good, service or asset. If Alice trades Bob 4 apples for an orange, the _____ of an orange is 4 apples. Inversely, the _____ of an apple is 1/4 oranges.

a. Price war
c. Price
b. Premium pricing
d. Price book

52. To _____ is to impose a financial charge or other levy upon a taxpayer by a state or the functional equivalent of a state.

_____es are also imposed by many subnational entities. _____es consist of direct _____ or indirect _____, and may be paid in money or as its labour equivalent (often but not always unpaid.)

a. 100-year flood
c. 1921 recession
b. 130-30 fund
d. Tax

53. The _____ , a component of the Federal Reserve System, is charged under United States law with overseeing the nation's open market operations. It is the Federal Reserve Committee that makes key decisions about interest rates and the growth jam of the United States money supply. It is the principal organ of United States national monetary policy.

a. Federal Open Market Committee
c. Federal Reserve Transparency Act
b. Fed Funds Probability
d. Primary Dealer Credit Facility

54. _____, 1st Baron Keynes was a renowned economist from Britain whose many ideas on economic and political theories as well as on many governments' monetary policies influenced America. He advocated a government that played an active role in the lives of people regarding business, economy, etc. In this role, the government would use fiscal measures to reduce the consequences of recessions, economic depressions and booms.

a. Adolf Hitler
c. Adolph Fischer
b. Adam Smith
d. John Maynard Keynes

55. In economics, the _____ is a historical inverse relation between the rate of unemployment and the rate of inflation in an economy. Stated simply, the lower the unemployment in an economy, the higher the rate of increase in nominal wages in the economy. Rate of Change of Wages against Unemployment, United Kingdom 1913-1948 from Phillips (1958)

Chapter 16. Changes in the Macroeconomy and Changes in Macroeconomic Policy 205

William Phillips, a New Zealand born economist, wrote a paper in 1958 titled The Relationship between Unemployment and the Rate of Change of Money Wages in the United Kingdom 1861-1957, which was published in the quarterly journal Economica.

 a. Lorenz curve
 b. Phillips curve
 c. Demand curve
 d. Cost curve

56. In economics, _____ is a rise in the general level of prices of goods and services in an economy over a period of time. When the general price level rises, each unit of currency buys fewer goods and services; consequently, _____ is also a decline in the real value of money--a loss of purchasing power in the medium of exchange which is also the monetary unit of account in the economy. A chief measure of general price-level _____ is the general _____ rate, which is the percentage change in a general price index (normally the Consumer Price Index) over time.
 a. Energy economics
 b. Opportunity cost
 c. Economic
 d. Inflation

57. A _____ is a hypothetical measure of overall prices for some set of goods and services, in a given region during a given interval, normalized relative to some base set. Typically, a _____ is approximated with a price index.

The classical dichotomy is the assumption that there is a relatively clean distinction between overall increases or decreases in prices and underlying, e;reale; economic variables.

 a. Price elasticity of supply
 b. Discretionary spending
 c. Discouraged worker
 d. Price level

58. In economics, _____ is a sustained decrease in the general price level of goods and services. _____ occurs when the annual inflation rate falls below zero percent, resulting in an increase in the real value of money -- a negative inflation rate. This should not be confused with disinflation, a slow-down in the inflation rate (i.e. when the inflation decreases, but still remains positive.)
 a. Price revolution
 b. Literacy rate
 c. Tobit model
 d. Deflation

59. _____ is a fee paid on borrowed assets. It is the price paid for the use of borrowed money , or, money earned by deposited funds . Assets that are sometimes lent with _____ include money, shares, consumer goods through hire purchase, major assets such as aircraft, and even entire factories in finance lease arrangements.
 a. Internal debt
 b. Insolvency
 c. Interest
 d. Asset protection

60. An _____ is the price a borrower pays for the use of money they do not own, for instance a small company might borrow from a bank to kick start their business, and the return a lender receives for deferring the use of funds, by lending it to the borrower. _____s are normally expressed as a percentage rate over the period of one year.

_____s targets are also a vital tool of monetary policy and are used to control variables like investment, inflation, and unemployment.

Chapter 16. Changes in the Macroeconomy and Changes in Macroeconomic Policy

a. Enterprise value
c. ACCRA Cost of Living Index
b. Arrow-Debreu model
d. Interest rate

61. A _____ is a public market for the trading of company stock and derivatives at an agreed price; these are securities listed on a stock exchange as well as those only traded privately.

The size of the world _____ was estimated at about $36.6 trillion US at the beginning of October 2008 . The total world derivatives market has been estimated at about $791 trillion face or nominal value, 11 times the size of the entire world economy.

a. Adam Smith
c. Stock market
b. Adolf Hitler
d. Adolph Fischer

62. A _____ is a type of economic bubble taking place in stock markets when price of stocks rise and become overvalued by any measure of stock valuation.

The existence of _____s is at odds with the assumptions of efficient market theory which assumes rational investor behaviour. Behavioral finance theory attribute _____s to cognitive biases that lead to groupthink and herd behavior.

a. Growth investing
c. Fill or kill
b. Scrip issue
d. Stock market bubble

63. In finance and economics _____ or nominal rate of interest refers to the rate of interest before adjustment for inflation (in contrast with the real interest rate); or, for interest rates 'as stated' without adjustment for the full effect of compounding (also referred to as the nominal annual rate.) An interest rate is called nominal if the frequency of compounding (e.g. a month) is not identical to the basic time unit (normally a year.)

The real interest rate includes compensation for the lender's lost value due to inflation, whereas the _____ excludes inflation.

a. London Interbank Offered Rate
c. Risk-free interest rate
b. Fixed interest
d. Nominal interest rate

64. The _____ is a group of three respected economists who advise the President of the United States on economic policy. It is a part of the Executive Office of the President of the United States, and provides much of the economic policy of the White House. The council prepares the annual Economic Report of the President.

a. Council of Economic Advisers
c. Hybrid renewable energy systems
b. Constrained Pareto optimality
d. Federal Reserve Bank Notes

65. _____ is an American economist and was the Chairman of the Federal Reserve of the United States from 1987 to 2006. He currently works as a private advisor and providing consulting for firms through his company, Greenspan Associates LLC.

First appointed Federal Reserve chairman by President Ronald Reagan in August 1987, he was reappointed at successive four-year intervals until retiring on January 31, 2006 after the second-longest tenure in the position.

Chapter 16. Changes in the Macroeconomy and Changes in Macroeconomic Policy 207

a. Adam Smith
b. Adolf Hitler
c. Adolph Fischer
d. Alan Greenspan

66. The _____ was an evolution of developed countries from an industrial/manufacturing-based wealth producing economy into a service sector asset based economy, brought about by globalization and currency manipulation by governments and their central banks. Some analysts claimed that this change in the economic structure of the United States had created a state of permanent steady growth, low unemployment, and immunity to boom and bust macroeconomic cycles. They believed that the change rendered obsolete many business practices.
a. 1921 recession
b. 130-30 fund
c. 100-year flood
d. New economy

67. _____ is a decrease in the rate of inflation. This phase of the business cycle, in which retailers can no longer pass on higher prices to their customers, often occurs during a recession. In contrast, deflation occurs when prices are actually dropping.
a. Stealth inflation
b. Mundell-Tobin effect
c. Reflation
d. Disinflation

68. Unemployment occurs when a person is available to work and seeking work but currently without work. The prevalence of unemployment is usually measured using the _____, which is defined as the percentage of those in the labor force who are unemployed. The _____ is also used in economic studies and economic indexes such as the United States' Conference Board's Index of Leading Indicators as a measure of the state of the macroeconomics.
a. AD-IA Model
b. ACCRA Cost of Living Index
c. Unemployment rate
d. ACEA agreement

69. The _____ is a concept of economic activity developed in particular by Milton Friedman and Edmund Phelps in the 1960s, both recipients of the Nobel prize in economics. In both cases, the development of the concept is cited as a main motivation behind the prize. It represents the hypothetical unemployment rate consistent with aggregate production being at the 'long-run' level.
a. Robertson lag
b. Romer Model
c. Real Business Cycle Theory
d. Natural rate of unemployment

70. _____ is generally measured by standards such as real (i.e. inflation adjusted) income per person and poverty rate. Other measures such as access and quality of health care, income growth inequality and educational standards are also used. Examples are access to certain goods (such as number of refrigerators per 1000 people), or measures of health such as life expectancy.
a. Standard of living
b. 130-30 fund
c. Remuneration
d. 100-year flood

71. _____, often called simply stagnation, is a prolonged period of slow economic growth (traditionally measured in terms of the GDP growth.) Under some definitions, 'slow' means significantly slower than potential growth as estimated by experts in macroeconomics. Under other definitions, growth less than 2-3% per year is a sign of stagnation.
a. Overcapitalisation
b. Anti-globalization
c. Economic stagnation
d. Anti-consumerism

Chapter 16. Changes in the Macroeconomy and Changes in Macroeconomic Policy

72. The _____ was a period in the late 18th and early 19th centuries when major changes in agriculture, manufacturing, mining, and transportation had a profound effect on the socioeconomic and cultural conditions in Britain. The changes subsequently spread throughout Europe, North America, and eventually the world. The onset of the _____ marked a major turning point in human society; almost every aspect of daily life was eventually influenced in some way.
    a. Adolf Hitler
    b. Adolph Fischer
    c. Adam Smith
    d. Industrial Revolution

73. In economics, _____ is the total supply of goods and services produced by a national economy during a specific time period. It is the total amount of goods and services in the economy available at all possible price levels.
    a. Aggregation problem
    b. Aggregate expenditure
    c. Aggregate demand
    d. Aggregate supply

74. The Federal Home Loan Mortgage Corporation (FHLMC) (NYSE: FRE) is a government sponsored enterprise (GSE) of the United States federal government. _____ has its headquarters in the Tyson's Corner CDP in unincorporated Fairfax County, Virginia.

    The FHLMC was created in 1970 to expand the secondary market for mortgages in the US.

    a. Financial Stability Board
    b. Mittelstand
    c. Bankruptcy of Lehman Brothers
    d. Freddie Mac

75. _____ is the prospect that a party insulated from risk may behave differently from the way it would behave if it were fully exposed to the risk. In insurance, _____ that occurs without conscious or malicious action is called morale hazard.

    _____ is related to information asymmetry, a situation in which one party in a transaction has more information than another.

    a. 130-30 fund
    b. 1921 recession
    c. 100-year flood
    d. Moral hazard

Chapter 17. The Future of Macroeconomics

1. _____s is the social science that studies the production, distribution, and consumption of goods and services. The term _____s comes from the Ancient Greek oá¼°κονομῖα from oá¼¶κος (oikos, 'house') + vÏŒμος (nomos, 'custom' or 'law'), hence 'rules of the house(hold)'. Current _____ models developed out of the broader field of political economy in the late 19th century, owing to a desire to use an empirical approach more akin to the physical sciences.
   a. Energy economics
   b. Economic
   c. Opportunity cost
   d. Inflation

2. In economics, a model is a theoretical construct that represents economic processes by a set of variables and a set of logical and/or quantitative relationships between them. The _____ is a simplified framework designed to illustrate complex processes, often but not always using mathematical techniques. Frequently, _____s use structural parameters.
   a. AD-IA Model
   b. ACEA agreement
   c. ACCRA Cost of Living Index
   d. Economic model

3. _____, 1st Baron Keynes was a renowned economist from Britain whose many ideas on economic and political theories as well as on many governments' monetary policies influenced America. He advocated a government that played an active role in the lives of people regarding business, economy, etc. In this role, the government would use fiscal measures to reduce the consequences of recessions, economic depressions and booms.
   a. Adam Smith
   b. Adolph Fischer
   c. Adolf Hitler
   d. John Maynard Keynes

4. _____ is a branch of economics that deals with the performance, structure, and behavior of a national or regional economy as a whole. Along with microeconomics, _____ is one of the two most general fields in economics. It is the study of the behavior and decision-making of entire economies.
   a. Nominal value
   b. Macroeconomics
   c. Tobit model
   d. New Trade Theory

5. _____ and Keynesian Theory) is a macroeconomic theory based on the ideas of 20th-century British economist John Maynard Keynes. _____ argues that private sector decisions sometimes lead to inefficient macroeconomic outcomes and therefore advocates active policy responses by the public sector, including monetary policy actions by the central bank and fiscal policy actions by the government to stabilize output over the business cycle.

The theories forming the basis of _____ were first presented in The General Theory of Employment, Interest and Money, published in 1936.

   a. Market failure
   b. Deflation
   c. Rational choice theory
   d. Keynesian economics

6. The _____ says that it is naïve to try to predict the effects of a change in economic policy entirely on the basis of relationships observed in historical data, especially highly aggregated historical data.

The basic idea pre-dates Lucas's contribution, but in a 1976 paper he drove home the point that this simple notion invalidated policy advice based on conclusions drawn from estimated system of equation models. Because the parameters of those models were not structural - that is, not policy-invariant - they would necessarily change whenever policy - the rules of the game - was changed.

a. Peak-load pricing
b. Demand management
c. Dahrendorf hypothesis
d. Lucas critique

7. _____ is the view within monetary economics that variation in the money supply has major influences on national output in the short run and the price level over longer periods and that objectives of monetary policy are best met by targeting the growth rate of the money supply.

_____ today is mainly associated with the work of Milton Friedman, who was among the generation of economists to accept Keynesian economics and then criticize it on his own terms. Friedman and Anna Schwartz wrote an influential book, Monetary History of the United States 1867-1960, and argued that 'inflation is always and everywhere a monetary phenomenon.' Friedman advocated a central bank policy aimed at keeping the supply and demand for money at equilibrium, as measured by growth in productivity and demand.

a. Complexity economics
b. Marginal revenue productivity theory of wages
c. Monetarism
d. Historical school of economics

8. The _____ is a concept of economic activity developed in particular by Milton Friedman and Edmund Phelps in the 1960s, both recipients of the Nobel prize in economics. In both cases, the development of the concept is cited as a main motivation behind the prize. It represents the hypothetical unemployment rate consistent with aggregate production being at the 'long-run' level.

a. Real Business Cycle Theory
b. Romer Model
c. Robertson lag
d. Natural rate of unemployment

9. In economics, the _____ is a historical inverse relation between the rate of unemployment and the rate of inflation in an economy. Stated simply, the lower the unemployment in an economy, the higher the rate of increase in nominal wages in the economy. Rate of Change of Wages against Unemployment, United Kingdom 1913-1948 from Phillips (1958)

William Phillips, a New Zealand born economist, wrote a paper in 1958 titled The Relationship between Unemployment and the Rate of Change of Money Wages in the United Kingdom 1861-1957, which was published in the quarterly journal Economica.

a. Cost curve
b. Demand curve
c. Lorenz curve
d. Phillips curve

10. _____ is an assumption used in many contemporary macroeconomic models, and also in other areas of contemporary economics and game theory and in other applications of rational choice theory.

Since most macroeconomic models today study decisions over many periods, the expectations of workers, consumers, and firms about future economic conditions are an essential part of the model. How to model these expectations has long been controversial, and it is well known that the macroeconomic predictions of the model may differ depending on the assumptions made about expectations

a. Potential output
b. Minimum wage
c. Balanced-growth equilibrium
d. Rational expectations

11. _____ Theory (or _____ Theory) is a class of macroeconomic models in which business cycle fluctuations to a large extent can be accounted for by real (in contrast to nominal) shocks. (The four primary economic fluctuations are secular (trend), business cycle, seasonal, and random.) Unlike other leading theories of the business cycle, it sees recessions and periods of economic growth as the efficient response to exogenous changes in the real economic environment.
   a. Balanced-growth equilibrium
   b. Monetary policy reaction function
   c. SIMIC
   d. Real business cycle

12. The term _____ refers to economy-wide fluctuations in production or economic activity over several months or years. These fluctuations occur around a long-term growth trend, and typically involve shifts over time between periods of relatively rapid economic growth (expansion or boom), and periods of relative stagnation or decline (contraction or recession.)

   These fluctuations are often measured using the growth rate of real gross domestic product.

   a. Tobit model
   b. Business cycle
   c. Consumer theory
   d. Nominal value

13. In economics, _____ is the total demand for final goods and services in the economy (Y) at a given time and price level. It is the amount of goods and services in the economy that will be purchased at all possible price levels. This is the demand for the gross domestic product of a country when inventory levels are static.
   a. Aggregate demand
   b. Aggregate expenditure
   c. Aggregation problem
   d. Aggregate supply

14. _____ is a school of contemporary macroeconomics that strives to provide microeconomic foundations for Keynesian economics. It developed partly as a response to criticisms of Keynesian macroeconomics by adherents of New Classical macroeconomics.
   a. Keynesian theory
   b. Law of demand
   c. Mainstream economics
   d. New Keynesian economics

15. Economics:

   - _____,the desire to own something and the ability to pay for it
   - _____ curve,a graphic representation of a _____ schedule
   - _____ deposit, the money in checking accounts
   - _____ pull theory,the theory that inflation occurs when _____ for goods and services exceeds existing supplies
   - _____ schedule,a table that lists the quantity of a good a person will buy it each different price
   - _____ side economics,the school of economics at believes government spending and tax cuts open economy by raising _____

   a. Production
   b. Variability
   c. Demand
   d. McKesson ' Robbins scandal

16. An _____ is a person who has possession of an enterprise and assumes significant accountability for the inherent risks and the outcome. It is an ambitious leader who combines land, labor, and capital to create and market new goods or services. The term is a loanword from French and was first defined by the Irish economist Richard Cantillon.
   a. ACEA agreement
   b. Entrepreneur
   c. ACCRA Cost of Living Index
   d. Expansionary policies

17. _____ in economics and business is the result of an exchange and from that trade we assign a numerical monetary value to a good, service or asset. If Alice trades Bob 4 apples for an orange, the _____ of an orange is 4 apples. Inversely, the _____ of an apple is 1/4 oranges.
   a. Price book
   b. Premium pricing
   c. Price
   d. Price war

18. In economics, _____ is the total supply of goods and services produced by a national economy during a specific time period. It is the total amount of goods and services in the economy available at all possible price levels.
   a. Aggregate supply
   b. Aggregation problem
   c. Aggregate expenditure
   d. Aggregate demand

19. In economics, a _____ is a sudden event that increases or decreases demand for goods or services temporarily. A positive _____ increases demand and a negative _____ decreases demand. Prices of goods and services are affected in both cases.
   a. Robertson lag
   b. War economy
   c. Lucas-Islands model
   d. Demand shock

20. The _____ or gross domestic income (GDI), a basic measure of an economy's economic performance, is the market value of all final goods and services produced within the borders of a nation in a year. _____ can be defined in three ways, all of which are conceptually identical. First, it is equal to the total expenditures for all final goods and services produced within the country in a stipulated period of time (usually a 365-day year.)
   a. Gross domestic product
   b. Market structure
   c. Countercyclical
   d. Monopolistic competition

21. In economics, _____ refers to the highest level of real Gross Domestic Product output that can be sustained over the long term. The existence of a limit is due to natural and institutional constraints. If actual GDP rises and stays above _____, then (in the absence of wage and price controls) inflation tends to increase as demand exceeds supply.
   a. Monetary policy reaction function
   b. Fundamental psychological law
   c. Potential output
   d. Monetary conditions index

22. An _____, in economics, is the amount by which the real Gross domestic product exceeds potential GDP. The real GDP is also known as GDP 'adjusted for inflation', 'constant prices' GDP or 'constant dollar' GDP, because it measures the aggregate output in a country's income accounts in a given year, expressed in base-year prices. On the other hand, the potential GDP is the quantity of real GDP when a country's economy is at full-employment.
   a. ACCRA Cost of Living Index
   b. ACEA agreement
   c. AD-IA Model
   d. Inflationary gap

23. A _____ is an event that suddenly changes the price of a commodity or service. It may be caused by a sudden increase or decrease in the supply of a particular good. This sudden change affects the equilibrium price.

Chapter 17. The Future of Macroeconomics

a. Demand shock
c. Friedman rule
b. Supply shock
d. SIMIC

24. In statistics, a _____ is a value that allows data to be measured over time in terms of some base period ussually through a price index in order to distinguish between changes in the money value of GNP which result from a change in prices and those which result from a change in physical output. It is the measure of the price level for some quantity. A _____ serves as a price index in which the effects of inflation are nulled.
    a. Market microstructure
    c. Contingent employment
    b. Blanket order
    d. Deflator

25. _____ is the period of time that an individual spends at paid occupational labor. Unpaid labors such as housework are not considered part of the working week. Many countries regulate the work week by law, such as stipulating minimum daily rest periods, annual holidays and a maximum number of working hours per week.
    a. 130-30 fund
    c. Working time
    b. 1921 recession
    d. 100-year flood

26. In economics, the _____ or marginal physical product is the extra output produced by one more unit of an input (for instance, the difference in output when a firm's labour is increased from five to six units.) Assuming that no other inputs to production change, the _____ of a given input (X) can be expressed as:

    _____ = $\Delta Y/\Delta X$ = (the change of Y)/(the change of X.)

    -
        ○
            ■ Pending approval by Thomas Sowell***

In neoclassical economics, this is the mathematical derivative of the production function.... Note that the 'product' (Y) is typically defined ignoring external costs and benefits.

   a. Factor prices
   c. Labor problem
   b. Productive capacity
   d. Marginal product

27. In microeconomics, _____ is quite simply the conversion of inputs into outputs. It is an economic process that uses resources to create a good or service that is suitable for exchange. This can include manufacturing, storing, shipping, and packaging.
    a. Red Guards
    c. Solved
    b. MET
    d. Production

28. The _____ is the central banking system of the United States. Created in 1913 by the enactment of the Federal Reserve Act (signed by Woodrow Wilson), it is a quasi-public and quasi-private (government entity with private components) banking system that comprises (1) the presidentially appointed Board of Governors of the _____ in Washington, D.C.; (2) the Federal Open Market Committee; (3) twelve regional Federal Reserve Banks located in major cities throughout the nation acting as fiscal agents for the U.S. Treasury, each with its own nine-member board of directors; (4) numerous other private U.S. member banks, which subscribe to required amounts of non-transferable stock in their regional Federal Reserve Banks; and (5) various advisory councils. Since February 2006, Ben Bernanke has served as the Chairman of the Board of Governors of the _____.

Chapter 17. The Future of Macroeconomics

a. Federal Reserve System
c. Federal Reserve System Open Market Account
b. Term auction facility
d. Monetary Policy Report to the Congress

29. _____ is the process by which the government, central bank (ii) availability of money, and (iii) cost of money or rate of interest, in order to attain a set of objectives oriented towards the growth and stability of the economy. Monetary theory provides insight into how to craft optimal _____.

_____ is referred to as either being an expansionary policy where an expansionary policy increases the total supply of money in the economy, and a contractionary policy decreases the total money supply.

a. 100-year flood
c. Monetary policy
b. 1921 recession
d. 130-30 fund

30. The _____ is the upward-sloping relationship between the inflation rate and the unemployment rate. When the inflation rate rises, a central bank wishing to fight inflation will raise interest rates to reduce output and thus increase the unemployment rate. The _____ is a function of the Taylor Rule, the Investment-Spending Curve (IS Curve) and Okun's Law

The _____ has the equation:

$u = u_0 + \Phi(\pi - \pi t)$

Where Φ is a parameter that tells us how much unemployment rises when the central bank raises the real interest rate r because it thinks that inflation is too high and needs to be reduced.

a. Marginal propensity to import
c. Monetary policy reaction function
b. Secular basis
d. Value added

31. _____ refers to a business or organization attempting to acquire goods or services to accomplish the goals of the enterprise. Though there are several organizations that attempt to set standards in the _____ process, processes can vary greatly between organizations. Typically the word '_____' is not used interchangeably with the word 'procurement', since procurement typically includes Expediting, Supplier Quality, and Traffic and Logistics (T'L) in addition to _____.
a. 100-year flood
c. Free port
b. 130-30 fund
d. Purchasing

32. _____ is the number of goods/services that can be purchased with a unit of currency. For example, if you had taken one dollar to a store in the 1950s, you would have been able to buy a greater number of items than you would today, indicating that you would have had a greater _____ in the 1950s. Currency can be either a commodity money, like gold or silver, or fiat currency like US dollars.
a. Compliance cost
c. Genuine progress indicator
b. Human Poverty Index
d. Purchasing power

33. In economics, an _____ or spillover of an economic transaction is an impact on a party that is not directly involved in the transaction. In such a case, prices do not reflect the full costs or benefits in production or consumption of a product or service. A positive impact is called an external benefit, while a negative impact is called an external cost.

Chapter 17. The Future of Macroeconomics

a. Existence value
c. Environmental impact assessment
b. Environmental tariff
d. Externality

34. _____ is the electoral problem resulting from competition between two or more candidates or political parties from the same or approximate location in the political ideological spectrum or space against an opposing candidate or political party from the other side of the political ideological spectrum or space. The resulting fragmentation of political support may result in electoral defeat. _____s, and thus political calculations attempting to avoid them, appear most frequently in elections involving executives and representatives from single member districts.
   a. 1921 recession
   c. 100-year flood
   b. Coordination failure
   d. 130-30 fund

35. A trade union or _____ is an organization of workers who have banded together to achieve common goals in key areas and working conditions. The trade union, through its leadership, bargains with the employer on behalf of union members (rank and file members) and negotiates labor contracts (Collective bargaining) with employers. This may include the negotiation of wages, work rules, complaint procedures, rules governing hiring, firing and promotion of workers, benefits, workplace safety and policies.
   a. Business valuation standards
   c. Basis of futures
   b. Demand-side technologies
   d. Labor union

36. The term _____s refers to wages that have been adjusted for inflation. This term is used in contrast to nominal wages or unadjusted wages.

The use of adjusted figures is in undertaking some form of economic analysis.

   a. Federal Wage System
   c. Living wage
   b. Real wage
   d. Profit sharing

37. In economics, _____ is inflation that is very high or 'out of control', a condition in which prices increase rapidly as a currency loses its value. Definitions used by the media vary from a cumulative inflation rate over three years approaching 100% to 'inflation exceeding 50% a month.' In informal usage the term is often applied to much lower rates. As a rule of thumb, normal inflation is reported per year, but _____ is often reported for much shorter intervals, often per month.
   a. 130-30 fund
   c. 100-year flood
   b. Hyperinflation
   d. 1921 recession

38. A _____ or labor union is an organization of workers who have banded together to achieve common goals in key areas and working conditions. The _____, through its leadership, bargains with the employer on behalf of union members (rank and file members) and negotiates labor contracts (Collective bargaining) with employers. This may include the negotiation of wages, work rules, complaint procedures, rules governing hiring, firing and promotion of workers, benefits, workplace safety and policies.
   a. Guaranteed investment contracts
   c. Consumer goods
   b. Trade union
   d. Case-Shiller Home Price Indices

39. _____, is an economic theory that suggests consumers internalise the government's budget constraint and thus the timing of any tax change does not affect their change in spending. Consequently, _____ suggests that it does not matter whether a government finances its spending with debt or a tax increase, the effect on total level of demand in an economy will be the same. It was proposed, and then rejected, by the 19th-century economist David Ricardo.

216 Chapter 17. The Future of Macroeconomics

  a. Quasi-market
  c. Municipalization
  b. Social discount rate
  d. Ricardian equivalence

40. A _____ is a public market for the trading of company stock and derivatives at an agreed price; these are securities listed on a stock exchange as well as those only traded privately.

The size of the world _____ was estimated at about $36.6 trillion US at the beginning of October 2008 . The total world derivatives market has been estimated at about $791 trillion face or nominal value, 11 times the size of the entire world economy.

  a. Adolf Hitler
  c. Adam Smith
  b. Adolph Fischer
  d. Stock market

41. A _____ is a type of economic bubble taking place in stock markets when price of stocks rise and become overvalued by any measure of stock valuation.

The existence of _____s is at odds with the assumptions of efficient market theory which assumes rational investor behaviour. Behavioral finance theory attribute _____s to cognitive biases that lead to groupthink and herd behavior.

  a. Growth investing
  c. Scrip issue
  b. Stock market bubble
  d. Fill or kill

42. _____ is that which is owed; usually referencing assets owed, but the term can also cover moral obligations and other interactions not requiring money. In the case of assets, _____ is a means of using future purchasing power in the present before a summation has been earned. Some companies and corporations use _____ as a part of their overall corporate finance strategy.
  a. Collateral Management
  c. Hard money loan
  b. Debenture
  d. Debt

43. Market _____ is a business, economics or investment term that refers to an asset's ability to be easily converted through an act of buying or selling without causing a significant movement in the price and with minimum loss of value. Money, or cash on hand, is the most liquid asset. An act of exchange of a less liquid asset with a more liquid asset is called liquidation.
  a. Liquidity
  c. 130-30 fund
  b. 1921 recession
  d. 100-year flood

44. _____ is a broad label that refers to any individuals or households that use goods and services generated within the economy. The concept of a _____ is used in different contexts, so that the usage and significance of the term may vary.

Typically when business people and economists talk of _____s they are talking about person as _____, an aggregated commodity item with little individuality other than that expressed in the buy/not-buy decision.

Chapter 17. The Future of Macroeconomics

a. 1921 recession
c. 130-30 fund
b. 100-year flood
d. Consumer

45. _____ is a common concept in economics, and gives rise to derived concepts such as consumer debt. Generally _____ is defined by opposition to production. But the precise definition can vary because different schools of economists define production quite differently.

a. Foreclosure data providers
c. Federal Reserve Bank Notes
b. Cash or share options
d. Consumption

46. In economics, the _____ is the term used to refer to the environment in which bonds are bought and sold between a central bank ' its regulated banks. It is not a free market process.

- To intervene in the 'business cycle', a central bank may choose to go into the _____ and buy or sell government bonds, which is known as _____ operations to increase reserves.

a. Open market
c. ACCRA Cost of Living Index
b. Outside money
d. Inside money

47. _____ are the means of implementing monetary policy by which a central bank controls its national money supply by buying and selling government securities, or other financial instruments. Monetary targets, such as interest rates or exchange rates, are used to guide this implementation.

Since most money is now in the form of electronic records, rather than paper records such as banknotes, _____ are conducted simply by electronically increasing or decreasing ('crediting' or 'debiting') the amount of money that a bank has, e.g., in its reserve account at the central bank, in exchange for a bank selling or buying a financial instrument.

a. AD-IA Model
c. ACEA agreement
b. ACCRA Cost of Living Index
d. Open market operations

48. The _____ problem (often 'double _____') is an important category of transaction costs that impose severe limitations on economies lacking money and thus dominated by barter or other in-kind transactions. The problem is caused by the improbability of the wants, needs or events that cause or motivate a transaction occurring at the same time and the same place.

In-kind transactions have several problems, most notably timing constraints.

a. RFM
c. Going concern
b. Buy-sell agreement
d. Coincidence of wants

49. A variety of measures of _____ and output are used in economics to estimate total economic activity in a country or region, including gross domestic product (GDP), gross national product (GNP), and net _____

There are three main ways of calculating these numbers; the output approach, the income approach and the expenditure approach. In theory, the three must yield the same, because total expenditures on goods and services must equal the total income paid to the producers (Gnational income), and that must also equal the total value of the output of goods and services (GNP.)

a. Gross world product
b. GNI per capita
c. National income
d. Volume index

50. _____ use double-entry accounting to report the monetary value and sources of output produced in a country and the distribution of incomes that production generates. Data are available at the national and industry levels.

The NIPA summarizes national income on the left (debit, revenue) side and national product on the right (credit, expense) side of a two-column accounting report.

a. National income and product accounts
b. Gross private domestic investment
c. Net national product
d. Current account

51. _____ refers to the actions that governments take in the economic field. It covers the systems for setting interest rates and government deficit as well as the labour market, national ownership, and many other areas of government.

Such policies are often influenced by international institutions like the International Monetary Fund or World Bank as well as political beliefs and the consequent policies of parties.

a. Economic policy
b. AD-IA Model
c. ACCRA Cost of Living Index
d. ACEA agreement

52. In economic models, the _____ time frame assumes no fixed factors of production. Firms can enter or leave the marketplace, and the cost (and availability) of land, labor, raw materials, and capital goods can be assumed to vary. In contrast, in the short-run time frame, certain factors are assumed to be fixed, because there is not sufficient time for them to change.

a. Price/performance ratio
b. Diseconomies of scale
c. Productivity world
d. Long-run

53. _____ is the increase in the amount of the goods and services produced by an economy over time. It is conventionally measured as the percent rate of increase in real gross domestic product, or real GDP. Growth is usually calculated in real terms, i.e. inflation-adjusted terms, in order to net out the effect of inflation on the price of the goods and services produced.

a. ACEA agreement
b. ACCRA Cost of Living Index
c. AD-IA Model
d. Economic growth

54. The term _____ refers to government debt, expenditures and revenues, or to finance (particularly financial revenue) in general.

- _____ deficit is the budget deficit of federal or local government
- _____ policy is the discretionary spending of governments. Contrasts with monetary policy.
- _____ year and _____ quarter are reporting periods for firms and other agencies.

a. Bucket shop
c. Drawdown
b. Fiscal
d. Procter ' Gamble

55. In economics, _____ is the use of government spending and revenue collection to influence the economy.

_____ can be contrasted with the other main type of economic policy, monetary policy, which attempts to stabilize the economy by controlling interest rates and the supply of money. The two main instruments of _____ are government spending and taxation.

a. Sustainable investment rule
c. Fiscalism
b. 100-year flood
d. Fiscal policy

56. The _____ was a worldwide economic downturn starting in most places in 1929 and ending at different times in the 1930s or early 1940s for different countries. It was the largest and most important economic depression in the 20th century, and is used in the 21st century as an example of how far the world's economy can fall. The _____ originated in the United States; historians most often use as a starting date the stock market crash on October 29, 1929, known as Black Tuesday.

a. Great Depression
c. Jarrow March
b. British Empire Economic Conference
d. Wall Street Crash of 1929

57. A _____ is a package or set of measures introduced to stabilise a financial system or economy. The term can refer to policies in two distinct sets of circumstances: business cycle stabilization and crisis stabilization.

Stabilization can refer to correcting the normal behavior of the business cycle.

a. New International Economic Order
c. Stabilization policy
b. Capacity Development
d. Volunteers for Economic Growth Alliance

58. In economics, _____ is a rise in the general level of prices of goods and services in an economy over a period of time. When the general price level rises, each unit of currency buys fewer goods and services; consequently, _____ is also a decline in the real value of money--a loss of purchasing power in the medium of exchange which is also the monetary unit of account in the economy. A chief measure of general price-level _____ is the general _____ rate, which is the percentage change in a general price index (normally the Consumer Price Index) over time.

a. Economic
c. Energy economics
b. Inflation
d. Opportunity cost

59. In economics, the _____ functional form of production functions is widely used to represent the relationship of an output to inputs. It was proposed by Knut Wicksell (1851-1926), and tested against statistical evidence by Charles Cobb and Paul Douglas in 1900-1928.

For production, the function is

Y = AL$^\alpha$K$^\beta$,

where:

- Y = total production (the monetary value of all goods produced in a year)
- L = labor input
- K = capital input
- A = total factor productivity
- α and β are the output elasticities of labor and capital, respectively. These values are constants determined by available technology.

Output elasticity measures the responsiveness of output to a change in levels of either labor or capital used in production, ceteris paribus. For example if α = 0.15, a 1% increase in labor would lead to approximately a 0.15% increase in output.

a. Growth accounting
c. Social savings
b. Demand-pull theory
d. Cobb-Douglas

60. In economics, a _____ is a monetary-policy rule that stipulates how much the central bank would or should change the nominal interest rate in response to divergences of actual inflation rates from target inflation rates and of actual Gross Domestic Product (GDP) from potential GDP. It was first proposed by the by U.S. economist John B. Taylor in 1993. The rule can be written as follows:

$$i_t = \pi_t + r_t^* + a_\pi(\pi_t - \pi_t^*) + a_y(y_t - \bar{y}_t).$$

In this equation, i_t is the target short-term nominal interest rate (e.g. the federal funds rate in the US), π_t is the rate of inflation as measured by the GDP deflator, π_t^* is the desired rate of inflation, r_t^* is the assumed equilibrium real interest rate, y_t is the logarithm of real GDP, and $\bar{y}_t$ is the logarithm of potential output, as determined by a linear trend.

a. Fed Funds Probability
c. Term Securities Lending Facility
b. Federal Reserve Banks
d. Taylor rule

61. _____ refers to the objective and subjective components of the believability of a source or message.

Traditionally, _____ has two key components: trustworthiness and expertise, which both have objective and subjective components. Trustworthiness is a based more on subjective factors, but can include objective measurements such as established reliability.

a. 130-30 fund
c. 100-year flood
b. 1921 recession
d. Credibility

62. In economics, _____ is the total amount of money available in an economy at a particular point in time. There are several ways to define 'money', but standard measures usually include currency in circulation and demand deposits.

_____ data are recorded and published, usually by the government or the central bank of the country.

a. Veil of money
c. Neutrality of money
b. Velocity of money
d. Money supply

63. In economics, a _____ is a function that specifies the output of a firm, an industry, or an entire economy for all combinations of inputs. A meta-_____ compares the practice of the existing entities converting inputs X into output y to determine the most efficient practice _____ of the existing entities, whether the most efficient feasible practice production or the most efficient actual practice production. In either case, the maximum output of a technologically-determined production process is a mathematical function of input factors of production.
a. Constant elasticity of substitution
c. Post-Fordism
b. Short-run
d. Production function

64. A _____ is an expression that compares quantities relative to each other. The most common examples involve two quantities, but any number of quantities can be compared. _____s are represented mathematically by separating each quantity with a colon, for example the _____ 2:3, which is read as the _____ 'two to three'.
a. Ratio
c. Y-intercept
b. 130-30 fund
d. 100-year flood

222 Chapter 17. The Future of Macroeconomics

65. A _____ is:

- Rewrite _____, in generative grammar and computer science
- Standardization, a formal and widely-accepted statement, fact, definition, or qualification
- Operation, a determinate _____ for performing a mathematical operation and obtaining a certain result (Mathematics, Logic)
    - Unary operation
    - Binary operation
- _____ of inference, a function from sets of formulae to formulae (Mathematics, Logic)
- _____ of thumb, principle with broad application that is not intended to be strictly accurate or reliable for every situation. Also often simply referred to as a _____
- Moral, an atomic element of a moral code for guiding choices in human behavior
- Heuristic, a quantized '_____' which shows a tendency or probability for successful function
- A regulation, as in sports
- A Production _____, as in computer science
- Procedural law, a _____ set governing the application of laws to cases
    - A law, which may informally be called a '_____'
    - A court ruling, a decision by a court
- In the U.S. Government, a regulation mandated by Congress, but written or expanded upon by the Executive Branch.
- Norm (sociology), an informal but widely accepted _____, concept, truth, definition, or qualification (social norms, legal norms, coding norms)
- Norm (philosophy), a kind of sentence or a reason to act, feel or believe
- 'Rulership' is the concept of governance by a government:
    - Military _____, governance by a military body
    - Monastic _____, a collection of precepts that guides the life of monks or nuns in a religious order where the superior holds the place of Christ
- Slide _____

- '_____,' a song by Ayumi Hamasaki
- '_____,' a song by rapper Nas
- '_____s,' an album by the band The Whitest Boy Alive
- _____s: Pyaar Ka Superhit Formula, a 2003 Bollywood film
- ruler, an instrument for measuring lengths
- _____, a component of an astrolabe, circumferator or similar instrument
- The _____s, a bestselling self-help book
- _____ Project (Run Up-to-date Linux Everywhere), a project that aims to use up-to-date Linux software on old PCs
- _____ engine, a software system that helps managing business _____s
- Ja _____, a hip hop artist
    - R.U.L.E., a 2005 greatest hits album by rapper Ja _____
- '_____s,' a KMFDM song

a. Technocracy
b. Demand
c. Procter ' Gamble
d. Rule

Chapter 17. The Future of Macroeconomics

66. The term financial crisis is applied broadly to a variety of situations in which some financial institutions or assets suddenly lose a large part of their value. In the 19th and early 20th centuries, many _____ were associated with banking panics, and many recessions coincided with these panics. Other situations that are often called _____ include stock market crashes and the bursting of other financial bubbles, currency crises, and sovereign defaults.
- a. General equilibrium
- b. Microeconomics
- c. Financial crises
- d. Georgism

67. In algebra, a _____ is a function depending on n that associates a scalar, det(A), to an n×n square matrix A. The fundamental geometric meaning of a _____ is a scale factor for measure when A is regarded as a linear transformation. _____s are important both in calculus, where they enter the substitution rule for several variables, and in multilinear algebra.

For a fixed nonnegative integer n, there is a unique _____ function for the n×n matrices over any commutative ring R. In particular, this function exists when R is the field of real or complex numbers.

- a. 130-30 fund
- b. 100-year flood
- c. 1921 recession
- d. Determinant

68. In economics, the concept of the _____ refers to the decision-making time frame of a firm in which at least one factor of production is fixed. Costs which are fixed in the _____ have no impact on a firms decisions. For example a firm can raise output by increasing the amount of labour through overtime.
- a. Hicks-neutral technical change
- b. Productivity model
- c. Product Pipeline
- d. Short-run

69. In economics, the term _____ refers to the microeconomic analysis of the behavior of individual agents such as households or firms that underpins a macroeconomic theory (Barro, 1993, Glossary, p. 594.)

Most early macroeconomic models, including early Keynesian models, were based on hypotheses about relationships between aggregate quantities, such as aggregate output, employment, consumption, and investment.

- a. Fiscal adjustment
- b. Technology shock
- c. Minimum wage
- d. Microfoundations

Chapter 1

1. a	2. b	3. c	4. d	5. b	6. d	7. c	8. d	9. d	10. d
11. d	12. d	13. d	14. a	15. d	16. b	17. b	18. c	19. d	20. b
21. a	22. d	23. c	24. b	25. a	26. d	27. d	28. d	29. a	30. d
31. d	32. a	33. b	34. a	35. d	36. a	37. c	38. d	39. d	40. d
41. d	42. b	43. d	44. d	45. d	46. b	47. d	48. b	49. b	50. b
51. c	52. b	53. a	54. b	55. d	56. d	57. d	58. d	59. d	60. a
61. b	62. b	63. d	64. b	65. c	66. d	67. d	68. a	69. a	70. b
71. d	72. d	73. d	74. b	75. d	76. d	77. c	78. c	79. a	80. d
81. c	82. b	83. d	84. a	85. a	86. c	87. d	88. c	89. b	90. c
91. d	92. d	93. a	94. c	95. d	96. c	97. a	98. c		

Chapter 2

1. d	2. b	3. a	4. d	5. d	6. b	7. d	8. c	9. d	10. d
11. c	12. c	13. d	14. d	15. d	16. d	17. c	18. d	19. b	20. b
21. d	22. b	23. c	24. d	25. d	26. a	27. b	28. b	29. a	30. d
31. d	32. c	33. b	34. d	35. b	36. d	37. b	38. b	39. b	40. a
41. d	42. a	43. a	44. a	45. d	46. d	47. d	48. b	49. d	50. d
51. c	52. c	53. d	54. a	55. a	56. a	57. b	58. d	59. d	60. d
61. c	62. c	63. b	64. d	65. d	66. d	67. c	68. a	69. d	70. d
71. c	72. a	73. d	74. d	75. b	76. d	77. a	78. b	79. d	80. b
81. d	82. b	83. c	84. d	85. d	86. a	87. b	88. d	89. d	90. d
91. d	92. d	93. a							

Chapter 3

1. d	2. d	3. d	4. c	5. a	6. d	7. a	8. c	9. d	10. b
11. d	12. b	13. a	14. c	15. b	16. a	17. d	18. a	19. b	20. a
21. d	22. a	23. b	24. d	25. d	26. d	27. b	28. d	29. d	30. a
31. a	32. d	33. d	34. d	35. c	36. b	37. b	38. b	39. d	40. d
41. d	42. b	43. d	44. c	45. b	46. d	47. b	48. d	49. b	50. d
51. c									

Chapter 4

1. a	2. d	3. d	4. d	5. d	6. d	7. c	8. a	9. c	10. a
11. a	12. a	13. d	14. a	15. a	16. a	17. d	18. b	19. d	20. d
21. a	22. d	23. d	24. d	25. a	26. d	27. b	28. d	29. d	30. a
31. a									

ANSWER KEY

Chapter 5

1. d	2. d	3. d	4. a	5. c	6. d	7. d	8. c	9. d	10. d
11. a	12. d	13. d	14. d	15. d	16. d	17. a	18. b	19. d	20. c
21. d	22. c	23. a	24. d	25. b	26. a	27. d	28. c	29. d	30. c
31. a	32. a	33. a	34. d	35. d	36. a	37. d	38. b	39. a	40. d
41. d	42. c	43. c	44. d	45. a	46. c	47. d	48. d	49. b	50. b
51. b	52. b	53. d	54. d	55. a	56. d	57. d	58. b	59. c	60. b
61. b	62. d	63. a	64. d	65. b	66. d	67. d	68. d	69. b	70. d
71. b	72. d	73. c							

Chapter 6

1. d	2. b	3. d	4. b	5. d	6. c	7. d	8. d	9. a	10. b
11. a	12. a	13. d	14. c	15. a	16. d	17. c	18. a	19. d	20. a
21. b	22. d	23. d	24. d	25. d	26. b	27. d	28. b	29. b	30. d
31. b	32. d	33. d	34. c	35. d	36. b	37. d	38. c	39. b	40. c
41. b	42. c	43. a	44. a	45. d	46. c	47. d	48. d	49. c	50. d
51. b	52. a	53. b	54. d	55. d	56. d	57. a	58. b	59. a	60. d
61. d	62. b	63. d	64. d	65. c	66. a	67. b	68. d	69. d	70. d
71. c	72. d	73. d	74. c	75. c	76. b	77. b	78. d	79. c	80. d
81. a	82. b								

Chapter 7

1. b	2. a	3. c	4. d	5. d	6. b	7. a	8. b	9. a	10. d
11. c	12. d	13. d	14. d	15. a	16. d	17. b	18. d	19. d	20. c
21. a	22. d	23. b	24. b						

Chapter 8

1. d	2. d	3. d	4. b	5. d	6. c	7. b	8. a	9. d	10. d
11. d	12. d	13. b	14. c	15. c	16. d	17. c	18. d	19. a	20. b
21. d	22. a	23. d	24. b	25. d	26. d	27. b	28. b	29. d	30. a
31. d	32. a	33. d	34. d	35. b	36. d	37. c	38. a	39. d	40. c
41. b	42. d	43. d	44. c	45. c	46. d	47. a	48. b	49. d	50. c
51. d	52. b	53. c	54. c	55. d	56. b	57. d	58. b	59. c	60. b
61. c	62. d	63. c	64. d	65. b					

Chapter 9

1. b	2. b	3. d	4. b	5. a	6. d	7. d	8. d	9. d	10. d
11. b	12. d	13. d	14. b	15. d	16. d	17. c	18. c	19. d	20. b
21. d	22. a	23. d	24. c	25. b	26. a	27. d	28. d	29. b	30. d
31. d	32. a	33. d	34. a	35. d	36. c	37. d	38. a	39. d	40. b
41. a	42. d	43. d	44. c	45. d	46. d	47. d	48. c	49. d	50. a
51. a	52. c	53. a	54. b	55. c	56. d	57. c			

Chapter 10

1. d	2. b	3. d	4. d	5. d	6. d	7. c	8. c	9. d	10. b
11. d	12. d	13. d	14. c	15. d	16. c	17. a	18. b	19. d	20. b
21. a	22. c	23. b	24. b	25. d	26. d	27. a	28. a	29. d	30. d
31. a	32. d	33. d	34. c	35. a	36. d	37. a	38. d	39. d	40. c
41. a	42. d	43. c	44. b	45. d	46. d				

Chapter 11

1. d	2. d	3. d	4. c	5. b	6. c	7. d	8. a	9. c	10. d
11. a	12. d	13. a	14. d	15. c	16. d	17. c	18. d	19. d	20. c
21. d	22. d	23. d	24. b	25. a	26. c	27. a	28. a	29. d	30. d
31. b	32. c	33. a	34. a	35. b	36. a	37. b	38. d	39. d	40. b
41. c	42. d	43. c	44. d						

Chapter 12

1. b	2. b	3. c	4. a	5. d	6. c	7. d	8. d	9. c	10. a
11. d	12. c	13. a	14. b	15. c	16. a	17. d	18. c	19. d	20. d
21. c	22. d	23. d	24. a	25. d	26. d	27. c	28. b	29. d	30. b
31. d	32. a	33. a	34. d	35. d	36. d	37. c	38. c	39. c	40. a
41. d	42. c	43. b	44. d	45. b	46. b	47. c	48. d	49. a	50. d
51. b									

Chapter 13

1. c	2. a	3. d	4. c	5. d	6. d	7. d	8. a	9. d	10. d
11. d	12. d	13. d	14. c	15. d	16. a	17. d	18. c	19. d	20. d
21. d	22. d	23. d	24. d	25. a	26. d	27. a	28. d	29. d	30. a
31. d	32. b	33. d	34. b	35. d	36. d	37. b	38. b	39. d	40. d
41. d	42. d	43. d	44. d	45. d	46. d	47. b	48. a	49. d	50. d
51. c	52. d	53. a	54. d	55. b	56. d	57. d	58. c	59. d	60. a
61. d	62. b	63. c	64. b	65. d	66. a	67. d	68. c	69. d	70. d
71. d	72. a	73. d	74. c						

Chapter 14

1. d	2. b	3. d	4. d	5. d	6. a	7. c	8. d	9. d	10. d
11. d	12. a	13. d	14. d	15. c	16. d	17. a	18. d	19. d	20. a
21. b	22. b	23. d	24. a	25. b	26. a	27. b	28. b	29. d	30. b
31. a	32. d	33. c	34. a	35. d	36. d	37. b	38. a	39. d	40. a
41. b	42. d	43. a	44. d	45. d	46. d	47. d	48. b	49. a	50. b

ANSWER KEY

Chapter 15

1. c	2. a	3. d	4. d	5. d	6. b	7. d	8. d	9. d	10. d
11. d	12. b	13. c	14. d	15. d	16. a	17. d	18. c	19. b	20. d
21. d	22. c	23. b	24. d	25. d	26. c	27. a	28. c	29. a	30. c
31. d	32. d	33. d	34. a	35. b	36. d	37. b	38. c	39. b	40. d
41. d	42. c	43. d	44. d	45. d	46. a	47. c	48. c	49. c	50. d
51. c	52. b	53. d	54. d	55. a	56. a	57. d	58. d	59. d	60. d
61. d	62. d	63. d							

Chapter 16

1. d	2. d	3. c	4. b	5. d	6. c	7. d	8. d	9. d	10. a
11. d	12. d	13. d	14. b	15. c	16. d	17. a	18. d	19. d	20. c
21. c	22. c	23. d	24. a	25. d	26. d	27. b	28. b	29. c	30. d
31. d	32. d	33. a	34. d	35. d	36. a	37. b	38. b	39. d	40. d
41. b	42. c	43. c	44. d	45. d	46. a	47. c	48. d	49. a	50. b
51. c	52. d	53. a	54. d	55. b	56. d	57. d	58. d	59. c	60. d
61. c	62. d	63. d	64. a	65. d	66. d	67. d	68. c	69. d	70. a
71. c	72. d	73. d	74. d	75. d					

Chapter 17

1. b	2. d	3. d	4. b	5. d	6. d	7. c	8. d	9. d	10. d
11. d	12. b	13. a	14. d	15. c	16. b	17. c	18. a	19. d	20. a
21. c	22. d	23. b	24. d	25. c	26. d	27. d	28. a	29. c	30. c
31. d	32. d	33. d	34. b	35. d	36. b	37. b	38. b	39. d	40. d
41. b	42. d	43. a	44. d	45. d	46. a	47. d	48. d	49. c	50. a
51. a	52. d	53. d	54. b	55. d	56. a	57. c	58. b	59. d	60. d
61. d	62. d	63. d	64. a	65. d	66. c	67. d	68. d	69. d	

www.ingramcontent.com/pod-product-compliance
Lightning Source LLC
Chambersburg PA
CBHW081350230426
43667CB00017B/2784